FOUNDATIONS OF
MORAL AND POLITICAL
PHILOSOPHY

FOUNDATIONS OF MORAL AND POLITICAL PHILOSOPHY

Edited by

Ellen Frankel Paul, Fred D. Miller Jr, and Jeffrey Paul

BASIL BLACKWELL

British Library Cataloguing in Publication Data
Foundations of moral and political philosophy.
  1. Politics. Ethical aspects.
  I. Paul, Ellen Frankel II. Bowling Green State University, Social Philosophy and Policy Centre.
  172

  ISBN 0-631-17305-6

U.S. Library of Congress Cataloguing in Publication Data Card No. 8977686

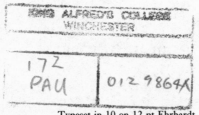
Typeset in 10 on 12 pt Ehrhardt
by SB Datagraphics Ltd, Colchester
Printed in Great Britain by Whitstable Litho, Kent.

CONTENTS

INTRODUCTION

Questions regarding the foundations of ethics and politics have intrigued philosophers ever since Socrates first pointed out their importance. Many philosophers have agreed with the ancient Greeks that we cannot obtain the knowledge we need to lead the best lives as individuals or to pursue the wisest public policies unless we are guided by a correct normative theory providing basic definitions, analyses, or explications of concepts such as "good" and "bad," and "right" and "wrong," and basic judgments or principles regarding good things and right actions. However, the task of providing a correct account of the foundations of moral and political philosophy is both difficult and perplexing. Earlier in this century, philosophers generally despaired of success – and many even regarded the task as misguided – on the grounds that values or norms were not a proper object of knowledge or even of cognitive discourse, so that the quest for the foundations of such knowledge or discourse was simply quixotic. However, the past two decades have witnessed an enthusiastic revival of interest on the part of moral and political philosophers concerning such foundations, which promises to continue unabated through the rest of this century. It is a field of great ferment and diversity, as reflected by the nine philosophers who have written essays for this volume.

These contributors offer new insights and approaches to the central questions of the foundations of moral and political philosophy. These include: is it possible to provide a rational justification of normative concepts, principles, or discourse? Further, what form would such a justification take: would it involve the derivation of normative or evaluative claims from prior non-normative premises (if so, how would it avoid the charge of fallacious reasoning), or, alternatively, would such a justification terminate in normative premises with no further justification (if so, how would it avoid the charge of arbitrariness)? Supposing that one could provide such a rational justification, what sort of motivation would it provide for acting accordingly? That is, could it provide an answer to the traditional problem, "Why should I be moral?" Is it irrational for someone to be immoral rather than moral? Further, is it reasonable for philosophers to suppose that they could provide a rational justification of basic moral principles, in the light of widespread disagreement about such principles among apparently rational people? Is an ethical and political norm or value, instead, the sort of thing that must evolve within a specific historical tradition or a specific social community, so that no justification in abstraction from this tradition or community is possible? What specific form should the foundational principles take: should they be fundamentally concerned with the consequences of individual actions or public policies (as in consequentialist theories) or with the character of these actions or policies (as in deontic theories of justice and rights)? Should they represent norms or values as absolute for all agents, or as relative to individual agents? Finally, should we assume that the foundations of moral *and* political philosophy are the same or admit of the same sorts of justification? Should those who establish basic rules or basic policies act upon the same normative principles and justifications as ordinary decision makers? These are among the important questions addressed by our contributors.

Judith Jarvis Thomson discusses the methodology of moral theory in her paper, with special attention to just what the data for moral theory are. Her essay "The No Reason Thesis" suggests that some of our moral beliefs cannot be false, and that most (if not all) disagreements on moral questions spring from what she calls a *failure to connect*: that is, a failure when making moral judgments to use relevant propositions appropriately. The idea that some of our moral beliefs cannot be false is offered in rebuttal to the thesis that there is no reason to suppose any moral judgment true, as well as to the weaker thesis that no statement of fact entails any moral statement. Thomson argues that if the weaker thesis is false, then the stronger thesis must be false as well. Her analysis of the way moral theorizing has to work is thus central to her exploration of the foundations of morality.

Jean Hampton explores, conversely, the foundations of *immorality*: her "The Nature of Immorality" concentrates on three areas of inquiry. Why do people behave immorally? What is it for someone to be culpable of wrongdoing? And what do we mean when we accuse someone of having an evil character? Theories which analyze immorality in terms of the immoral agent's ignorance, indifference, or incontinence are examined; however, all three explanations are found wanting, for none of them can explain the phenomenon of moral culpability. Hampton then develops a fourth theory – which she calls the *defiance theory* – which rests on an analysis of immorality as rooted in the defiance of the authority of morality. After noting the way that this theory is consistent with certain of our intuitions about the nature of culpability, she then discusses certain passages in the philosophy of Kant and the stories of the Bible that are illuminated by the defiance theory. The essay concludes with a discussion of issues that must be resolved in order for the defiance theory to give us a complete account of immorality.

T.H. Irwin, in his essay, focuses on a recurrent contender for the basis of moral and political judgments: tradition. In "Tradition and Reason in the History of Ethics," Irwin focuses on the historicism of Alasdair MacIntyre, as exemplified in his recent book *Whose Justice? Which Rationality?* It is MacIntyre's argument that there is no such thing as justice-as-such or rationality-as-such; rather, specific visions of justice and rationality are intimately tied to particular cultural and historical settings. Irwin criticizes Macintyre's general arguments about the nature of rationality and justification, as well as the relevance and accuracy of his historical examples. Irwin argues that MacIntyre's general arguments entail a position much closer to relativism than MacIntyre would likely want to occupy, and that MacIntyre's historical examples (particularly those derived from Aristotle and John Rawls) rest on doubtful claims about interpretation. What this adds up to, Irvin suggests, is that the gap between different views about justice and rationality is not as wide as MacIntyre claims.

Russell Hardin, in "Ethics and Stochastic Processes," addresses one special class of problems in moral and political philosophy: questions of public policy which affect large numbers of people. Hardin begins by arguing that traditional moral theories do not readily fit major policy issues; the goal of public policy, generally, is not to save our souls, change our characters, or enable us all to act as ends in ourselves, but rather is usually the more mundane one of saving lives and preserving health. Theories, then, that focus on the rightness of actions will have special difficulties with large-scale stochastic problems, which commonly involve externalities. Public policies that are meant to deal with such problems seem inherently to be directed at consequences and to imply tradeoffs between individuals. Hardin's consequentialism informs his consideration of vaccination policy (such as policy against smallpox before it was eradicated): some people die because they are vaccinated, but far more would have died had there been no vaccination program. His conclusion is that we cannot reason about vaccination policy in the same way that we might reason about, say, lying – that is, we aren't allowed the luxury, on the level of public policy, of arguing that things are right and wrong independent of their likely consequences.

Eric Mack's essay, on the other hand, is devoted in part to demonstrating that consequentialism is morally unsatisfactory. In "Moral Individualism: Agent-Relativity and Deontic Restraints," Mack argues that moral theory and practice must be based on an appreciation of *deontic restraints* – by which he means moral restraints on actions which are, roughly speaking, grounded in the character of those actions and not merely in the disvalue of their results. The recognition of deontic restraints, Mack says, is one complementary part of a rational and practical response to other individuals as separate reason-possessing and value-pursuing entities – the other part being the acknowledgment of the relativity of value among different agents. Acknowledging that different agents will have different values, Mack argues, stands as an admission of the individualist conception of the good and a crucial part of the objection to consequentialism from the integrity of persons; acknowledging the existence of deontic restraints stands as an admission of the individualist conception of the right and a crucial part of the objection to consequentialism from justice. He thus concludes that deontic restraints serve two functions: they represent respect for individuals as separate possessors of different reasons, and they provide protection for each individual's pursuit of different values by marking operational boundaries.

Holly M. Smith's "Two-Tier Moral Codes" examines one aspect of modeling right conduct as based upon a law-like moral code composed of neutral rules and principles. She begins by noting that cognitive shortcomings often prevent agents from using otherwise attractive moral codes as guides for action. These cognitive handicaps include such things as incapacity to understand the code, incorrect or absent information about the world which must be correct for the code to deliver the right answer, and limited time or ability to perform the calculations or follow the mental rules which the code requires. Smith analyzes the responses of the moral theorists who have been concerned with the attendant difficulties of complex moral codes, and divides them into three kinds: those which hold that codes that ever fail to guide action correctly must be rejected, those which hold that such failures are the moral responsibility of the agent and so are properly corrected by that agent's improvement, and those which hold that defective codes must be supplemented by auxiliary ones which will be invulnerable to the defects in question. Smith concentrates on a variant of the third response, which she calls "Esoteric Moralities." Esoteric Moralities consist of a set of first-tier principles providing the correct theoretical account of right and wrong conjoined with a set of second-tier principles to be used by cognitively limited decision-makers. (Under such a system, those who use the second-tier rules are unaware of the existence and true moral authority of the rules of the first tier.) Smith explores several possible objections to a two-tier moral system, but does not find them compelling. She concludes, however, that the implementation problems involved would be insurmountable.

Stephen L. Darwall's "Motive and Obligation in the British Moralists" also contains close readings of historical conceptions of the nature of moral action. Darwall's essay sketches in some detail the fundamental changes in the concept of obligation as it evolved over the early modern period in British moral thought (with particular attention to the Earl of Shaftesbury), as well as this concept's importance to the seventeenth-century natural law theorists. He pays particular attention to the nature of obligation as it developed in the direction of the view that moral obligation is one sort of motivational force – a view, of course, that is a major presence in moral thought today. Darwall also suggests that an unappreciated source for the views of the British moralists was a doctrine of Immanuel Kant's – a doctrine which may seem surprising in the context of British ethics – that rational agents are obligated by self-imposed motives through a form of practical thinking that is necessary for moral autonomy.

Peter Railton argues that we can derive important moral truths from the way that we use language. Railton, in "Naturalism and Prescriptivity," first notes that the way we talk about a person's good or well-being displays two facets – one prescriptive, the other descriptive. Since the era in moral philosophy of G. E. Moore's "open question" argument, Railton argues, two approaches to the interpretation of moral language have predominated: non-naturalism (Moore's own position, which takes the descriptive character of talk about the good to be fundamental, and seeks to accommodate the question of prescription by treating good as a unique, irreducibly normative, and non-natural property) and non-cognitivism (which takes the prescriptive character of moral talk as fundamental, and treats whatever descriptive content it may contain as derived). However, he considers (and clarifies) a third possibility: that discussion about a person's good may have genuine, descriptive content, but of a natural, reducible kind. Railton then uses his idea of reductive naturalism to indicate a strategy by which the naturalist might attempt to accommodate the prescriptive portion of talk about a person's good.

Allan Gibbard's "Communities of Judgment" provides an account of how one might derive moral truths from norms in various communities. First, Gibbard sketches a theory of normative judgment: normative statements express speakers' acceptance of norms, and accepting a norm is explained as a state which helps to solve the problem of social coordination. Groups, on this view, move towards normative consensus through mutual influence and demands for consistency. Gibbard then explores the way this account might apply when different groups tend towards different consensuses. Perhaps groups might abandon other groups, or attempt to repress them, but they may ultimately have to find collectively agreeable norms in order to accommodate their disagreements, and the chief aim of Gibbard's essay is to explore how such accommodative norms might work. These sorts of norms could have two kinds of roles: they might be accepted at face value and foster social coordination in widespread discussion, but they might be treated simply as instruments needed for accommodation if they do not jibe with local norms.

From tradition to language, from communitarianism to natural rights, the contributors to this volume have provided a variety of bases on which moral and political theory might rest.

CONTRIBUTORS

Judith Jarvis Thomson is Professor of Philosophy at MIT. She has written a number of articles on topics in ethics and metaphysics, some of which have been reprinted in her collection *Rights, Restitution, & Risk*. Her book *Acts and Other Events* is a study in the ontology of action. Her article in this volume is part of the introduction to her forthcoming book (Harvard University Press) on the theory of rights.

Jean Hampton is Associate Professor of Philosophy at University of California, Davis, and has taught at UCLA and the University of Pittsburgh. She is the author of *Hobbes and the Social Contract Tradition,* and (with Jeffrie Murphy) *Forgiveness and Mercy* (both published by Cambridge University Press). Her interests range over topics in political philosophy, ethics, and the philosophy of law. The paper in this volume is part of her research on theories of moral culpability, legal *mens rea,* and the role of retributive punishment in a liberal state. Another focus of her current research is contemporary moral and political contractarian theory.

T. H. Irwin is Professor of Philosophy at Cornell University. He is the author of *Plato's Moral Theory* (Clarendon Press, 1977), *Plato's Gorgias* (Clarendon Press, 1979), *Aristotle's Nicomachean Ethics* (Hackett, 1985), *Aristotle's First Principles* (Clarendon Press, 1988), and *Classical Thought* (Oxford University Press, 1989).

Russell Hardin is Mellon Foundation Professor of Political Science, Philosophy, and Public Policy Studies at the University of Chicago. He is the author of *Morality within the Limits of Reason* (University of Chicago Press, 1988) and *Collective Action* (Johns Hopkins University Press, 1982) and co-editor of *Nuclear Deterrence : Ethics and Strategy* (University of Chicago Press, 1985). He is also the editor of *Ethics.* His articles on rational choice, moral and political philosophy, and nuclear defense policy have appeared in many journals and books. He is a Fellow of the American Association for the Advancement of Science.

Eric Mack is an Associate Professor of Philosophy, and a member of the faculty of the Murphy Institute of Political Economy, at Tulane University. He has published a wide range of articles in moral, political, and legal philosophy in journals such as *Ethics, Philosophical Studies,* and *Philosophy and Public Affairs,* as well as in numerous anthologies. He has edited several books, including Herbert Spencer's *The Man Versus The State* (Liberty Press, 1982).

Holly M. Smith is Professor of Philosophy and Head of the Philosophy Department at the University of Arizona. Having previously taught at the

University of Pittsburgh, the University of Michigan, and the University of Illinois at Chicago Circle, her publications focus on normative theory and applied ethics. She is currently working on a book exploring how moral theories ought to accommodate human cognitive shortcomings.

Stephen L. Darwall is Professor of Philosophy at the University of Michigan. He is the author of *Impartial Reason*, a work that criticizes instrumental theories of rationality and develops a substantive account of practical reason, according to which ethical conduct is rational. His other writings span a variety of topics in moral psychology and moral and political philosophy. More recently, his research interests have turned towards the history of ethics. He is currently working on a book on British moral philosophy in the late seventeenth and early eighteenth centuries.

Peter Railton is Associate Professor of Philosophy at the University of Michigan, Ann Arbor. He received his Ph.D. from Princeton in 1980. His principal areas of research are ethics and the philosophy of science, and his work has appeared in *Philosophy and Public Affairs, Philosophical Review, Ethics,* and *Philosophy of Science,* as well as other journals. He has also written papers in applied ethics and value theory for the Center for Philosophy and Public Policy and the National Research Council of the National Academy of Sciences.

Allan Gibbard is Professor of Philosophy at the University of Michigan, Ann Arbor, and has been there since 1977. Previously, he taught at the University of Chicago and the University of Pittsburgh, having received his Ph.D. from Harvard University. He is the author of numerous articles on topics in ethical theory, especially on the structure of utilitarianism and the nature of normative judgments. He has also published in economics journals on the theory of social choice. He is presently finishing a book on moral judgments, and more broadly on judgments of what it makes sense to do and to feel.

THE NO REASON THESIS

By Judith Jarvis Thomson

I

Moral theorists often say such things as "But surely A ought to do such and such," or "Plainly it is morally permissible for B to do so and so," and do not even try to prove that those judgments are true. Moreover, they often rest weight on the supposition that those judgments are true. In particular, they often rest theories on them: they take them as data.

Others object. They say that nobody is entitled to rest any weight at all on judgments such as those. They say, not that the judgments are false, but that there is no reason to believe them true. They say, more generally, that there is no reason to think of any moral judgment that it is true. I will call this The No Reason Thesis.

Is there reason to think The No Reason Thesis true? There are lots of arguments for it in the literature, but I want to focus on one of them in particular. I think that the one I will focus on lies behind all the others, but no matter if it does not: I suggest that if this argument fails, they all fail.

I should perhaps confess that my interest in The No Reason Thesis does not arise out of an interest in moral epistemology. What interests me is rather the method of moral theorizing I mentioned. I want to try to defend it.

II

The argument I have in mind comes to us in the modern era from Hume. Hume had said, in a passage most of us probably know by heart now:

> In every system of morality, which I have hitherto met with, I have always remark'd, that the author proceeds for some time in the ordinary way of reasoning, and establishes the being of a God, or makes observations concerning human affairs; when of a sudden I am surpriz'd to find, that instead of the usual copulations of propositions, *is*, and *is not*, I meet with no proposition that is not connected with an *ought*, or an *ought not*. This change is imperceptible; but is, however, of the last consequence. For as this *ought*, or *ought not*, expresses some new relation or affirmation, 'tis necessary that it shou'd be observ'd and explain'd; and at the same time that a reason should be given, for what seems altogether inconceivable, how this new relation can be a deduction from others, which are entirely different from it.[1]

---

[1] David Hume, *A Treatise of Human Nature*, ed. L.A. Selby-Bigge (London: Oxford University Press, 1973), p. 469.

That is, moralists begin by telling us that the world is this way and is not that way. They then say "So people ought to do this and ought not do that." But the conclusion they draw "expresses some new relation or affirmation"; and it seems "altogether inconceivable" that it should be deducible from what preceded it, which is "entirely different from it."

There has been dispute as to what Hume actually meant by saying these things, and it is arguable that he did not mean what he has in our century been taken to mean; what matters for our purposes is what the passage seemed to say, and indeed, seemed to be right in saying: namely, that no statement to the effect that a person ought or ought not do a thing can be "a deduction from" any statement about what is in fact the case. Or, as I shall put the point: no statement to the effect that a person ought or ought not do a thing *is entailed by* any statement about what is in fact the case.

I should perhaps stop to say a word about my use of the phrases "is entailed by" and (in the active mode) "entails." I will throughout say that a statement Q is entailed by a statement P (and that P entails Q) if and only if, if P is true, then so must Q also be true.[2]

And why merely "ought" and "ought not"? Why not also "right" and "wrong," "good" and "bad," and so on? Are these not also "new relations or affirmations"? So it seemed right to say, more generally, that no moral judgment at all is entailed by any statement about what is in fact the case.

We might call this The Fact-Value Thesis. The Fact-Value Thesis says (in the active mode) that no statement of fact entails any moral judgment. The No Reason Thesis certainly appears to be considerably stronger: it says that there is no reason at all to think any moral judgment true. How is one to get from The Fact-Value Thesis to The No Reason Thesis? One popular route (more popular some years ago than it is nowadays) passed through a certain diagnosis of the source of The Fact-Value Thesis. You begin with the fact that you have already shown *that* The Fact-Value Thesis is true. (How did you show this? By appeal to Hume, by pointing in one or another way to the fact that, as Hume put it, a moral concept "expresses some new relation or affirmation."[3]) Then what you do is to ask *why* The Fact-Value Thesis is true – what explains its being a truth. And you offer the following answer: having a moral belief is merely having an attitude, and making a moral assertion is merely displaying that attitude (as a smile is a display of an attitude), and moral 'judgments' therefore have no truth-value (as smiles have no truth-value). Certainly, if that answer is correct, then its being correct would explain why The Fact-Value Thesis is true, for if moral 'judgments' have no truth-value, then *a fortiori* no statement of fact entails a moral judgment.

---

[2] I think it arguable that this is how Hume meant us to understand "a deduction from." Whatever precisely Hume may have had in mind in the passage quoted in the text above, it is surely plain that he did not mean to be drawing our attention merely to the fact that "ought" is not obtainable from "is" within (as it might be) first-order logic.

[3] Or you might have appealed to G.E. Moore's 'open question' argument from *Principia Ethica* (London: Cambridge University Press, 1966), pp. 15ff. See also A.J. Ayer's *Language, Truth and Logic* (New York: Dover Publications, 1952), ch. VI.

Moreover, if that is why The Fact-Value Thesis is true, then The No Reason Thesis is also true, for if moral 'judgments' have no truth-value, then *a fortiori* nothing really is reason to think them true. That diagnosis of the source of The Fact-Value Thesis, therefore, takes us all the way to The No Reason Thesis.

This is not the only possible route along which a philosopher might think he or she could travel from The Fact-Value Thesis to The No Reason Thesis, but it was, as I say, a popular one. In the first place, moral beliefs (if they can properly be called beliefs) plainly do connect with attitudes: people who believe people ought not do a thing do typically (always?) have an unfavorable attitude towards the doing of it. Second, what property could it be thought that we ascribe to a person or to a kind of act when we say that the person ought not engage in an act of that kind? There seems to be nothing discoverable by looking, as the presence of redness is discoverable by looking, or by listening, as the presence of sounds is discoverable by listening, or by any other form of perception, which wrongness could be thought to consist in. (If there were, then moral judgments would be entailed by statements of fact, which The Fact-Value Thesis denies.) But then doesn't a hard-headed empiricist do better to say that there is no such property as wrongness, and thus that 'ascriptions of wrongness' are not *really* ascriptions of anything? And if they are not ascriptions of anything, what more plausible than to think that they are mere displays of attitudes?

All this has been very abstract. Consider the disputes about capital punishment. I say "disputes," since there are several of them. Many people argue that we ought to make it impermissible for the death penalty to be imposed on anyone, for any crime, even for murder, even for a particularly despicable murder, even for a second commission of a particularly despicable murder. Others disagree. Now some of those arguments issue from disagreements as to the facts. One side believe it wrong to impose the death penalty *because* they believe it does not deter more effectively than long prison terms; the other side believe it acceptable to impose the death penalty *because* they believe it does deter more effectively than long prison terms. In the case of these arguments, one is inclined to think that the difference of opinion on the moral matter would end if the two sides came to agreement on the facts.

But in the case of other disputes about capital punishment, that is not so. A, we may imagine, believes that we ought to make it impermissible for the death penalty to be imposed on anyone, for any crime, even for murder, even for a particularly despicable murder, even for a second commission of a particularly despicable murder, and believes this *not* because he has a belief of fact of the kind I mentioned above: A believes this because he believes that a community (like an individual) must never intentionally kill a person who is in captivity, and who thus currently constitutes no threat to others, and who can be kept from constituting a threat to others by less drastic means than killing. B, by contrast, believes it permissible for the death penalty to be imposed on those who are properly convicted of particularly despicable crimes in that he thinks they deserve death for their crimes, and that by executing them, the community demonstrates its respect for their victims and its commitment to the belief that the crimes in question really are particularly despicable. Indeed, we may suppose B to believe that the community's failure to execute them (on proper conviction) would precisely show a lack of respect for their victims and a lack of commitment to its moral beliefs.[4] It is plausible to think that *this* dispute about capital punishment is purely moral: that is, we may plausibly think that A and B are in complete agreement on all the relevant matters of fact while nevertheless disagreeing as to the moral permissibility of capital punishment.

It is worth noticing in passing that it was not necessary to invent people with wild or crazy moral views in order to invent what looks for all the world like a purely moral dispute. We did not even need to look across cultures; A and B are our neighbors here at home.

How is the dispute between A and B to be settled? Friends of The Fact-Value Thesis say it cannot be settled by convicting either one of the parties to the dispute of an inconsistency between his beliefs of fact on the one hand and his moral belief about capital punishment on the other hand – for if The Fact-Value Thesis is true, then no statement reporting all of the relevant matters of fact believed by both A and B entails either that capital punishment is permissible or entails that it is not permissible. And isn't that plausible?

One who takes the step from The Fact-Value Thesis to The No Reason Thesis says that the dispute between A and B cannot be settled at all. A thinks capital punishment permissible, B thinks it impermissible, but neither has any reason at all for thinking this – for as The No Reason Thesis says, there is no reason to think of any moral judgment that it is true. And isn't that plausible too? For if The No Reason Thesis is true, it would be no wonder that our deepest differences over capital punishment have proved so resistant to settlement.

There are of course a great many moral judgments that are not at all in dispute among our neighbors here at home, judgments (for example) to the effect that it is on the whole not a good thing to lie, cheat, maim people, or cause them pain. But mightn't it occur to us that agreement on those matters would also be no wonder, given our common background and education? Perhaps we need to invent a person with wild or crazy moral views if we are to invent a purely moral dispute about our most favored moral views. But can't we?

It is a good question whether the procedure for getting from The Fact-Value Thesis to The No Reason Thesis that I described above really does get us there. That procedure is suspect, in a number of ways. More generally, I know of no clear way of proving that if The Fact-Value Thesis is true, then so also is The No Reason Thesis.

On the other hand, I am myself inclined to think that if The Fact-Value Thesis is true, then we would be right to be suspicious of the idea that there is reason to believe that some moral judgment is true. After all, if no statement of fact P entails a moral judgment Q, then even a statement of fact P that is a 'complete' report of all of the facts of our world does not entail Q: that means that the totality of all of the facts of our world is compatible with Q's not being true. What, then, is supposed to be reason to think that Q really is true?

[4] Hitler tends to turn up as an example in defense of this view.

I suggest that we bypass the question whether one can get from The Fact-Value Thesis to The No Reason Thesis, and, if so, how. Many (indeed, I think most) philosophers who accepted The Fact-Value Thesis did take that step, and we can at a minimum understand why they thought they were entitled to. Moreover, what we will focus on below is The Fact-Value Thesis itself. If The Fact-Value Thesis is false, then it matters not a bit how one might pass from it to The No Reason Thesis. Indeed, if The Fact-Value Thesis is false, then The No Reason Thesis is also false, and we need not attend to any of the many considerations that have been brought forward in support of it.

III

I hope it will be clear that I have not been trying to prove The No Reason Thesis, or even The Fact-Value Thesis. I have wanted only to bring out what lies behind them, and to do this as convincingly as I could. For I think Hume was entirely right to be struck by that sudden shift from "is" to "ought" in the writings of the moralists, and, indeed, that he made a major contribution to philosophy in showing it to us. I think, moreover, that his modern followers also made a major contribution to philosophy in bringing out, explicitly, the threat to moral confidence that lurks in what Hume showed us. At the very least, the burden of proof nowadays lies on the defender of moral confidence. One way in which that burden has been picked up comes out as follows.

Disputes about capital punishment are in a number of ways particularly well-suited to the purposes of one who wishes to convince us of the truth of The Fact-Value Thesis and The No Reason Thesis. In the first place, there are ongoing unsettled disputes about capital punishment, and it is plausible to think that some of them really are purely moral.

Second, and more important, the considerations that people bring to bear in support of their views about capital punishment are relatively easy to divide into the factual on the one hand and the moral on the other.[5]

But a number of people have entirely rightly drawn attention to the fact that much of our moral thinking is neither purely factual nor purely moral, and some have offered that fact as an objection to The Fact-Value Thesis.[6] Philippa Foot, for example, invited us to take note of such predicates as "rude".[7] She said:

> I think it will be agreed that in the wide sense in which philosophers speak of evaluation, 'rude' is an evaluative term. . . . [I]t expresses disapproval, is meant to be used when action is to be discouraged, implies that other things being equal the behavior to which it is applied will be avoided by the speaker, and so on.

[5] That is not true of many other current moral disputes, such as the disputes about abortion. The question whether the fetus is a person – which most participants take seriously – is neither straightforwardly factual, nor straightforwardly moral.

[6] A different kind of straddle judgment (that is, judgment which is neither purely moral nor purely factual) was drawn attention to by Arthur N. Prior in "The Autonomy of Ethics," reprinted in his collection of essays *Papers in Logic and Ethics* (Amherst: University of Massachusetts Press, 1976).

[7] See her "Moral Arguments," reprinted in her collection of essays *Virtues and Vices* (Oxford: Basil Blackwell, 1978). My quotations are all from p. 102 of that edition.

It seems right to think that saying about (as it might be) Bloggs that he behaved rudely is making an unfavorable moral judgment about him. On the other hand, a bit of behavior is rude if it meets certain conditions of fact. Foot suggests that a bit of behavior is rude just in case it "causes offence by indicating lack of respect"; whether or not that is correct as an account of what rudeness *is*, it does seem right to think that if Bloggs interrupted a lecture at a scholarly meeting with an insult, then it follows that he acted rudely. In short, Foot says, some moral judgments are entailed by some statements of fact, namely those moral judgments to the effect that someone has been rude.

There is a range of concepts here, of which the concept 'rude' is only one. Bernard Williams helpfully gives them the name "thick ethical concepts";[8] among the examples he gives are the concepts 'treachery', 'brutality', 'courage', and 'cowardice'. It seems right to think that saying about Bloggs that he behaved treacherously is making a moral judgment about him. On the other hand, a bit of behavior is treachery if it meets certain conditions of fact. Treachery is breach of trust, and it does seem right to think that if Bloggs sold his country's secrets to the enemy during wartime, then it follows that he acted treacherously. Similar points hold of ascriptions of brutality, courage, and cowardice. So anyone who agrees with Foot about rudeness will very likely want to say that here are further moral judgments which are entailed by statements of fact.

Williams gives two further examples of thick ethical concepts which seem to me to be different, namely the concepts 'promise' and 'lie.' It does seem right to think that saying about Bloggs that he behaved rudely or treacherously, or brutally, and so on, is making a moral judgment about him; does it seem right to think that saying about him that he made (or broke) a promise, or that he told a lie, is making a moral judgment about him? That is less clear. To borrow Foot's language, these do not seem to be evaluative terms; they do not seem to express disapproval. Certainly if I merely say Bloggs made a promise, I express no disapproval; and even though disapproval may well be in place where Bloggs broke a promise or lied, to say he broke a promise or lied does not seem to have already expressed that disapproval.

Nevertheless, it is arguable that Foot's concept 'rude' and all of Williams's sample thick ethical concepts (including 'promise' and 'lie') do have something important in common, a something in virtue of which they all yield counter-cases to The Fact-Value Thesis. What I have in mind is hinted at in the passage by Foot that I quoted above, and comes out as follows. It seems right to think that there are statements of fact about Alfred's current circumstances (as it might be: lecturer, scholarly meeting, serious faces all round, and so on) that entail

(1)   Alfred will be acting rudely if he shouts "Boo!"

(1) does not entail "Alfred ought not shout 'Boo!'," for, as Foot says, "there are occasions when a little rudeness is in place"; but it seems right to think that (1) entails

---

[8] Bernard Williams, *Ethics and the Limits of Philosophy* (Cambridge: Harvard University Press, 1985), pp. 129, 140.

(2)   Other things being equal, Alfred ought not shout "Boo!"

And isn't (2) a moral judgment? No doubt "Other things being equal, Alfred ought not shout 'Boo!'" is a weak moral judgment – weaker by far than "Alfred ought not shout 'Boo!'" All the same, if an author "proceeded for some time in the ordinary way of reasoning," telling us about what is in fact the case, and then suddenly said "So other things being equal, one ought not do such and such," should we not be as much struck by the appearance of a "new relation or affirmation" as Hume told us we should be if our author had suddenly said the stronger "So one ought not do such and such"? But if (2) is a moral judgment, then since (2) is entailed by (1) and (1) is entailed by a statement of fact, there are moral judgments that (by transitivity) are entailed by statements of fact, and The Fact-Value Thesis is false.

This little argument does not presuppose that (1) is itself a moral judgment: where one draws the line between fact and value does not matter to this argument – indeed, it is among the central points which those struck by the thick ethical concepts want to make by appeal to them precisely that there is a continuum between fact and value.

And a similar argument is constructable for each of Williams's sample thick ethical concepts, including 'promise' and 'lie'. It seems right to think that

(1′)   Bert promised to pay Smith five dollars

is entailed by some statements of fact. (1′) does not entail "Bert ought to pay Smith five dollars," for Bert might already have paid. Or Bert might not already have paid, but might desperately need the five dollars to buy food for his starving wife, child, dog, or cat. And so on. But it seems right to think that (1′) entails

(2′)   Other things being equal, Bert ought to pay Smith five dollars.[9]

No doubt (2′) is not as strong a moral judgment as "Bert ought to pay Smith five dollars," but (2′) surely is a moral judgment all the same. If so, then since (2′) is a moral judgment and is entailed by (1′), and (1′) is entailed by some statements of fact, there are moral judgments that (by transitivity) are entailed by statements of fact; and (we now have a second demonstration that) The Fact-Value Thesis is false. And this whether or not (1′) is, itself, a moral judgment.

What should we make of these arguments? Four things call for attention. In the first place, consider

(1″)   If Charles rings David's doorbell he will thereby cause David pain.

(Think of poor David as wired up to his own doorbell.) There really is no better reason to think (1) entails (2), and (1′) entails (2′), than there is to think (1″) entails

[9] Compare John Searle's route from fact to value in his "How to Derive 'Ought' From 'Is'," *Philosophical Review*, vol. 73 (1964), pp. 43–58. Searle begins with what is on any view a statement of fact, "Jones uttered the words 'I hereby promise to. . .'," and at the end arrives at what is on any view a moral judgment, "Jones ought to. . . ." He breaks the step from premise to conclusion into a series of sub-steps. It is certainly plausible to think that by the time we reach "Other things being equal, Jones ought. . . .," we have already reached a moral judgment.

I should say, however, that I do not here endorse Searle's *explanation* of what makes those sub-steps acceptable.

(2″)   Other things being equal, Charles ought not ring David's doorbell.

If (2) and (2′) are moral judgments, so surely is (2″). But (1″) is not merely entailed by some statement of fact, it is, on any view, *itself* a statement of fact. "Causes a person pain" is not a thick ethical concept, for surely it is not an ethical concept at all. Thus we need not have attended to the thick ethical concepts in order to find counter-cases to The Fact-Value Thesis:[10] counter-cases to that thesis lie ready to hand in considerably simpler moral considerations.

But second, if we are to take these ideas seriously, hadn't we better take a closer look at that phrase "other things being equal"? What role does it play in (2), (2′), and (2″)? People do very often use "other things being equal" in moral discourse, and such discourse would be the poorer if this phrase were not available to us. But what exactly do we mean by it?

It seems to me that there are two ways in which the phrase is used in moral discourse. One is epistemic and relatively weak. Take, for example, something rather more general than we have looked at so far:

(3″)   Other things being equal, one ought not cause others pain.

On the epistemic, relatively weak, way of using "other things being equal," (3″) means something like

> If one would cause a person pain by doing a thing, then there is reason to think one ought not do it

or, slightly stronger,

> The fact that one would cause a person pain by doing a thing is itself reason to think one ought not do it.

I say this is relatively weak since, while it reports an evidential connection, it leaves open what the source of that evidential connection is.

A second (and I think more common) way in which the phrase is used in moral discourse is metaphysical and relatively strong. On this second way of using it, (3″) means something that can be expressed as follows:

> "Causes a person pain" is a wrong-making feature of an act.

I say this is relatively strong since, while it entails the weaker reading, it in addition purports to point to the source of the evidential connection. I say only that it "purports" to do this, since we lack an account of what exactly it is for a feature of an act to be a wrong-making feature of it; but as I see it, that is not so much an objection to reading (3″) in this way as rather a philosophical problem to be solved.[11] I will bypass that problem here: I will suppose that what (3″) says is

---

[10] And the fact that the thick ethical concepts lend themselves to this kind of argument against The Fact-Value Thesis is not a fact about them by means of which they can be distinguished from concepts – such as 'causes a person pain' – which I take not to be ethical concepts at all, and *a fortiori* not to be thick ethical concepts.

[11] The notion at work here is presumably the obverse of Ross's 'prima facie duty'. (See W.D. Ross, *The Right and the Good* (Oxford: Clarendon Press, 1930) Nobody regards Ross as having made that notion satisfactorily clear; everyone, I think, has a sense of what notion it is that he was trying to make clear.

An act's being an instance of 'causes a person pain' is favorably relevant to its being wrongful,

leaving open how precisely that relevance is to be understood.

Let us turn back now to, for example,

(2″)   Other things being equal, Charles ought not ring David's doorbell.

I will suppose, analogously, that what that says is

There is something that actually is the case, that is favorably relevant to its being the case that Charles ought not ring David's doorbell.

But doesn't

(1″)   If Charles rings David's doorbell, he will thereby cause David pain

entail that? How *could* it be the case that if Charles rings David's doorbell he will cause David pain, but that nevertheless there is nothing at all that actually is the case that is favorably relevant to its being the case that Charles ought not ring David's doorbell?

Another way to put the point comes out as follows.

(3″)   Other things being equal, one ought not cause others pain

is surely true: an act's being an instance of 'causes a person pain' *is* favorably relevant to its being wrongful. An act's being an instance of 'causes a person pain' is not conclusive proof that it is wrongful, for surely it could be, and in some cases is, permissible to cause pain. (As, for example, where the victim will die if not caused pain, and prefers pain to death.) But that fact about an act is certainly favorably relevant to its being wrongful.

More strongly, (3″) is surely a necessary truth: it not merely is, but could not have failed to be, the case that an act's being an instance of 'causes a person pain' is favorably relevant to its being wrongful. Some people like to express such claims as follows: there is no possible world in which an act's being an instance of 'causes a person pain' is irrelevant to the question whether it is wrongful. (Perhaps you think of a possible world in which people like pain? I doubt that there can be such a world, in light of what pain is. If there is, then you are invited to replace "pain" by "excruciating pain" throughout. There certainly is no possible world in which people like excruciating pain. No doubt a person might on occasion welcome excruciating pain, for example, because he or she wants to do penance for past sins. But supplying oneself with some excruciating pain would not constitute doing penance if excruciating pain were not a pretty awful business – and thus if it were not the case that an act's being an instance of "causes a person excruciating pain" was favorably relevant to its being wrongful.)

But if (3″) is a necessary truth, then (1″) really does entail (2″). I do not say merely that if (3″) is a necessary truth, then the conjunction of (1″) with (3″) entails (2″); the conjunction of (1″) with (3″) entails (2″) whether or not (3″) is a necessary truth. What I say is that if (3″) is a necessary truth then (1″), by itself, entails (2″). But that is surely right. If (3″) is a necessary truth, then it really could not be the case that Charles would cause David pain by ringing his doorbell, though there is nothing at all the case that is favorably relevant to its being wrongful for Charles to do this.

Similarly for the arguments we looked at that involve thick ethical concepts. That Bert promised to pay Smith five dollars is favorably relevant to its being the case that he ought to do this, and could not have failed to be.

(3′)   Other things being equal, one ought to do what one promised

is not merely a truth, it could not have failed to be a truth. To promise is to bind, or commit, oneself to another to do a thing; how could the fact that you bound yourself to do a thing fail to be favorably relevant – merely favorably relevant! – to its being the case that you ought to do it? If so, then (1′) entails (2′). Again, that Alfred would be acting rudely if he shouted "Boo!" is favorably relevant to its being the case that he ought not do this, and could not have failed to be.

(3)   Other things being equal, one ought not act rudely

is not merely a truth; it could not have failed to be a truth. Rudeness is of less moral moment than causing pain and breach of promise, but it is not nothing, and could not have failed to be something. (We distort the content of morality if we think it concerns itself only with evils.) If so, then (1) entails (2).

It pays to remind ourselves here of the fact that skepticism about morality has two sources. One – I think it the more interesting one – issues from a concern about how morality can be thought to mesh with the world at all. That is the one I have been speaking to here. I have suggested that there are necessary connections between facts and weak moral judgments to the effect that there is something actually the case that is favorably relevant to the truth of a strong moral judgment to the effect that someone ought or ought not do a thing. That *is* a step forward if it is true. (For some obscure reason, people do not on the whole even ask whether it is true. There is a widespread view – indeed, it seems to be a view deeply lodged in us – that morality had better be simple, so that morality is suspect if we cannot go the whole way from facts to strong moral judgments in one step.) It *is* a step forward, since if there really are necessary connections between facts and weak moral judgments to the effect that there is something actually the case that is favorably relevant to the truth of a strong moral judgment to the effect that someone ought or ought not do a thing, then morality really does mesh with the world.

The second source of skepticism – I think it the less interesting one – issues from a concern about how strong moral conclusions to the effect that someone ought or ought not do a thing can be arrived at by the weighing of the various considerations that are favorably or unfavorably relevant to the truth of those strong moral conclusions. No doubt there is much that is of interest here. I say this is less interesting only because we are familiar from other areas of investigation with models of the weighing of considerations. That a thing looks like cheese is not conclusive proof that it is, but its looking like cheese is one consideration among others, such as what it tastes like, and how it affects the stomach, and so on, all of this having to be weighed in settling whether the stuff really is cheese.

I said earlier that four things called for attention. The first was that if arguments involving the thick ethical concepts yield counter-cases to The Fact-Value Thesis, so also do arguments involving concepts such as 'causes a person pain' that are not ethical concepts at all, and *a fortiori* are not thick ethical concepts. The second was that we needed an account of the role played by "other things being equal" in the sentences we have been looking at. The third is that once we take seriously the possibility that some statements of fact really do entail some moral judgments, we can surely find even simpler candidates than the ones we have been looking at: we not only need not have attended to the thick ethical concepts, we need not have restricted ourselves to weak moral judgments of the form "Other things being equal, one ought (or ought not) do such and such." Consider

(1‴)   Edward plans to torture a baby to death for fun.

Doesn't that entail

(2‴)   Edward ought not do what he plans to do?

(1‴) is a statement of fact, and (2‴) is not merely a moral judgment, it is – unlike (2), (2′), and (2″) – a strong moral judgment. But how *could* it fail to be the case that Edward will do something he ought not do if he proceeds to torture a baby to death for fun?

We might have put this point in another way. Consider

(3‴)   One ought not torture babies to death for fun.

Surely (3‴) is true. It is not merely true that, other things being equal, one ought not torture babies to death for fun; one just plain ought not do it – no matter what the circumstances. Indeed, (3‴) is surely a necessary truth. How on earth could it fail to be the case that a person who has tortured a baby to death for fun has acted impermissibly in doing so? Suppose we made the amazing discovery that torturing a baby to death for fun actually causes the crops to improve. (You are invited to invent the causal mechanism.) Would that incline us to think that perhaps we live in a world in which (3‴) is false? We would certainly not ignore this amazing discovery, but we would equally certainly not meet it by thinking we had been mistaken about the moral status of torturing babies to death for fun: we would instead try to figure out how to short-circuit the causal mechanism, so as to be able to obtain the same effect from a different cause. But, of course, if (3‴) is a necessary truth, then we can easily produce a very simple counter-case to The Fact-Value Thesis, for if (3‴) is a necessary truth, then (1‴) entails (2‴).

Overheated examples in ethics are tiresome (one feels one's lapels are being clutched), and I apologize for this one. Still, if what is wanted are places at which morality meshes with the world, then melodrama is useful: it supplies places at which facts mesh directly with strong moral judgments to the effect that a person ought or ought not do a thing.

The fourth and last thing I wished to call attention to comes out as follows. I have suggested that (1), (1′), (1″), and (1‴) entail (2), (2′), (2″), and (2‴). Saying so comes to the same as saying that certain rather more general statements, such as

    (3″)   Other things being equal, one ought not cause others pain

and

    (3‴)   One ought not torture babies to death for fun,

are necessary truths, and I have suggested that these *are* necessary truths – I have suggested that they not only are true but could not have failed to be. But people who take a certain view of what makes a truth be a necessary truth are sure to find this objectionable. The view I have in mind is that a statement is a necessary truth if and only if it is "analytic": roughly, true by virtue of the meanings of the words used to make it. For suppose that view is correct. Then necessary truths must surely be trivial. But how could a triviality license a step from facts to value, that being a step which is surely anything but trivial?

Again, the likes of (3″) and (3‴) certainly appear to be, themselves, moral judgments. But a moral judgment is not a triviality. How then can it be a necessary truth?[12]

What we should think of the view that a statement is a necessary truth if and only if it is analytic is a larger issue than I can deal properly with here, and probably a larger issue than I am competent to deal properly with anywhere. But some things do seem to be clear. Perhaps a statement S is a necessary truth if and only if *in some sense* it is true by virtue of the meanings of the words used to make it; but that leaves open that S cannot be certified as a truth by looking in a dictionary, and that S is decidedly non-trivial. "All bachelors are unmarried" can be certified as a truth by appeal to a dictionary, and is trivial. So presumably also for "Whatever is red is colored." But this is not so of any of the candidate necessary truths that are of interest to philosophers. Kripke argues, very convincingly, that a great many statements one might not have thought necessary truths – such as "Water is H_2O," "Gold is the element with atomic number 79," and "The table in my attic was made out of a chunk of wood" [the table in my attic was in fact made out of a chunk of wood] – really are necessary truths, and one certainly cannot conclude that he is mistaken on the ground that they are not trivial and were not certified as truths by appeal to a dictionary.[13]

In any case, the fourth and last thing I wished to call attention to is that in agreeing that the sample arguments we looked at really are counter–cases to The Fact-Value Thesis, I am also committing myself to the view that there are necessary truths that are non-trivial – the likes of (3″) and (3‴), for example. Since it seems to me that the likes of (3″) and (3‴) are moral judgments, I am also

---

[12] Compare R.M. Hare: "it might be said that a principle of conduct was impossible to reject, if it were *self-contradictory* to reject it. But if it is self-contradictory to reject a principle, this can only be because the principle is analytic. But if it is analytic, it cannot have any content; it cannot tell me to do one thing rather than another." *The Language of Morals* (New York: Oxford University Press, 1965), p. 41.

[13] See Saul A. Kripke, *Naming and Necessity* (Cambridge: Harvard University Press, 1980).

committing myself to the view that there are moral judgments that are non-trivial necessary truths.[14] But these things seem to me to be right.

IV

We certainly act as if we thought of many of our moral beliefs as necessary truths; we often respond to moral proposals as if they were intended to have the status of necessary truths, and think ourselves entitled to reject them when they do not. When I put

(3‴) One ought not torture babies to death for fun

to my students (who are rightly suspicious of moralizing), they do not ask me whether I have examined all actual past instances of people who tortured babies to death for fun; what they do is to try to invent a possible scenario, an imaginary, even a contra-causal scenario, in which someone tortured a baby to death for fun and yet was not acting wrongly in doing so. When (to provoke discussion) I tell my students that lying is wrong, they tell me I am mistaken; but no one feels a need to draw my attention to an instance of non-wrongful lying last week in New Jersey – they feel it enough to refute me if they can invent a possible instance of non-wrongful lying. As of course they can.

That is not true of our attitudes towards all of our moral beliefs, and it is not true of our responses to just any moral proposal. If I were to put the following moral judgment to my students

Bloggs acted wrongly this morning

they would not invent scenarios in which Bloggs did not act wrongly this morning. They would rightly view me as having made an assertion that rests heavily on the truth of an array of suppositions of fact – facts, in particular, about what Bloggs did this morning – and they would ask what those facts are.

Similarly for some moral judgments that are markedly more general than "Bloggs acted wrongly this morning." I might think, and therefore tell my students, that engaging in a certain activity K is morally quite all right, and I am not moved to give up that view by invented scenarios – I am moved to give up that view only

---

[14] I should think it could be said, not merely that (3) through (3‴) are moral judgments that are non-trivial necessary truths, but also that it is not at all clear how their negations could be accommodated into what would be recognizable as a moral code.

In passing, that there are moral judgments that are non-trivial necessary truths is arguably something that Hume would have denied. As I said in note 2 above, it is surely plain that Hume was not, in the well-known passage I quoted, drawing our attention merely to the fact that "ought" is not obtainable from "is" within (as it might be) first-order logic; it is arguable that he would have denied that there is *any* necessary connection between "ought" and "is." Hume went on to say:

> But as authors do not commonly use this precaution, I shall presume to recommend it to the readers; and am persuaded, that this small attention wou'd subvert all the vulgar systems of morality, and let us see, that the distinction of vice and virtue is not founded merely on the relations of objects, nor is perceiv'd by reason. (*Treatise*, pp. 469–70)

Statements whose truth is "perceiv'd by reason" are statements whose truth (if they are true) we can come to know of *a priori*, and – following Kripke (in *Naming and Necessity*) – we nowadays distinguish between the *a priori* and the necessary. But it is arguable that Hume did not.

when a student brings home to me that as a matter of fact engaging in K causes harm, a fact I had not been aware of.

Moreover, some moral judgments are given a different status by different people. We took note earlier of the fact that a person, say Bloggs, might believe that capital punishment is permissible because of its being (as he thinks) a more effective deterrent than long prison terms, and would give up that moral belief if he were convinced that this is not so. We might put it that Bloggs gives his moral belief that capital punishment is permissible the status of a contingent truth.

As we also imagined, however, B believes capital punishment permissible on quite different grounds: *he* believes on the one hand that those who commit particularly despicable crimes deserve the death penalty, and on the other hand that the community which does not impose that penalty fails to display respect for the victims of those crimes and also fails to display an appropriately strong commitment to its own moral beliefs. Shall we say that B gives his moral belief that capital punishment is permissible the status of a necessary truth? Well, it depends. We need to hear more about B before we can say that about him. For example, would he give up his belief about capital punishment if he became convinced that people do not react to a failure to impose that penalty in the way in which he takes them to react?

It pays to take note of this possibility because it reminds us that the bearing of facts on moral beliefs may be relatively indirect. As we know, some people believe capital punishment permissible because they believe it a more effective deterrent than long prison terms; in their case, there is a question of fact – about deterrence – that has an immediate and direct bearing on their moral belief about capital punishment. But a question of fact might have a less direct bearing on a person's moral belief about capital punishment. If B would give up his moral belief if he were convinced that attitudes towards capital punishment are not what he takes them to be, then there is a question of fact – about attitudes – that has a bearing on his moral belief about capital punishment, but only via its having a bearing on his moral beliefs about what communities ought to do to display an appropriately strong commitment to their own moral beliefs.

And it pays to be reminded of this, because what it issues from is very important indeed: namely, that moral judgments do not face the facts one by one. What each of us confronts the world of facts with is a battery of interconnected moral beliefs. It is because of this that a discovery of fact may bear on a moral belief indirectly, by virtue of bearing on another, linked, moral belief. We will come back to this in the following section.

On the other hand, it might be that B would not give up his belief about capital punishment if he became convinced that people do not react to a failure to impose that penalty in the way in which he takes them to react – it might be that he would reply that this just shows people do not react as they ought to react. And it might be, more generally, that he neither is nor would be moved by any discovery of fact. Then he does give his moral belief that capital punishment is permissible the status of a necessary truth. In this respect he differs from Bloggs, who gives his the status of a contingent truth.

From the point of view of the question whether capital punishment is permissible, of course, it makes no difference whether Bloggs or B or anyone else gives his or her moral belief about it the status of a necessary truth. That one or the other side in disputes about capital punishment do give their moral belief about it this status does not show that they are right to do so. It does not even show that their belief is true, and *a fortiori* does not show that their belief is a necessary truth.

How *is* it to be decided which view on this matter is true?

V

Is capital punishment permissible? To ask that question is to be asking what we should believe.

Some people think capital punishment is permissible if and only if it is a more efficient deterrent than a life sentence. This raises two questions. Is capital punishment a more efficient deterrent than a life sentence? That is a question of fact. It has turned out to be a peculiarly difficult question to answer, but it is not of interest for our purposes. The second question is markedly more interesting. Is capital punishment permissible if and only if it is a more efficient deterrent than a life sentence? That is a moral question.

We know that many people would say no in answer to this moral question. Here is B, for example. B would say that it does not matter whether capital punishment does (or does not) deter more efficiently than a life sentence. How so? B would reply that those who commit particularly despicable crimes deserve the death penalty, whether or not they would have been (and whether or not anyone else would be) deterred by the prospect of its imposition on them. And he would add that the community which does not impose that penalty fails to display respect for the victims of those despicable crimes and also fails to display an appropriately strong commitment to its own moral beliefs.

A, we know, would reject this. A, we imagined, believes capital punishment impermissible on the ground that a community (like an individual) must never intentionally kill a person who is in captivity, and who thus currently constitutes no threat to others, and who can be kept from constituting a threat to others by less drastic means than killing him. So A would say that B is right to think that it does not matter whether capital punishment does (or does not) deter more efficiently than a life sentence, but he would argue that B's reasons for believing that capital punishment is permissible are not good reasons, or, anyway, are not good enough reasons for believing it permissible.

Should we agree with A? Should we instead agree with B? Or should we instead think that the question whether capital punishment is permissible *is* settled by the answer to the question how efficiently it deters and thus think that maybe A is right that capital punishment is impermissible, maybe B is right that capital punishment is permissible, but that both are mistaken in the reasons they have for thinking this? And there are other possibilities for us too.

For my own part, I agree with A and B that the question whether capital punishment is permissible is not settled by the answer to the question how efficiently it deters, but I am on the fence about their reasons for the conclusions they draw. One thing that is plain, however, is that whether we are on the fence or off it, we have a pretty good idea how both A and B would argue if they came to argument with each other. I said earlier that it was plausible to think that the dispute between them is a purely moral dispute;[15] but to have reached a point at which it has become clear that a dispute between two people is a purely moral dispute is by no means to have arrived at a point after which there is nothing more to be done. I also said earlier that the disputes about capital punishment are particularly well-suited to the purposes of one who wishes to convince us of the truth of The Fact-Value Thesis and The No Reason Thesis. But there is one way in which they are ill-suited to those purposes, for purely moral disputes about capital punishment are disputes in which there is a considerable amount of room for good and bad reasoning *inside morality itself*.

A, for example, is likely to zero in on that concept 'desert', and try to bring out that B's views about it are incoherent. He is also likely to accuse B of condoning a state's using people as means by which to express its attitudes. And so on. B is likely to respond that there is no more incoherence in the idea of deserving death than there is in the idea of deserving a term in jail, and ask why imposing a term in jail is any the less a use of a person. And so on. What the parties to a purely moral dispute do is to search for common moral ground, that is, for something which is in both their 'moral codes', which can be brought to bear on the issue in hand to settle it. The options here are vastly richer than one might think from an examination of the arguments for The No Reason Thesis.

Let me first bring out what I mean by a person's moral code. Each of us who has grown to the status of adult has a battery of moral beliefs, many of them more or less loosely stitched together by non-moral beliefs. For example, most of us, I should think, believe that it is, other things being equal, wrong to break promises, lie, cheat, cause harm, and so on. We might (or might not) in addition have the non-moral belief that lying very often causes harm, and we might (or might not) therefore have the further moral belief that, when lying is wrong, it is wrong because it causes harm. For another example, we might have the non-moral belief that Bloggs kicked his little brother for fun this morning, and we might therefore have the further moral belief that Bloggs did something he ought not have done this morning. But I suspect that no one's moral beliefs are more than *very* loosely stitched together in the ways I point to here.

A person (it might be Bloggs) knows that he believes $P_1, P_2, \ldots$, for a great many statements P; indefinitely many further statements follow from them, and in the case of a great many of them, say $Q_1, Q_2, \ldots$, Bloggs does not know that they follow from $P_1, P_2, \ldots$ Should we choose to say that what Bloggs believes includes all and only those statements Bloggs knows he believes? Or should we instead choose to say that what Bloggs believes includes also all those statements that follow

---

[15] I said this because I am inclined to think it rare that disputants on this issue disagree because they disagree about whether human acts have causes. If a pair of disputants on this issue do disagree because they disagree about whether human acts have causes, then while their dispute is presumably not settleable by appeal to evidence about human acts (or anything else), the dispute between them is not purely moral. But it is, I think, far more common for disputants about capital punishment to agree that acts have causes, and to disagree only about the moral significance to be attached to that fact.

from the statements Bloggs knows he believes? This is a matter for choice: there is no theoretically interesting ground for choosing one way or the other. Let us make the former choice: that is, let us so use "believes" that what Bloggs believes includes all and only those statements he knows he believes. So, for example, if Bloggs knows he believes that he has no sisters or half-sisters, and that his first cousins are all doctors, and that Alice is a daughter of his paternal grandmother's only daughter, then all the same it remains an open question whether Bloggs believes that Alice is a doctor. For while that follows from what he knows he believes, he could simply have failed to notice that it does, and we are so using "belief" that if Bloggs does not know he believes that Alice is a doctor, then he does not believe that she is.

How could Bloggs have failed to draw the conclusion that Alice is a doctor? There is a range of phenomena we might call "failing to connect."[16] One species of it is failing to notice that statements one knows one believes commit one to the truth of others. This is very common when the deduction is complex, as where proving the conclusion from the premises would be difficult. (It really does take a minute or two to see that what Bloggs knows he believes does commit him to Alice's being a doctor.) But it is also common where the deduction is simple but one has strong motives for failing to draw the conclusion, and we might in such cases speak not merely of failing to connect, but of positive "walling-off." A man might, for example, know he believes that blacks are human beings, possessed of all such rights as are possessed by human beings, but refuse (typically unconsciously) to draw the conclusion that certain discriminatory practices he himself engages in are impermissible. The more profitable it is to a man that he keep certain of his beliefs walled-off from the conclusions that follow from them (if only to avoid internal discomfort), the harder it is to get him to see that that is what he is doing.

A second species of failing to connect is failing to notice the possibility that statements one knows one believes have something in common. Three subspecies are familiar to all of us. First, Bloggs might know he believes that one ought not eat bananas, and that one ought not eat apples, and that one ought not eat pears, and he might also know he believes that these are kinds of fruit, but never have asked himself whether the prohibition extends to all kinds of fruit. This would be failure to notice the possibility of generalizing. Again, second, Bloggs might know he believes that one ought not torture babies, and that one ought not torture little children, and that one ought not torture the mentally retarded, but never have asked himself whether that is because one ought not torture the innocent. This would be failure to notice the possibility of explaining. Third, Bloggs might know he believes that he owes Jones five dollars, and know he believes that he ought to pay Jones the five dollars, but not have asked himself whether owing someone something just is its being the case that one ought to supply it. This would be failure to notice the possibility of simplifying. These three subspecies obviously overlap, for some generalizations explain, and some explanations simplify. And here, too, there might be positive walling-off: a failure to generalize, explain, or simplify – like a failure to draw conclusions – might be motivated.

---

[16] The term comes, of course, from E.M. Forster's *Howard's End* (Harmondsworth: Penguin Books, 1941).

Underlying this entire range of phenomena is something deeper, which we might call simply "failing to attend." There are many things we know we believe that we just are not constantly attending to. Now that I think on the matter, I am aware that I have a great many beliefs about theft, but I am not canvassing them now. Indeed, five minutes ago I was not conscious of having any at all, since it did not occur to me to think about theft then. That could hardly be thought of as a failure on my part, since I did not then have, and do not now have, the slightest need to be clear on what I think about theft. What is of great interest, however, is that this can happen even when I do need to be clear on what I think about theft, as where I am asked to say what I think about it: one can, for one or another reason, simply fail to attend to things one really knows one believes. A given instance of failing to connect may be due to mere lack of intelligence or imagination; most instances of failing to connect are probably due to failing to attend.

My examples of failing to connect have included failing to draw a moral conclusion, failing to connect one moral belief with another, and failing to connect a moral belief with a non-moral belief. Let us refer to the totality of a person's moral beliefs as that person's "moral code." We may fail to connect within our moral code; we may also fail to connect across the boundary of our moral code.

Now as I said, what the parties to a purely moral dispute try to do is to search for common moral ground – that is, for something which is in both their moral codes – which can be brought to bear on the issue in hand to settle it. That means that what X tries to do is to convict Y of failing to connect, either within Y's own moral code, or across its boundary. It is because there is the possibility of success in doing this that one side can surprise the other, and that one side can learn from the other, even if discovery of fact is not in question. Moreover, it is because there is the possibility of success in doing this that one side can be convinced by the other, and that moral arguments can be settled.

It must of course be granted that if one of the parties, X, does succeed in demonstrating that the other party, Y, did fail to connect, either within or across the boundary of Y's moral code, that would not show that any particular given belief of Y's is false: it would show only that Y's totality of beliefs as a whole is defective. What it will strike Y as right to revise in his or her beliefs would remain to be seen – it will turn on such matters as the relative weights Y had attached, or now thinks it right to attach, to his different beliefs. And if X is not satisfied with the revision offered by Y, it would be up to X to begin the process all over again.

VI

It is largely because there is such a thing as failing to connect that there is such a thing as moral progress.

People's views about capital punishment, for example, have changed over several generations. There was a time (not really all that long ago) at which it was widely thought appropriate to attach the death penalty to what we now regard as relatively minor crimes, such as petty theft, and at which it was widely thought appropriate for the criminal to be executed in public. Even those who favor capital punishment nowadays do not favor attaching the death penalty to theft, and do not favor public executions.[17]

No doubt these changes have a complex variety of sources. Among them, however, are surely these: an increase in the value placed on a human life, and of the respect due to it. But these are nothing new. Such changes can easily be seen as a product of the recognition that there had been a failure to connect.

I said only "largely," however, since truly dramatic changes in moral beliefs across generations probably issue from matters of fact as well as from recognition that there had been a failure to connect. I have in mind here changes in the facts themselves as well as changes that consist in discoveries of fact – as, for example, where resources expand, or where technology makes new activities possible. A dramatic change, however, is not one that consists in replacement of an old code by an entirely new one. (How is 'an entirely new moral code' supposed to differ from an old one? How would we recognize that it is a moral code? What could possibly make us think it true?) A dramatic change in moral beliefs is one that involves a major reorganization in moral thinking, which may involve an expanding or a shrinking or both, but which finds its justification in parts of the moral thinking that preceded it.

It will be noticed that I said only "changes" in moral beliefs across generations: I did not say "progress." There is no a priori reason why such changes should be for the better. Consider, for example, a tribe whose moral code consists in the belief that one ought to do whatever the gods enjoin, together with such consequences as they believe follow from that, in light of their beliefs about what in fact the gods do enjoin. We now convince them that as a matter of fact, there are no gods. This will provoke a deep change in their moral code, but there are any number of possibilities. For example, they might retain some of their moral beliefs – as, for example, that one ought not eat bananas – while either retaining them as mere clutter, or supplying some new common source(s) for them. Or again, they might take the view that morality permits everything. Indeed, they might not undergo a change in moral code, for they might instead reject morality altogether. We might plausibly view some of these possible changes as progress, but not just any.

What then does mark a change as progress? Whatever marks such change in an individual as progress. Suppose, for example, that B were convinced by A that B should give up his belief that capital punishment is permissible. Would that be progress in B? To ask this is to ask whether B should make this shift. And to ask that is to ask for the kind of discussion I described in the preceding section.

VII

And a discussion of that kind may end in stalemate. Sometimes it ends in stalemate for an entirely uninteresting reason: that is, one of the parties demonstrates that the other really is misrepresenting the facts or is failing to connect, but the other party cannot be got to see this. Sometimes the discussion

---

[17] Nor do they favor execution by ghastly means. But that, I fancy, is due more to a change in conception of how much pain and humiliation may be caused in the name of a public purpose than to a change in conception of what warrants killing.

ends in stalemate for a more interesting reason: that is, neither party is able to demonstrate that the other is misrepresenting the facts or is failing to connect. Are there moral disputes in which the discussion ends in stalemate for the most interesting reason? – that is, not only can neither of the parties demonstrate one of these failings in the other, but there is no such failing in either? This seems to be a real possibility. The dispute between A and B about capital punishment may itself be an example of which this is true. In light of the history of moral beliefs about capital punishment – that is, in light of the direction of the changes in moral belief about it that have taken place over time – I think this exceedingly unlikely to be the case, but it might be.

Very well, suppose it is. What does that show? We would have to grant that there are (at least) two moral codes, one containing that capital punishment is permissible, the other that it is not, such that there really is no more reason to prefer one than there is to prefer the other.

But that does not for a moment show that there is something suspect about morality generally. In particular, it does not lend support to The No Reason Thesis or even to The Fact-Value Thesis. That there are equally well supported moral codes (if there are) does not show that there is no reason to believe about any given moral judgment that it is true. For some moral judgments could not have been false, and others flow from them in complex ways that we learn of when we recognize that we had been failing to connect.

VIII

The method of argument that consists in an attempt to get another person either to represent the facts correctly or to connect in ways he or she had been failing to connect in, or both, is the method we all use in ordinary life when we try to convince others of the truth of our moral beliefs. Moral theorists[18] use the very same method[19] when trying to convince readers of the truth of their moral theories.

Moral theorists differ from participants in moral dispute in ordinary life in three ways, and the first of them is merely a matter of degree, lying in the fact that a theorist's theory is a more general moral judgment than is the judgment typically at issue in dispute in ordinary life.

The second difference lies in the overall direction in which the argument proceeds. The theorist defends his or her theory by showing that it explains a body of less general moral judgments, the participant in ordinary moral dispute defends his or her moral judgment by showing that it can be explained by a body of more general moral judgments. But there is in both cases backing and filling – moving from more to less general and back again to more general – along the way.

The third difference lies in the difference in their aims, and *therefore* in what anchors the process: what is taken as a datum. The participants in ordinary dispute

---

[18] I should perhaps say explicitly that the people I have in mind by "moral theorists" do not include those who are primarily interested in moral epistemology or moral metaphysics.

[19] The method I described is very like the process Rawls describes as the effort to reach "reflective equilibrium," with this proviso: on Rawls's account of the matter, everything is provisional, everything is open to revision, whereas I am suggesting that some moral judgments are necessary truths, and hence not open to revision. See *A Theory of Justice* (Cambridge: Harvard University Press, 1971) pp. 20, 48–51.

typically aim only at convincing each other, and are therefore typically content to take as data what is in fact agreed between them, even if they are aware that what is in fact agreed between them might well be rejected by third parties. Theorists aim at convincing the universe, and therefore try to be sure that what they take as data would be accepted by all – indeed for preference, what cannot be imagined false. It is most unlikely that a very general moral theory – one that tries to answer all moral questions – could be defended only by appeal to such data. (How, for example, is the theory's stand on capital punishment to be defended?) But there is no reason why a theory could not be more modest, taking no stand on (or taking a stand on, while explicitly leaving open for the universe to disagree on) what cannot be defended in that way. The extent of what can be defended in that way may be surprisingly large, however, since connecting is a creative enterprise whose results can greatly surprise us.[20]

Philosophy, Massachusetts Institute of Technology

[20] I am grateful to the other contributors to this volume for helpful criticism. I owe thanks also to Jonathan Bennett, David Brink, Derek Parfit, and Warren Quinn, who made helpful criticisms of earlier versions.

THE NATURE OF IMMORALITY

By Jean Hampton

This article is concerned with the nature of individual moral failure. This has not been a standard issue for exploration in moral philosophy, where questions surrounding moral success have been more popular: in particular, the questions "What is it to do the moral thing (i.e., how do I identify moral success)?" and "Why am I supposed to do the moral thing (i.e., what is morality's authority)?" I want to change the subject and pursue answers to three importantly related questions about people's failure to be moral.

First, I want to explore an issue in moral psychology: why do people behave immorally? I suspect this question has been largely ignored by philosophers because they have thought it a question for psychologists, and one that, at any rate, has an easy surface answer. Isn't it our immorality simply the result of our excessive self-interest? Yet we shall see in what follows that this answer is not nearly good enough, and that philosophers have a lot to contribute in determining what would *count* as a satisfactory answer. We shall also see that different meta-ethical theories purporting to explain the authority of moral action implicitly assume different and often mutually inconsistent accounts of why (and when) we fail to be moral, and our analysis will show that none of these accounts of moral failure is unproblematic.

Second, I am interested in a conceptual question, namely: "What is it for someone to be culpable for a moral wrongdoing?" It is not enough to answer this question by arguing for a theory (such as utilitarianism or contractarianism) which purports to identify morally wrong actions. Consider that a man-eating tiger can't be guilty of murder; a one-year-old who takes a piece of candy from a store isn't guilty of theft. Killing a human being or taking someone else's property only count as moral wrongs if they are performed by human beings over a certain age, and even then only when those human beings perform them in certain mental states. For example, they aren't wrongs if the person did them "by accident," or out of ignorance, or to avoid a greater moral harm. So there must be something about the way an agent is related to the harmful action he performs which makes him culpable for it. It is that relationship which I want to explore here. What must be true about the agent who performs one of these acts in order for that act to be a moral wrong for which the agent is culpable – such that he has, to use legal terminology, a *mens rea* or "guilty mind" regarding that act?

The first and second questions are related. Theories of moral failure, which attempt to answer the first question by offering an explanation of why moral failure occurs, offer an account of the agent's state of mind when he commits a crime. We shall see that some theories of moral failure which seem initially plausible will turn out to present an account of the wrongdoer's state of mind which we normally believe excuses someone from wrongdoing. One of the challenges of explaining immorality will be to arrive at an explanation of the reason behind moral failure which does not end up by dissolving the phenomenon to be explained.

Finally, I want to pursue a third question: what does it mean to say of someone that she has a "bad" or "immoral" or "evil" character? That a person commits immoral actions is not a sufficient condition for classifying *her* as immoral. Indeed, committing immoral acts might not even be a necessary condition for having an immoral character. So what are the necessary and sufficient conditions? And what is behind our judgment that immoral characters come in different degrees?

Again, we shall see that this third question is connected to the first question. A satisfactory theory of moral psychology must not only explain what happens when a person commits any single immoral act, but must also explain why certain human beings are persistently disposed to perform such acts, and also why some are disposed to perform particularly evil acts. Hence, implicit in that theory is an account of what immoral characters are, an account which, on inspection, may prove considerably less plausible than the original theory's explanation of single immoral acts.

My aim in this paper is neither to defend nor to attack the notion of immorality (although I myself have great allegiance to it), but rather to explicate the notion as it functions in our everyday judgments and practices. Some may value the explication as a clarification of what it is they wish to revise or reject; others (myself included) will see it as an analysis that aims to expose the bare bones of an idea critical to our moral life.

I. The Things That Are Said about Immorality

I begin by considering the second and third questions, and I will do so by trying to get straight our intuitions about culpability and immoral character. These intuitions are neither unassailable nor beyond revision, but they are a good place to begin our discussion. As a way of presenting them, I want to ask, in Aristotelian fashion, what sorts of things are typically said about people who are judged culpable for a wrongdoing, or who are themselves judged as immoral, vicious, or evil.

1. We say of a person who performs an immoral act that he did it voluntarily and can be held responsible for it: in a word, that he performed it "freely." These concepts are certainly not clear, but at the very least a voluntary and responsible action is held to be one that does not fall completely under an excusing condition. It was not, for example, done because of ignorance, or under duress, or because of some kind of reasonable mistake. Nor was it something done out of some kind of inner compulsion (e.g., an insane or epileptic action). It is frequently said that in order to distinguish a person culpable for her crimes from a kleptomaniac or an epileptic, one needs to be able to say of her that she "could have done otherwise."

2. A judgment of someone as having committed a moral wrong involves holding her "culpable" or "at fault," *blaming* as opposed to praising her. These judgments go along with what Strawson has called certain "reactive attitudes" towards the person, e.g., resenting her, being morally indignant at her action, or even hating (as opposed to loving) her.

3. We say that a person who committed a moral wrong "deserves" at the very least censure, and perhaps punishment, for her action, whereas we think the kleptomaniac should receive therapy and the physically diseased person medical treatment.

4. A judgment of oneself as culpable involves having certain reactive attitudes towards oneself and one's deeds, e.g., "faulting" oneself and feeling shame and guilt, as opposed to pride and moral satisfaction.

5. We believe of someone who has done something immoral that she not only could have but *should* have done otherwise.

6. We think some immoral actions result after a moral conflict, perhaps difficult and painful, manifesting the wrongdoer's "weak will."

7. We generally say that people are immoral because they are "selfish."

8. We blame and hold culpable – we resent or feel angry at – an individual *self.* As Nagel puts it, "When we blame someone for his actions we are not merely saying it is bad they happened, or bad that he exists: we are judging *him*, saying he is bad, which is different from his being a bad thing. This kind of judgment takes only a certain kind of object. Without being able to explain exactly why, we feel that the appropriateness of moral assessment is easily undermined by the discovery that the act or attribute, no matter how good or bad, is not under the person's control."[1] The importance of personal control in moral assessment is connected with our view that external and internal compulsions excuse, for we feel that when they determine the action, the person does not. And this seems to be because, as Nagel notes, the self which we judge is not something which can survive

> absorption into the class of events. Moral judgment of a person is judgment not of what happens to him, but of him. It does not say merely that a certain event or state of affairs is fortunate or unfortunate or even terrible. It is not an evaluation of a state of the world, or of an individual as part of the world. We are not thinking just that it would be better if he were different, or did not exist, or had not done some of the things he has done. We are judging *him*, rather than his existence or characteristics. The effect of concentrating on the influence of what is not under his control is to make this responsible self seem to disappear, swallowed up by the mere order of events.[2]

Yet what this self is and how it stands out from the class of events, is very unclear.

9. Finally, a person's performance of a single culpable act isn't enough to justify calling him 'immoral' or 'vicious' or 'evil'. Nor are these labels straightforwardly linked simply to the *number* of immoral acts a person commits. Instead they are linked with a perceived *disposition* to perform such acts, a disposition which betrays some kind of commitment to them. And the more immoral the actions, the worse the disposition in our eyes (and the more thorough the commitment to immorality seems).

[1] Thomas Nagel, "Moral Luck," in *Free Will*, ed. Gary Watson (Oxford: Clarendon Press, 1982), pp. 174–75.
[2] *ibid.*, p. 184.

These linguistic practices, beliefs, and emotions surrounding moral failure need conceptual underpinning and perhaps even revision. I will now discuss different theories of why we are immoral which, as we shall see, generate different conceptions of the nature of culpable wrongdoing and immoral character.

II. THE IGNORANCE AND INDIFFERENCE EXPLANATIONS

Theories of why people act immorally are importantly connected to theories purporting to explain why people *should* act morally. In her "Morality as a System of Hypothetical Imperatives,"[3] Philippa Foot presents the two major competing explanations of moral authority. One explanation regards a moral imperative as authoritative insofar as it is hypothetical: the reason we should act as the imperative dictates is that the action will further some interest or objective we (supposedly) have. The other explanation regards a moral imperative as authoritative insofar as it is categorical: it presents an action as necessary of itself, without regard to any other end. But as Foot discusses, the nature of the "inescapability" supposedly associated with categorical moral imperatives is terribly obscure. Kantian proponents of this view of moral authority insist that the imperative commands us whatever our interests or desires – indeed, that the imperative itself gives us a reason for acting. But none of this seems to make good sense; the Kantians, says Foot, may simply be giving moral imperatives a kind of "magic force,"[4] and the inescapability which these imperatives are supposed to have may be "merely the reflection of the way morality is taught,"[5] or perhaps, as Anscombe contends, only a psychological remnant of a (largely) abandoned divine law conception of morality.[6]

A singular virtue of the hypothetical imperative account of moral authority is that it does make sense. We understand how moral imperatives give us a reason for acting if those imperatives are supposed to be hypothetical. But how adequate is the conception of moral failure linked to this explanation of moral authority? Consider: if moral actions ought to be performed insofar as they further a particular interest or goal, then it is natural to say that people must fail to act morally either because they are *ignorant* of this means-end connection or because they *desire some other end* which dictates the performance of a different, immoral action. And on this view, we would have to analyze a person with a "bad" character in one of two ways: either as one who is consistently disposed to act badly because he is woefully ignorant of what is in his best interest, or else as one who is consistently disposed to act badly because he desires a goal which requires him to undertake bad actions on many occasions. Do either of these conceptions of the reason for immoral behavior provide an acceptable analysis of culpable wrongdoing and/or immoral human character?

Let us start with the *ignorance explanation*. There are two ways in which someone might be morally ignorant of the means-end connection between the virtues and

---

[3] Reprinted in Foot's *Virtues and Vices* (Berkeley: University of California Press, 1978), pp. 151–73.
[4] *ibid.*, p. 167.
[5] *ibid.*, p. 162.
[6] G.E.M. Anscombe, "Modern Moral Philosophy," in *Collected Works, Volume III: Ethics, Religion and Politics* (Minneapolis: University of Minnesota Press, 1981), p. 30.

what he has done. He can be ignorant of the fact that the virtues will realize the end
he desires, or he can be ignorant about what it is that he desires, mistakenly
identifying it as an object to which the vices rather than the virtues are appropriate
means. Socrates, who was attracted to the ignorance explanation of moral failure,
appears to think immoral people generally suffer from the second form of
ignorance. He claims in the *Protagoras* that "it is from defect of knowledge that men
err, when they do err, in their choice of pleasures and pains – that is, in their choice
of good and evil."[7] Likewise, in the *Meno* he insists that, "Obviously those who are
ignorant of the evil do not desire it, but only what they supposed to be good, though
it is really evil; so that those who are ignorant of it and think it good are really
desiring the good."[8] There is much to recommend this Socratic perspective, for
when we look at a person whom we call immoral or wicked, we generally see a
wretched and unhappy human being. Consider a man who rapes a woman in order
to achieve a sense of mastery over the world, or consider a woman who refuses to
admit she is an alcoholic and who drives home drunk every evening from her local
bar: such people, we say, "don't know how to live." *We* see the destruction which
their evil pursuits are bringing both on others and on themselves, but *they* don't see
or adequately appreciate either the disintegration of their own lives or the pain and
damage which they inflict on others. Hence it is natural to think of them as being in
error about what their good is. Perhaps this Socratic attitude towards wrongdoers
was recommended by Christ on the cross when he said of the people who were
unjustly executing him, "Lord, forgive them, for they know not what they do."

But the ignorance explanation is discordant with many of our intuitions about
immorality. For example, it is normally the case that people ignorant of how to do
something they very much want to do welcome instruction from someone more
knowledgeable. So it would seem that if wrongdoers acted immorally only because
they were ignorant of what they truly wanted (or of how to get it), they too would
welcome such moral instruction – even solicit it. Yet we know that, more than
likely, they will resist any advice or instruction offered, treating our moral
instruction with derision. What does that resistance mean? Socrates himself
implicitly recognized its existence when he argued that the education of the
wrongdoer had to involve punishment, which generally involves the infliction of
pain. That is a peculiar educational technique, and the fact that he would perceive
it as necessary suggests that he knew there was more needed to acount for
wrongdoing than mere ignorance, and that force was needed to, in some sense,
break down a certain kind of rebellion in the wrongdoer.

The ignorance explanation also fails to explain the kind of reactive attitudes we
have towards ourselves when we wrong others. Why should someone who has
harmed another out of ignorance of what is right (in either of the two senses we
defined) feel ashamed or guilty about what he has done? While some people do feel
guilty about harmful actions performed out of ignorance, we feel their guilt is
inappropriate. ("It's not your fault," we say, "you didn't know what you were

---

[7] Plato, *Protagoras*, 357d–e; trans. W.R.M. Lamb (Cambridge: Harvard University Press, 1924), p. 243.
[8] Plato, *Meno*, 77e; trans. W.R.M. Lamb (Cambridge: Harvard University Press, 1924), p. 289.

doing.") Moreover, while such a person may rightly *regret* both his action and his ignorance, it sounds very odd to say that he should be ashamed of either, unless his ignorance is itself something for which he is culpable. And even if it is, that doesn't help. If culpability is cashed out as moral ignorance, then the one who is negligently ignorant can trace that negligence to ignorance also. So how can shame "get started," as it were?

Finally, the ignorance explanation fails to explain the kind of anger we feel towards wrongdoers other than ourselves. Socrates himself pointed out that it is hard to be *indignant* about an action that someone performed in error; it doesn't seem appropriate to *resent* or be *angry at* wrongdoers who are ignorant. Socrates welcomed this defusing of anger; nonetheless, anger and indignation are clearly part of our standard reactions to immoral people and, many might argue, appropriately so, even if they should also be accompanied by compassion. How to make sense of these sorts of reactive judgments is unclear on the ignorance view.

Indeed, it is worth noting the way our intuitions seem to link ignorance with *innocence*, rendering inappropriate such emotional responses as resentment and indignation. As we noted in the last section, ignorance is something that we believe absolves one of blame – excuses one who committed the offense – by lessening or negating entirely one's responsibility for the action. And although Socrates's wrongdoers may not be ignorant that what they are doing is vicious, they are ignorant that what they are doing is wrong. And that ignorance seems to wholly or partially excuse them in our minds, for it seems to make it hard to say that they really *meant* to do what they did.

So this analysis of wrongdoers doesn't seem to make them "bad" enough; even if a person culpable of a wrongdoing is in some sense ignorant, he is also more than this: his "mistake" is worse than mere ignorant error. And it seems entirely incorrect to maintain that someone whose character we would call 'wicked' or 'evil' is (merely) ignorant in a big way.

If ignorance excuses, then knowledge must convict. So judgments of immorality must rest on the wrongdoer knowing something about the wrongness of his act which makes him culpable, and deserving of resentment on our part. But what does he know?'

If ethical imperatives are hypothetical imperatives, then perhaps he knows that virtuous activity is a means to a certain goal but *doesn't care*, because he doesn't share that goal. On this *indifference explanation* of immorality, wrongdoing is the result of a person desiring an object which he correctly identifies and which requires for its achievement the performance of that wrongful act. An immoral action is therefore done intentionally and deliberately, and not mistakenly out of ignorance, in order to achieve a certain goal. And on this view, a person with an immoral or wicked character is one whose desired goals, which are correctly identified, persistently (i.e., in many or most circumstances) dictate the performance of a vicious rather than a virtuous action.

This explanation of immorality accords with at least some of our intuitions. Basically decent people do seem to commit wrongdoings on occasion because of the way these actions help to achieve goals which these people appear to find genuinely attractive (e.g., a better job, a lot of money). And genuinely wicked people seem to be indifferent to and indeed contemptuous of the values of virtuous men and women, inflicting violence on others without regret in order to get what they want, and sometimes even because they *enjoy* the harm they cause.

Some will find this explanation of immorality disappointing. If, as this explanation says, a man who is culpable for a wrongdoing has a conception of the good and a conception of what actions he must take to achieve it which are different from those of a virtuous person and *which are not mistaken*, then we could never say of him that when he performed an immoral action which was an appropriate means to a goal he (quite correctly) desired that *he* had reason to do otherwise, because he simply didn't. He made no mistake; he didn't do anything that, according to his lights, was wrong. The notion of moral *wrong*doings vanishes, because no one who performs an immoral act ever has a better reason, on this view, to do otherwise. Contrast this view to the ignorance explanation, which does attempt to show how a wrongdoer has made a mistake, and has better reason to perform the virtuous action.

Therefore, on this indifference model, words such as "bad" or "evil" when applied to a person's action or character would have to be regarded as analogous to aesthetic labels, rather than labels which offered an "internal" criticism of the wrongdoer. That is, they would convey *our* displeasure and even hatred for the deeds of such people (and the goals which those deeds served), but they could not be used to convey to the wrongdoer that he "should have done otherwise" (i.e., had a better – maybe even the best – reason to act differently), and thus made a moral mistake (i.e., committed a moral wrong). Of course, as Foot says, immoral behavior "does not cease to offend against either morality or etiquette because the agent is indifferent to the purposes and to the disapproval he will incur by flouting them."[9] But it only offends *us*, who have these purposes; it doesn't offend the agent who performed them, and who therefore cannot be convinced that he made a mistake (except, perhaps, in failing to avoid being caught). The "should have done otherwise" judgment only has meaning, on this view, as an external judgment; it has no meaning from the agent's internal perspective.

Self-regarding reactive emotions such as guilt or shame also go unexplicated on this view. About what does or should a culpable person feel guilty? As long as his action was completely appropriate given his desire, why should he convict himself of any wrongdoing? Perhaps he should feel ashamed of the fact that he had this desire? But why? He might well appreciate that it was a desire that *we* wished he never had, but that fact, by itself, doesn't give him a reason to regret his having it. Of course, he might regret the desire for other reasons (e.g., if it gets him into unwanted trouble with those of us who disapprove of the behavior it prompts), but that regret is a function of *his* motivational system, not of ours.

So, as I noted above, the label 'immoral' can survive under this explanation if that label is a kind of external "aesthetic" evaluation of those for whom morality doesn't apply. Let us understand Externalism in ethics as the thesis that to know an action

[9] Foot, p. 162.

A is morally required is not necessarily to have a reason to do A. In contrast, let us understand Internalism as the thesis that to know that an action A is morally required is necessarily to have a reason to do A. Those philosophers (such as Socrates) who are internalists will insist that any immoral person is making a mistake when he acts immorally, because in fact he has reason to act otherwise. Externalists, however, will maintain that it is possible for an immoral person to be making no mistake acting immorally, so that she is only 'wrong' insofar as she fails to be moved by a reason – which she doesn't happen to have herself – to be moral. I do not want to debate the merits of either position. Suffice it to say here, however, that the indifference explanation of immorality commits one to holding what I will call the "radical externalist position" that *every* immoral person has *no* reason for being moral and is wrong only insofar as she acts contrary to our (moral) lights, not hers. The label 'immoral' becomes not an internal criticism but an external negative assessment.

Even if it is disappointing, is this account of immorality nonetheless acceptable? I want to argue that it isn't. While it might do as an explanation of immoral action by a few people (e.g., psychopaths), it cannot provide an explanation of what we call *immorality*, because it subtly undercuts the concept itself. Consider that if the reason for being moral is one that *all* people who commit wrongdoings do not have, then all of them are outside the system of hypothetical imperatives which dictate moral action. So in what meaningful sense do moral injunctions apply to these people? If we call them 'wrong' when they do not adhere to these injunctions, isn't that more like calling them 'distasteful' rather than 'immoral'? Indeed, I think it no accident that, in her paper, Foot repeatedly calls those who are indifferent to the goals dictating virtuous actions, and who thus have no reason to act morally, *amoral* rather than immoral. This label seems exactly right: amoral people are indeed people to whom moral injunctions do not apply. The indifference explanation of moral failure puts every wrongdoer beyond the reach of these injunctions, and so makes every wrongdoer amoral. Immorality collapses into amorality. But no matter how much we may desire amoral behavior, we still see it as different from evil, wickedness, badness, sin – words which refer to conduct that we are convinced the agent should not have engaged in from her point of view, proscribed by imperatives that are indeed applicable to her. The phenomenon of immorality therefore eludes the attempt to explain it as a function of an agent's indifference to the reasons for being moral. The problems of the indifference and ignorance accounts of immorality are ones that I think Aristotle appreciated long ago. For example, in the *Nichomachean Ethics*, Aristotle tosses and turns between the ignorance and indifference explanations, although the second explanation is more prominent in that work and is the one generally attributed to him.[10] Aristotle divides up wrongdoers into two categories: those whose wrongdoing is a sign that they are incontinent, and those whose wrongdoing is a sign that they are "wicked" (*mochtheros*). We will explore the first sort of wrongdoer later. For now, we are

---

[10] I am indebted to Julie Heath Elliott for discussions on Aristotle's view of wickedness, in which she persuaded me that he does not take a consistent position on what the wicked man is like.

interested in the second sort, the wicked people, or as Aristotle sometimes calls them, wrongdoers who are 'self-indulgent' or 'vicious', and whom he considers worse, from a moral point of view, than incontinent offenders. Aristotle insists that "incontinence and vice are different in kind; vice is unconscious of itself, incontinence is not."[11] The wicked person "is like a city that *uses its own laws*, but has wicked laws to use."[12] The idea seems to be that such people have a conception of the good which dictates the performance of vicious rather than virtuous action. Indeed, Aristotle depicts the wicked person as one who has a settled, stable disposition:

> ... the man who pursues the excesses, or pursues to excess necessary objects, and does so *by choice, for their own sake*, and not at all for the sake of any result distinct from this, is self-indulgent *for such a man is of necessity unlikely to repent*, and therefore incurable, since a man who cannot repent cannot be cured ...[13]

The wicked man *knows* he offends against our moral standards, but doesn't care. He refuses to repent.

Yet this portrait of the worst among us is one that Aristotle himself has trouble accepting. In a very interesting passage in Book IX of the *Nicomachean Ethics*, he writes that far from being conflict-free, such people are conflict-ridden, at variance with themselves, miserable, and wretched:

> And those who have done many terrible deeds and are hated for their wickedness even shrink from life and destroy themselves ... And having nothing lovable in them they have no feeling of love to themselves. Therefore also such men do not rejoice or grieve with themselves; for their soul is rent by faction, and one element in it by reason of its wickedness grieves when it abstains from certain acts, while the other part is pleased, and one draws them this way and the other that, as if they were pulling them in pieces. If a man cannot at the same time be pained and pleased, at all events after a short time he is pained because he was pleased, and he could have wished that these things had not been pleasant to him; for *bad men are laden with repentance*.[14]

Contrast this with the passage previously quoted in which he said that the wicked or self-indulgent man will not repent. In this passage, however, Aristotle suggests that wicked people do dislike not only what they have done, but also the conception of the good that their wrongful actions have served. Indeed, he suggests elsewhere in the *Nicomachean Ethics* that wicked men must be in error about what the good is, because "that which appears [to be good] to the good men is thought to be really so. If this is correct, as it seems to be, and virtue and the good men as such are the measure of each thing; those alone will be pleasures which appear to him, and those

---

[11] All references to the *Nicomachean Ethics* in the text will be to the translation by W.D. Ross in *The Basic Works of Aristotle*, ed. Richard McKeon (Chicago: Random House, 1941); the quote is from 1150b35.

[12] *ibid.*, 1152a23.

[13] *ibid.*, 1150a20–23. My emphasis.

[14] *ibid.*, 1166b10–30. My emphasis.

things pleasant which he enjoys."[15] And in Book III, he explicitly reverts to the Socratic explanation of the wicked person as ignorant of what constitutes the good: "Now every wicked man is ignorant of what he ought to do and what he ought to abstain from, and it is by reason of error of this kind that men become unjust and in general bad."[16]

In the end, Aristotle draws back from the indifference portrait, retreating to the ignorance analysis, because he is unable to accept the idea that the wicked person's life is outside the system of ethical imperatives. Yet to include that person inside the system appears to mean that one must be committed to an explanation of wrongdoing which invokes ignorance, and Aristotle cannot embrace this portrait unequivocally either. Shortly after the passage just quoted, in which wicked men are said to be ignorant, Aristotle insists that

> perhaps a man is the kind of man not to take care. Still they are themselves by their slack lives responsible for becoming men of that kind, and men make themselves responsible for being unjust or self-indulgent, in the one case by cheating and in the other by spending their time in drunken bouts and the like, for it is activities exercised on particular objects that make the corresponding character ... Now *not to know* that it is from the exercise of activities on particular objects that states of character are produced is the mark of a thoroughly senseless person.[17]

So he suggests that of course they do know what they are doing, in which case they can't claim ignorance as an explanation of the dissolution of their characters. These passages show that Aristotle is unsure about how to characterize wicked people; he is reluctant to place them outside the system of virtues, but he is also unpersuaded that such people are *merely* ignorant of the connection between the virtues and the good as Socrates had claimed.[18]

III. THE MANICHEAN EXPLANATION

What about Aristotle's other category of wrongdoer? If we understand immoral action as the product of incontinence, do we get a better portrait of what culpable actions and immoral characters are like?

Understanding wrongdoers as incontinent is, as Aristotle suspected, not appropriate for all wrongdoers; for example, it does not seem an appropriate description of the worst moral offenders, who appear to do evil not because they are "weak" but because they want to do it. Nonetheless, it does seem attractive as an explanation of the intermittent immorality of most of us, who tend to regret what we have done and who feel guilt and shame. This explanation of immorality can be used by the advocate of either of the two prominent theories of moral authority. No matter if moral imperatives are held to be authoritative because they are

---

[15] *ibid.*, 1176a15–19.

[16] *ibid.*, 1110b26–29.

[17] *ibid.*, 1114a3–11. My emphasis.

[18] Aquinas noted this vacillation, and proposed a way of reconciling the Aristotelian claims that wrongdoers were ignorant and yet knowledgeable of something that makes them culpable; see note 39.

hypothetical or categorical, this explanation holds that the wrongdoer *knows* they are authoritative but acts immorally anyway. As Aristotle puts it,

> of the people who are incontinent with respect to bodily enjoyments . . . he who pursues the excesses of things pleasant. *not by choice but contrary to his choice and judgment,* is called incontinent.[19]

The incontinent man is therefore "likely to repent."[20]

But if the incontinent person does not *choose* to do bad deeds, then why does he do them? Why doesn't his knowledge of their wrongness stop him from performing them? One popular (although controversial) explanation of the phenomenon which seems well-suited as an explanation of immorality is suggested by Aristotle, who maintains that the incontinent person's action is *caused* rather than chosen by something which usurps control of the will:

> we praise the rational principle of the continent man and of the incontinent, and the part of their soul that has such a principle, since it urges them aright and towards the best objects; but there is found in them also another natural element besides the rational principle, which fights against and resists that principle.[21]

St. Paul agrees; in a well-known passage of Romans, he presents his own immoral deeds as the result of incontinence, and the incontinence is explained as the result of a "bad" part of him wresting control away from his will:

> We know that the law is spiritual; but I am not: I am unspiritual, the purchased slave of sin. I do not even acknowledge my own actions as mine for what I do is not what I want to do, but what I detest. But if what I do is against my will, it means that I agree with the law and hold it to be admirable. But as things are, it is no longer I who perform the action, but sin that lodges in me. For I know that nothing good lodges in me – in my unspiritual nature I mean – for though the will to do good is there, the deed is not. The good which I want to do, I fail to do; but what I do is the wrong which is against my will and if what I do is against my will, clearly it is no longer I who am the agent, but sin that has its lodging in me.[22]

My evil action, says Paul, does not arise out of my will, but instead arises out of "sin that has its lodging in me." Paul cannot be the one who does the evil because Paul is the one who knows it is evil and detests it. So it must be an unspiritual nature within him which produces, against his will and after a struggle with it, his shameful deeds. Immorality is therefore presented as the result of a force within each human being which struggles with and overpowers that person's "true self," while good is the result of that "true self" prevailing over the "evil force."

---

[19] *ibid.,* 1148a4–10. My emphasis.
[20] *ibid.,* 1150b30.
[21] *ibid.,* 1102b15–18.
[22] Romans 7:14–20.

But what is this usurping part of us, this "sin that has its lodging in us"? Most philosophers have followed Aristotle in believing it to be passion or appetite: "The incontinent man acts with appetite but not with choice; while the continent man on the contrary acts with choice, but not with appetite."[23] For example, Plato argues in the *Republic* that each of us is constituted by three parts: the calculating or rational part, the desiring or irrational part, and the spirited part. And he maintains that when the desires become insubordinate and/or spirit is disengaged from its proper role as a servant of the rational part, the dictates of reason are assaulted and overpowered by one or both of these parts, such that bad actions result. Moreover, in the *Groundwork*, the second *Critique*, and *The Doctrine of Virtue* (but not, as we shall see, in *Religion Within the Limits of Reason Alone*), Kant is attracted to an explanation of immorality that makes it a product of the struggle between our reason and the (victorious) desires within us. Our will, says Kant, is connected with (in one place he says it is identical with)[24] the moral law within us. And he suggests (albeit without explicitly taking this position) that this moral law struggles with our desires to determine our action, so that we act rightly when the moral law wins the struggle, and we act wrongly (or at best only according to duty) when desires triumph.

> The impulses of nature ... are obstacles within man's mind to his observance of duty and forces (sometimes powerful ones) struggling against it. Man must, therefore, judge that he is able to stand up to them and subdue them by reason – not at some time in the future but at once (the moment he thinks of duty).[25]

Therefore, although Plato, Kant, and Paul would quarrel over how to understand the "forces of good" and the "forces of evil" within us, nonetheless all three philosophers are attracted to the same *type* of explanation of good and evil action, one with the following characteristics:

A. A human being is made up of parts which have motivational force.
B. Good action is motivated by one part (or parts), evil action is motivated by another part (or parts), and moral deliberation takes place when these parts within us struggle to determine the person's action.
C. The struggle between the parts is understood deterministically, such that the strongest force will always "win" in virtue of its strength, and "winning" here means determining the person's action.
D. The good part of us is identified with *us* (Paul's "true self," Plato's and Aristotle's rational principle, Kant's noumenal self), so that our bad actions are portrayed as something which *we* do not *choose*. "The incontinent man acts with appetite but not with choice."[26]

---

[23] Aristotle, 1111b12–15.
[24] *Groundwork of the Metaphysics of Morals*, trans. H.J. Paton (New York: Harper and Row, 1964), p, 80.
[25] *Doctrine of Virtue*, trans. Mary J. Gregor (Philadelphia: University of Pennsylvania, 1964), p. 37.
[26] Aristotle, 1111b12.

I shall call this the *Manichean explanation* of immorality.[27] Should we believe that some sort of Manichean explanation of immorality is correct, even if we are now unclear about which variant to adopt?

No – not if we want to preserve the concept of immorality. Recall what I listed as the first belief associated with our judgment of culpability: namely, that the agent was not in an excusing state (e.g., she wasn't acting in ignorance, or under duress, or under compulsion because of a physical illness). And I discussed the way in which these excusing conditions were linked with the idea that, if the self is found to be either distanced from or unconnected to a harmful action, blame is either mitigated or else entirely inappropriate. Would we be able to preserve this distinction between those who are culpable and those who are excused if we adopted a Manichean picture? That we could not was the central problem of the ignorance explanation of moral failure, and in a different way it is also the central problem of the Manichean explanation. On this picture, the strength of the evil force within the wrongdoer compelled the action. How is this compulsion different from the medical or psychological compulsion which we think excuses someone from wrongdoing? Since Aristotle and Kant speak of a wrongdoer's actions as *caused* by desire, and not chosen, it would seem the wrongdoer does not act freely in the way a moral person does. So shouldn't the wrongdoer plead that he is no different from the kleptomaniac or any other compulsive wrongdoer whom we now recognize and excuse?

A Manichean could try to resist this argument in a way suggested by J.J.C. Smart:[28] Smart insists that we can hold a bad schoolboy responsible for his mischievous actions, but not a stupid schoolboy for his bad exam (or presumably a kleptomaniac schoolboy for his stealing), because we think that the bad conduct of the first boy is still open to influence through positive or negative reinforcements. But this is not the sense of 'responsible' which the judgment of culpability presupposes; it is because the boy acted voluntarily and responsibly that one condemns his actions as immoral. It is what he was like when he committed the crimes that we focus on, and not the future flexibility of his character, when we call him "responsible." And we do not *excuse* people from our condemnation because of the future flexibility of their character, but rather because of the fact that their past action has somehow failed to warrant our condemnation.

Moreover, blame seems inappropriate on this view. We don't blame someone for being ugly or stupid, and we don't praise someone for being pretty or petite. But if good and bad actions are compelled in us by forces which exist in us for biological or social reasons, then why is our bad behavior any more culpable than our ugliness or our stupidity? Again, Smart has tried to answer this question. We blame the mischievous schoolboy for his action, according to Smart, and not the stupid schoolboy for his bad exam, because we see our condemnation as a way of conditioning the bad schoolboy such that he is no longer bad. The idea is that the

[27] See Allen Wood's use of this term to describe such an approach to immorality in his *Kant's Moral Religion* (Ithaca: Cornell University Press, 1970), p. 214. John Rawls also uses the term in this way in unpublished lectures on Kant, and it was he who first prompted me to think about the approach.
[28] See Smart's "Free Will, Praise and Blame," *Mind*, LXX, no. 279 (July 1961), pp. 291–306.

evil force within him can be weakened by our condemnation, whereas the intellectual level of the schoolboy would be unchanged by it. But even if Smart is right about the efficacy of censure, he has not captured the sense of blame and praise which is associated with our condemnation of a person as culpable. (And Smart himself seems to recognize this because he wants us to give up the word 'blame' and substitute the word 'dispraise' in its place.) There is no difference between our blame of a "flexibly" mischievous schoolboy and our blame of a "flexibly" mischievous dog – the blame is justified in both cases as a way of effecting a desirable change. Yet our notion of culpability is such that only certain adult human beings can be held blameworthy for their actions, not dogs or very small children. Moreover, our holding an adult culpable for her actions is because of what she has done in the past, not because of what we think we can get her to do in the future. And whereas Smart sees "blame" as a kind of punishment-like device, the standard view of culpability is that it precedes and is *a condition of* punishment.

Not only is blame problematic on this view: so also are a whole variety of reactive emotions surrounding judgments of culpability. I might be upset at the awful deeds which the evil force within the wrongdoer has compelled, but why should I be upset at *her*, hate *her*, resent *her*? I should only be angry at, hate, or resent the bad force, which is not supposed to be the real "her." Indeed, I should be supportive and approving of the good part of her – which is really her – sympathizing with her about the extent to which the more powerful evil forces are coercing her into unwanted action. So this explanation of immorality puts us in the position of having to commend and sympathize with, rather than criticize or upbraid, those who commit wrongs. It renders meaningless or inappropriate all angry reactive attitudes towards wrongdoers.

It also renders meaningless or inappropriate reactive attitudes towards ourselves when it is we who act immorally. If I commit a wrong, why should I be guilty about my wrongdoing if its performance was determined by the "bad" force within me? I might wish mightily that I had been *made* differently, such that these harmful actions were never triggered within me. ("If only my reason were made stronger," I might lament.) But I cannot be guilty about what *I* did not commit. Should I be ashamed? Of what? (The strength of my bad desires?) But if my good part is ineffective against these bad desires (because it is too weak, through no fault of its own, relative to them), I am helpless to prevent what I despise, so that, once again, shame is inappropriate.

Much of this discussion sounds as if it has been lifted from a tract against compatibilism, but it is not the determinism in the view which makes it problematic. Even if the struggle between the parts of the self were understood indeterministically, like a "fight" between two quantum mechanical particles, the outcome of the struggle would only be a matter of chance, and immoral actions would be made random and capricious. And how are we to blame or praise people whose evil or good actions are random? Hence, the source of the problems with the Manichean account of moral failure is that, however the struggle between the motivations is understood, it makes immoral action a product of a brute motivational force: e.g., desire, or appetite, or whatever is identified as "the sinful part within us." And you can't *convict* a brute motivational force; you only convict a person who has chosen to do what she did.

So it is the fact that the Manichean explanation removes the self from the commission of the crime which makes the view inadequate. For this reason, Donald Davidson rejects a view of this sort as an explanation of incontinence, for "it is not clear how we can ever blame the agent for what he does: his action merely reflects the outcome of a struggle within him. What could *he* do about it?"[29] Who is this "he" which looks weakly on while the good and bad forces rage within him? That is the "he" which Davidson and the rest of us think it does make sense to blame and hold accountable, and the "thing" (which is like no other natural entity) that Nagel notes we praise or resent or punish or find to be at fault. It also the "he" which is probably fooling itself into thinking that its bad actions were caused rather than chosen. Kant notes about St. Paul's attribution of our evil acts to some kind of evil spirit external to our will that "we would not be led astray by [this spirit] at all were we not already in secret league with him."[30] Kant's point is that even if the passions are snakes seducing us into sin, they can only succeed if we let them do so.

Hence, if we want to explain immorality as something for which we are responsible, blameworthy, and culpable, we must show it to be chosen by a self (where it may even be that the self's choices are determined).[31] Or, to quote Dante, we need an explanation of an immoral person as someone who "*lets* desire pull reason from her throne."[32] However, we have already discussed the ignorance and indifference accounts of moral failure, which do incorporate a self understood as a unitary chooser but are unsuccessful. So what other way is there to explain immorality as a "bad choice"?

IV. THE DEFIANCE EXPLANATION

Our examination of the failure of the three common explanations of immorality teaches us a great deal about what a successful explanation of immorality must include if it is going to capture central elements of our notion of immorality. First, *contra* the Manichean view, the immoral action must be something chosen by a self, and not caused by a self-part. Second, *contra* the ignorance explanation, the immoral action must not be chosen in ignorance that it is morally wrong. And third, *contra* the indifference explanation, the choice of the immoral action must be made in the knowledge that the moral injunction against the action is supposed to apply to oneself (so that one is inside the scope of morality). Can an explanation of immorality successfully include all of these features?

[29] "How is Weakness of the Will Possible?", in *Essays in Action and Events* (Oxford: The Clarendon Press, 1980), p. 35.

[30] See Kant's *Religion Within the Limits of Reason Alone*, trans. Theodore M. Greene and Hoyt H. Hudson, ed. John Silber (New York: Harper and Brothers, 1960), pp. 52–53.

[31] So nothing in this paper aims to show that compatibilism is wrong: the compatibilist's challenge is to show how the idea that actions are chosen by the self is compatible with those choices being determined.

[32] *Inferno*, Canto V, quoted by Davidson, p. 35. This is also the approach to explaining immorality which Augustine (himself an opponent of the Manichees) took: "As [God] is the creator of all nature so he is the giver of all power, but not of will. Evil wills are not derived from him, since they are contrary to nature, which is from him." *City of God*, bk. v, sec. 9; quoted from the translation by J.W.C. Wand (London: Oxford, 1963), p. 98.

The difficulty with doing so is that an explanation with these three features seems to represent the agent who makes the immoral choice as irrational. Bill Cosby, in a comedy routine, says that when he confronts his errant children after their wrongdoings, they admit that when they did the bad thing they knew they shouldn't be doing it. "So why," he asks his audience, "did they do it? There is only one explanation: brain damage."

Cosby's joke turns on our inability to comprehend the rationale behind knowing what is right but choosing to do wrong. Perhaps all this means is that the phenomenon of immorality is mysterious. But those people, such as myself, who are unsympathetic to philosophical mysteries will argue that any explanation of immorality that gives rise to such a mystery is a failure, because it fails to make immoral action intelligible. Still, I think it is possible to develop further this explanation of immorality along lines that will generate an intelligible account of immoral action that actually fits with many of our considered convictions about what such action is like. The explanation I will develop is naturally linked with the idea that the authority of moral imperatives comes from the fact that they are categorical. I call it the *defiance explanation*, and it is very old, deeply entrenched in the Judeo-Christian tradition, and implicit in the tale of Adam and Eve, which is supposed to be an explanation of the origin of human evil.

Consider that tale: God, who made heaven and earth, also made Adam, and placed him in a bountiful garden called Eden, in which there grew a tree of the knowledge of good and evil. About the latter, God specifically issues a command: "You may eat from every tree in the garden but not from the tree of knowledge of good and evil: for on the day that you eat from it, you will certainly die."[33] Thereafter, Eve was made and although "they were both naked, the man and his wife, ... they had no feeling of shame towards one another."[34] Life, however, did not proceed smoothly; the story continues:

> The serpent was more crafty than any wild creature that the Lord God had made. He said to the woman, 'Is it true that God has forbidden you to eat from any tree in the garden?' The woman answered the serpent, 'We may eat the fruit of any tree in the garden, except for the tree in the middle of the garden: God has forbidden us either to eat or to touch the fruit of that: if we do, we shall die.' The serpent said, 'Of course you will not die. God knows that as soon as you eat it, your eyes will be opened and you will be like gods knowing both good and evil.' When the woman saw that the fruit of the tree was good to eat, and that it was pleasing to the eye and tempting to contemplate, she took some and ate it. She also gave her husband some and he ate it. Then the eyes of both of them were opened and they discovered that they were naked: so they stiched fig-leaves together and made themselves loincloths.[35]

[33] Genesis 2:16–18.
[34] Genesis 2:24–26.
[35] Genesis 3:1–7.

When God found out what they had done he was furious; he angrily condemned the serpent, the woman, and the man, and punished all three of them for their actions.

How does this tale explain the origin of human immorality?[36] Consider that Adam and Eve's guilt is associated with doing something which was expressly forbidden by God. The command not to eat of the fruit of the tree of knowledge is portrayed as authoritative: not in the sense of being hypothetical, but solely because it is God's command. It is authoritative in and of itself just because He made it and He is the supreme commander who *must* be obeyed (don't ask why; God doesn't have to justify himself). Nonetheless it is interesting that God links that command with what looks like a sanction – death is threatened to anyone who eats the fruit.

Why didn't Adam and Eve obey that command? Were they somehow acting out of ignorance? The author certainly proposes this explanation of their moral failure, for the knowledge of good and evil which is, as we discussed, a necessary component of culpability only comes *after* they've eaten the fruit. It would seem that before the apple was eaten, they could not be morally culpable because they did not have the requisite knowledge of right and wrong to make that guilt possible. After the apple was eaten, that knowledge was gained and they "fell into sin." This is how Herbert Morris understands the story's point.[37]

But I want to argue that the Genesis author finally abandons this ignorance explanation of immorality and presents a very different account of its source. As we discussed, we generally think that if I don't know that I am doing something wrong (and if my moral ignorance is not the result of negligence), then I am thereby excused from full culpability. So if I am Eve and I have *no* moral knowledge, then all of my actions and decisions in this state – including my choice to eat the fruit – would not be subject to moral blame. But this means the ignorance explanation of Eve's fall cannot make her culpable for her fall. And if she isn't culpable for her fall, then she cannot be considered culpable for any of the immoral actions performed after, and as a result of, that fall.

---

[36] It can't explain the origin of evil itself, however. After all, the snake was already evil, and who made the snake?

[37] See Morris's "Lost Innocence," from *Guilt and Innocence* (Berkeley: University of California Press, 1976), pp. 139–61. Morris is one of the few philosophers who appreciates how philosophically interesting the Adam and Eve tale is, and I am indebted to him for suggesting to me its relevance to the task of explaining immorality. He contends about Adam and Eve that

> in disobeying God each was, if one accepts that they were required to obey, guilty, in an attenuated sense, of at a minimum, disobedience, and being guilty of this, they were no longer innocent of wrongdoing. Being guilty and no longer innocent in this sense, however, does not seem to imply, given their child-like nature at the time of disobedience and their ignorance of good and evil, moral culpability in disobeying. In the act of disobedience, then, there was moral innocence. And any vices manifested in this act would also have been those of innocent persons. In eating of the tree, however, each acquired knowledge; and it is this knowledge, not the fact of their disobedience nor any moral culpability in disobeying nor the presence of any vice in disobeying, that must in some way account for their losing innocence. (p. 141)

Morris is essentially trying to differentiate conduct which is wrong but morally innocent from conduct which is wrong but morally culpable. Whether or not this first category exists is a question I shall not pursue here. But I do want to question whether the eating of the fruit by Adam and Eve falls into this category.

There is no doubt, however, that the author of the story wants to see Eve and Adam as culpable for eating the fruit, and thus for their descent into sin, as well as for their immoral actions subsequent to that descent. God has very strong reactive attitudes towards them; not only does he blame them for eating the fruit, but he is also presented as furiously indignant with them for what they did, sentencing them to terrible punishments. Even more interesting, the story makes clear that Eve and Adam decide to eat the fruit *knowing that God forbade it*. So it seems they had at least some moral knowledge already, i.e., the knowledge that it was wrong to eat of the tree, and then *defied* the prohibition in a way that resulted in their being held culpable and, finally, punished. They did not ignorantly stumble into evil but chose it, with their eyes open, knowing they should not.[38]

So I would argue that, in the end, the Genesis author explains the source of human immorality as, to use Milton's words in *Paradise Lost*, a "foul revolt." This defiance explanation of immorality is, despite some similarities, importantly different from both the ignorance and indifference explanations discussed earlier.

On the indifference model, the wrongdoer is presented as someone for whom the moral imperatives have no authority whatsoever. Such a person doesn't have to rebel against the authority of morality because she is already free of its rule (although, in the guise of the law, it might exercise power over her in a way that she regrets). Compare a person from one nation-state who doesn't have to rebel against the authorities of another nation-state which has no authority over her; similarly, the indifference explanation of immorality presents immoral people as citizens of a different "moral realm" from the rest of us. But on the defiance model, the wrongdoer is presented as someone who recognizes that *prima facie* she is supposed to be subject to the same moral commands we are. She sees herself as inside the scope of moral injunctions: she feels the claims of its authority upon her. Nonetheless she *resists* and challenges that subjugation, like a political rebel in a civil war, in an effort to make her own desires authoritative.

I want to be precise about what the defiance is. It is a certain kind of choice. But it is not the choice to do an action knowing that it is wrong (i.e., knowing that it is prohibited by a moral injunction). This choice is not even sufficient for us to consider a person culpable for an action, since she might have performed it under duress or in a situation of dire necessity. (A bank teller who hands over her money to a gunman is not culpable for her action because we do not think that the injunction against contributing to a theft is authoritative for her in the circumstances.) Instead, the defiance that makes her culpable is her choice to do an action which she knows to be wrong, i.e., prohibited by a moral injunction, and where she knows this injunction claims to be the ruling principle of her choices. The word 'claims' here is important. She doesn't know that this injunction must be

---

[38] There is, however, one way to read the story so as to make something like the distinction Morris wants, but retain the idea that Eve was culpable. On this reading, Eve had knowledge of, and defied, God's authority, but such knowledge does not count as *moral* knowledge, something which she only attained after she ate the fruit. She therefore acted wrongly, but she did not commit a moral wrong. Indeed, on this view, her wrongdoing would presumably be worse than a moral wrongdoing, insofar as she defied a higher authority than morality. It is, on this reading, this (non-moral) defiance which makes here (non-morally) culpable.

authoritative over her; she knows only that it claims to be authoritative (where the demands of society or family or certain styles of reasoning might be thought to generate that claim). It is this claim that she resists, repudiates, fights off, as she chooses to do otherwise than it directs. The injunction is therefore not something that she can be merely indifferent towards, because she understands that she is supposed to be governed by it, so that its rulership must be fought off. One might say that the immoral person is attempting to establish herself as *amoral*; if her rebellion succeeds, she will show herself to be outside the scope of its imperatives. But by the very act of flouting the moral injunction, she understands that she is supposed to be inside its scope and rejects its power over her.

Let us return to the Bill Cosby joke. Does this explanation of immorality give us a better account of what is happening in the mind of the immoral person than Cosby's imputation of temporary brain damage? It does, in two ways. First, it pinpoints the mental act that constitutes the guilty mind: namely, the flouting of the authoritative command. Second, it suggests a reason for the flouting. Rebels reject the rulership of commanders not only when they perceive the commander to be directing them to act in a way that harms their interests but also when they think they can "get away" with the rebellion (either because it is possible to evade the bad consequences of the rebellion, or because they believe its costs will be outweighed by its benefits). So Eve takes the fruit and flouts God's commands, both because she is confident that getting the knowledge it promises is more desirable than remaining in her present state and because she is confident that she will be able to "handle" God if he is displeased by her defiance. As the text says, she sets herself up to be a rival god, directing her own actions and taking orders from her own will. In just this way, immoral people see moral commands as the enemy of their interests (believing neither Hobbesian claims that the commands are really precepts of enlightened self-interest, nor Kantian claims that they arise from one's own rational will), and such people expect that the authority of these commands is something they can successfully defy.

This account of the nature of immorality therefore fits with the idea that moral imperatives are authoritative because they are categorical. Knowingly defying moral imperatives whose authority is hypothetical doesn't seem to make any sense;[39] why would I resist doing an action if I know I should do it, insofar as it would help me to achieve my conception of the good? But if no such connection is made between moral actions and a person's good, if, instead, moral actions are presented simply as authoritative in and of themselves and suggestive of actions which can and frequently do *conflict* with one's self-interest, then the defiance explanation suggests itself naturally. Immorality is simply a rebellion against a kind

---

[39] However, Aquinas seemed to think it did. Although Aquinas's natural laws were derived from God, they were nonetheless hypothetical imperatives. In considering why people do not follow them, he seemed to be struck by Aristotle's uncertainty as to whether wrongdoers were ignorant that their deeds were wrong or aware of that fact. He attempts to reconcile the Aristotelian position by maintaining that wrongdoers are ignorant, but not in a way that excuses them, for their ignorance is willful – they know they should learn what the good is, but refuse. So, in the end, Aquinas makes defiance, rather than ignorance, the ultimate source of wrongdoing. Yet why someone would defiantly refuse to learn the good is never explained. See *Summa Theologica*. first part of the second part, question 6, article 8, "Does Ignorance Render An Act Involuntary?"

of authority which one may very well dislike, given the way it often opposes one's own interests. I would argue that Kant implicitly assumed this account in his *Religion Within The Limits of Reason Alone*, where immorality is explained as arising from "insubordination" by one who defies the Moral Law and puts the satisfaction of his own desires ahead of doing his duty.[40] And in the Judeo-Christian tradition, immoral people are frequently presented as rebels; for example, in Christian mythology the most evil person of them all is the Devil, who is also depicted as the most thoroughly rebellious of God's creatures.

Either in a secular or non-secular version, I would argue that this account of immorality fits well with the things we say and feel about immoral people. For example, it explains the way in which "selfishness" is supposed to be a reason for immorality. The immoral person is a rebel who sets herself up as the supreme authority for her actions, defying the claim which morality is supposed to exercise. It is not what morality commands but what *she* wants which will prevail. And her pursuit of what she wants frequently results in harm to other people – whom the moral commands were protecting. It also explains how immorality comes in degrees: the more extensive the rebellion against morality, the worse the rebel, and the more negative our judgment of him.

Another virtue of this account is that it explains the kinds of reactive attitudes we have towards wrongdoers. Insofar as it presents immoral actions as chosen by a person rather than caused by a motivation, it makes sense to respond negatively to the person who made the choices. We who are (supposedly) on the side of morality find the wrongdoer's rebellious choices offensive. She is not someone to be pitied, but someone to be resented, resisted, fought against, or even despised because of her allegiance. She has sided with that which is the enemy of the authority we see ourselves as respecting and serving.

This account of immorality makes our criticisms of her not external (which is all they could be on the indifference model) but internal, so that this account presupposes an internalist thesis about moral reasons. Because the wrongdoer is rebelling against the moral authority of morality, she knows that *prima facie* she is subject to it. Insofar as we repudiate her rebellion, we say that she should have acted otherwise not only from *our* standpoint but also from *her* standpoint, because we think that she, like us, has reason to be moral. Her action does not show her to be

---

[40] According to Kant, a person is the author of evil deeds and his own evil character when he orders the incentives to action (*Anlagen*) incorrectly. They are ordered correctly when the moral law (which he believes can motivate us to act) is placed first, such that nothing is performed which that law does not sanction. But immorality results from an ordering in which the moral law is subordinate to the desires:

> man (even the best) is evil only in that he reverses the moral order of the incentives when he adopts them into his maxim. He adopts indeed, the Moral Law along with the law of self-love; yet when he becomes aware that they cannot remain on a par with each other but that one must be subordinated to the other as its supreme condition, he makes the incentive of self-love and its inclinations the condition of obedience to the moral law; whereas, on the contrary, the latter, as the supreme condition of the satisfaction of the former, ought to have been adopted into the universal maxim of the will. (*Religion Within the Limits of Reason Alone*, pp. 31–32.)

So the immoral person is the one who *sides with* his own inclinations over morality; insofar as he reverses the proper order of the incentives, he rebels against the authority of the moral law, and it is in virtue of that rebellion that he is condemned.

making any simple-minded mistake about what she ought to do; on the contrary, she knows exactly what she ought to do. Instead, we criticize her because we see her as mistaken in thinking she can successfully overthrow moral injunctions and live solely as she chooses. "She can't get away with it," we insist (a thought that often motivates retributive punishment).[41]

Note also that this account leaves room for a distinction between being immoral and being (merely) morally mistaken. If someone accepts that she should be moral (because it will enable her to realize, rather than damage, her "true nature"), but doesn't know how to be moral and makes a mistake, she is only *morally mistaken*, not immoral. She is immoral only if (as Kant suggested) she *defies* morality's claim that it offers more for her than immorality, believing that what it offers her is different from (and seemingly less satisfying than) what morality offers.

Connected to the internal sense of "should have done otherwise" are the emotions of guilt and shame, and these emotions are nicely explicated on the defiance view. Moral rebels are often defeated, as Eve and Adam were when their rebellion was discovered and punished by God. And if the moral commands really do have categorical authority, then with defeat may come the awareness that one's immoral actions were the result of an unjustified and unjustifiable rebellion against morality. This awareness can thus produce shame, a kind of misery over what one is (a traitor to the right cause) and guilt, a kind of misery over the unjustified and unjustifiable harm one has caused to others.

Finally, this account fits well with our reactive attitudes towards wrongdoers other than ourselves. Our anger at them is a function of the fact that we see them as knowingly aligning themselves against morality. We despise their allegiance. Their knowledge that they are violating an authority that is supposed to rule them is the knowledge which makes them culpable. Our anger, however, is defused if we discover that their action did not arise out of this hateful allegiance, e.g., if it was performed in ignorance of the prohibition against it, or by accident. In fact, it is striking how many of the excusing conditions seem to pick out those states of mind in which there could be no real rebellion against moral authority and, hence, no culpability. People who do wrong out of ignorance, or mental illness, or because of a mistake do not challenge morality's authority. And those who act wrongly because they are coerced into doing so do not initiate a rebellion against this authority, but are forced to act against it in a way that they despise.

The natural way in which our everyday responses to ourselves and others are explicated by the defiance account of morality suggests that these responses might be generated by that account, perhaps implicit in our culture because of our Judeo-Christian heritage. But even if this is true, it is not an argument for it. If the defiance account of immorality is the theoretical source of the things that we say and feel about immoral people, then we must ask whether or not this account is one which, upon reflection, we can rationally embrace.

There are a number of problems one can raise with it. First, does it really fit the way we want to think about the "mildly immoral," who do wrong reluctantly,

---

[41] For more on the connection between this idea and retribution, see ch. 4 of my *Forgiveness and Mercy*, written with Jeffrie Murphy (Cambridge: Cambridge University Press, 1988).

neither shaking their fist at morality nor enjoying any challenge to it, perhaps beset by a bad conscience? Second, doesn't it fail to capture the way in which negligent people are immoral insofar as negligence is, by definition, immoral action that the agent doesn't intend to perform? Third, does it really do an acceptable job of representing the more evil among us, insofar as it makes their defiance something undertaken in ignorance of the fact that it cannot succeed, an ignorance that might be thought to undercut their culpability? And fourth, does it really incorporate an intelligible conception of morality's authority? Consider that in order to ensure that those who commit wrongs cannot be excused by reason of ignorance, the explanation must impute to people knowledge of morality's claim to hold authority over them. Yet it must also represent this authority as something they not only do not appreciate but want to overthrow. Now we understand how we human beings can have a human authority over us that we hate and wish to remove, but can we sensibly be said to respond to the authority of morality in this way? Interestingly, Kant did not want to impute to morality a hateful authority but an authority that all of us fully understand and are in awe of; however, if this is so, why do we defy it? It is as if, says Kant, we have a proof against the possibility of immorality when we reflect on morality's authority, and not an explanation of it:

> It is ... *inconceivable*, therefore, how the motivating forces of the sensuous nature should be able to gain ascendancy over a reason which commands with such authority. For if all the world were to proceed in conformity with the precepts of the law, we should say that everything comes to pass according to natural order, and no one would think of so much as inquiring after the cause.[42]

Kant ends up characterizing immorality as "inscrutable." But defenders of the defiance explanation will want to insist that immorality is perfectly understandable, given the attitude all of us human beings take towards what is in fact an unpleasant, even hateful, authority that commands us to forgo what is in our interest. What defenders of the defiance account owe the skeptics is an account of how morality can still have genuine authority over us and not simply mere power – for example, psychological power – given our distaste for (perhaps even hatred of) its commands.

Unlike the difficulties plaguing the other explanations of immorality, these four difficulties plaguing the defiance account are not obviously insurmountable, and I will attempt solutions of them in a forthcoming article.[43] But all of them, particularly the last one, highlight how problematic it is to explain why, and in what way, morality is authoritative for us. If immorality is a product of a person's defiance of its purported mastery over him, then the way to stop his immorality is to convince him either that its authority over him is good rather than hateful, or that if he rebels he must always lose. However, our belief in his inevitable defeat is based more on faith than on argument, and the idea that morality's rule is always

---

[42] *Religion Within the Limits of Reason Alone*, p. 52n. My emphasis.
[43] See "Mens Rea," in *Social Philosophy and Policy*, vol. 7, no. 2 (Spring 1990); this issue is forthcoming as *Crime, Culpability, and Remedy* (Oxford: Basil Blackwell, 1990).

attractive and never hateful is something that all of us who are prone to immoral acts on occasion have trouble sustaining. We await proof that we must always accept morality as our master.

Philosophy, University of California, Davis

TRADITION AND REASON IN THE HISTORY OF ETHICS

By T. H. Irwin

Introduction

Students of the history of ethics sometimes find themselves tempted by moderate or extreme versions of an approach that might roughly be called 'historicist'. This temptation may result from the difficulties of approaching historical texts from a 'narrowly philosophical' point of view. We may begin, for instance, by wanting to know what Aristotle has to say about 'the problems of ethics', so that we can compare his views with those of (say) Aquinas, Hume, Kant, Sidgwick, and Rawls, and then decide what is true or false in each theorist's position. But this narrowly philosophical attitude soon runs into difficulties, and writers on the history of ethics often warn us against it.

We quite often read, for instance, that the Aristotelian virtues called 'generosity' and 'justice' are not the same as the virtues that we call by these names; that an Aristotelian virtue is not the sort of thing that we count as a virtue; and that Aristotle's social, political, and cultural environment causes him to ask different questions, relying on different presuppositions, from those that would seem natural to us. We might infer that it is in some way naive, anachronistic, or unhistorical to treat Aristotle and ourselves as offering different answers to timeless questions; and a little further reflection may suggest to us that our own questions and presuppositions are no less historically limited and parochial than Aristotle's now appear to us to have been.

This general attitude to the history of ethics is what I mean in speaking of a 'historicist' approach. I do not intend this either as a term of abuse or as a precise technical term. I have sketched the position in general terms, because I think these general ideas convey a historicist position in its most attractive form (indeed, some people may think the position I have described is mere common sense). Particular versions of historicism seem to me to be hard to spell out convincingly, but it is important to recognize that the general (and perhaps somewhat vague) ideas may retain their appeal even for those who admit that they have not found a satisfactory way to articulate them.

Alasdair MacIntyre's book, *Whose Justice? Which Rationality?*,[1] is, among other things, an elaborate defense of a form of historicism about the history of ethics. He describes a 'narrowly philosophical' approach, in order to reject it:

> Historians of philosophy have often enough presented the historical context of each philosopher's life as mere background. They have been

---

[1] Notre Dame: Notre Dame University Press, 1988. Further references are given in the text in parentheses.

compelled by the way in which later philosophers comment upon earlier to recognize some types of historical sequence, but sometimes little more than this. So the development of philosophical thought has been presented as though relatively autonomous, as a socially disembodied enterprise concerned with relatively timeless problems. (p.390)

MacIntyre offers to explain why this 'disembodied' and narrowly philosophical approach needs to be replaced by a more historicist attitude to the history of ethics.

His book, therefore, raises an important issue about method in the study of the history of ethics. But MacIntyre's approach to this issue is especially interesting, insofar as it is not concerned simply with method in historical study. For his discussion of method and of history is part of a diagnosis of what is wrong in contemporary moral and political argument. He thinks the 'narrowly philosophical' attitude to the history of ethics also results in a mistaken view of the state of contemporary discussion, and that the right way to study the history of ethics is also the right way to approach contemporary questions. MacIntyre's claims are challenging and important. Even if, as I believe, they are not true, some discussion of them may throw some light on the fundamental issues that he raises.

My main aim in this paper is to examine MacIntyre's version of historicism and the case he makes for it; and I will eventually come back to the issue of historicism. The route will be a bit roundabout, however, for it requires some discussion of the central parts of MacIntyre's argument. The connection between his thesis about history and his thesis about contemporary questions is his conception of tradition and its role in rational inquiry. I therefore turn to his views on tradition.

I. JUSTICE, RATIONALITY, AND TRADITION

From the 'narrowly philosophical' point of view, we might ask what justice, say, really is, and what it really requires of us; and we might look for an answer to these questions in the hope of resolving contemporary disputes about justice. MacIntyre, however, believes that we should stop asking such questions, since they rest on the false presupposition that there is such a thing as justice-as-such; we will get nothing more out of such questions than insoluble disagreements. Instead, we should concentrate on the articulation and development of the different conceptions of justice embedded in different traditions.

He argues as follows (p. 2):

1. Claims about justice depend on claims about rationality.
2. Claims about rationality depend on traditions.
3. Hence claims about justice depend on traditions.

Here I focus mainly on the second claim. MacIntyre defends it by two main types of arguments:

(a) Relatively *a priori* arguments. He relies on general claims about the nature of rational justification, and its presuppositions; he takes these to show that justification is relative to presuppositions about rationality of the sort that are embedded in a tradition.

(b) Historical arguments. MacIntyre argues that study of the main traditions of moral philosophy shows us exactly what we should expect to find if we are convinced by his *a priori* argument – that different philosophers in different traditions have views about justice and rationality that differ widely enough to count as different justices and different rationalities.

Since MacIntyre's arguments go in these two directions, a critic needs to comment on both. I begin with the first type of argument.

MacIntyre remarks that in contemporary society we are confronted with many incompatible claims about what justice demands, and we lack an effective method to resolve the conflicts. In particular, theories of justice do not resolve the conflicts, since they defend conflicting conceptions of justice that support the conflicting claims about what justice requires. We might try to decide between theories of justice by asking which one should be acceptable to practically rational persons. But this question requires us to say what a practically rational person is like, and there turn out to be conflicting conceptions of practical rationality, no less than of justice.

We might turn to contemporary philosophy for help in resolving this conflict, but MacIntyre thinks that the predominant contemporary philosophical outlook will not help us. For it urges us to resolve conflicts about justice and practical rationality by taking up a 'neutral' point of view and accepting the answers that can be agreed on from this point of view:

> Rationality requires, so it has been argued by a number of academic philosophers, that we first divest ourselves of allegiance to any one of the contending theories and also abstract ourselves from all those particularities of social relationship in terms of which we have been accustomed to understand our responsibilities and our interests. Only by so doing, it has been suggested, shall we arrive at a genuinely neutral, impartial, and, in this way, universal point of view, freed from the partisanship and the partiality and onesidedness that otherwise affect us. (p. 3)

It is not clear – since MacIntyre gives no references – who is supposed to hold this view; in fact, I wonder whether any major theorist actually holds just this view.[2] At any rate, MacIntyre thinks this neutral point of view yields no agreement, and in any case is not the right point of view. He thinks it is a specifically liberal and individualist point of view that "illegitimately ignores the inescapably historically and socially context-bound character which any substantive set of principles of rationality, whether theoretical or practical, is bound to have" (p. 4). It follows that "disagreement arises concerning the fundamental nature of rationality and extends into disagreement over how it is rationally appropriate to proceed in the face of these disagreements" (p. 4).

Awareness of these disagreements may lead us into an unjustified (in MacIntyre's view) skepticism about the usefulness of rational argument. Such

---

[2] References constitute a major puzzle about this book. Sometimes very precise references and acknowledgements are given; sometimes no reference at all is given. No discernible principle seems to determine the presence or absence of references.

skepticism is a result of accepting an Enlightenment conception of rationality (p. 6). If we reject that conception, we may see a possible alternative:

> a conception of rational enquiry as embodied in a tradition, a conception according to which the standards of rational justification themselves emerge from and are part of a history in which they are vindicated by the way in which they transcend the limitations of and provide remedies for the defects of their predecessors within the history of that same tradition. (p. 7)

MacIntyre's view, then, is that attention to what we might call (it is not his phrase) 'traditional reason' – the conception of rationality that is inevitably the product of a tradition – is the only alternative to skepticism about the possibility of finding a true conception of practical reason that is strong enough to solve conflicts about justice.[3]

Traditional reason avoids the difficulties faced by the neutral and universal point of view, because it does not assume the impossible conditions that are involved in neutrality and universality. Within a tradition "the concept of rational justification which is at home in that form of enquiry is essentially historical. To justify is to narrate how the argument has gone so far" (p. 8). In such an inquiry we can identify and defend first principles. "But what justifies the first principles themselves, or rather the whole structure of theory of which they are a part, is the rational superiority of their particular structure to all previous attempts within that particular tradition to formulate such theories and principles" (p. 8). Since traditional reason is, to this extent, more modest than neutral and universal reason, it delivers results on issues where neutral and universal reason gets stuck in inconclusive arguments about first principles. Reflection on traditions shows us that there are "rationalities rather than rationality" and "justices rather than justice" (p. 9).

MacIntyre is well aware that his position may seem to be some form of relativism – that he may seem to be replacing the claim that a theory is true with the claim that it is "true within a tradition." He insists that this is not what he means, and he argues at length against the tendency to draw such conclusions from his views (ch. 18). Later on, I will discuss MacIntyre's attempt to avoid relativism. First, I take up some more elementary questions about his conception of a tradition, and about the specific ways he applies it to questions about justice.

II. What Is a Tradition?

MacIntyre does not say much in general terms about what a tradition of the relevant sort might be. He distrusts such attempts at general definition: "the concept of tradition-constrained and tradition-constitutive rational enquiry cannot be elucidated apart from its exemplifications" (p. 10). His book offers a fairly lengthy discussion of four traditions (Aristotelian, Thomist, Scottish, and liberal).

---

[3] By 'strong enough', I mean that the conception is full and definite enough to determine one view about practical reason and justice and to exclude others. Acceptance of the Principle of Non-Contradiction provides a partial conception of rationality, but not a strong enough conception to support one conception of justice against another (p. 4).

The existence of a tradition is meant to explain something about the unquestioned premises, assumptions, and presuppositions of a theory, and something about why the theory is addressed to these questions and not to others. Insofar as a particular theorist has to take something for granted in these areas, MacIntyre wants to appeal to a tradition. I assume, however, that he does not think you can generate a tradition just by deciding to take some things for granted; if I put forward my own strange theory with strange presuppositions, that is not enough to create a tradition. As MacIntyre thinks of it, a tradition seems to involve more than one person; to this extent it is like an institution. It also seems to involve more than one person for more than one generation. In a degenerate case, a pretentious school, say, may deliberately try to conceal its embarrassingly recent foundation by inventing a number of traditions overnight; but since it does this precisely to convey an impression of antiquity and stability, the degenerate case indicates that a tradition normally involves some degree of antiquity and stability.

It is less clear whether MacIntyre thinks a succession of philosophers sharing roughly the same unquestioned assumptions constitutes a tradition. Perhaps I can offer an example that MacIntyre does not discuss. We might suggest (for the sake of argument) that the Presocratics constitute a tradition, because they share a number of assumptions about knowledge, method, and cosmology that affect the shape and scope of their inquiries. But (let us suppose) these common features are purely intellectual; they are not significantly affected by any social, political, or institutional framework.

MacIntyre does not seem to believe that the Presocratics (as I have described them) could constitute a tradition. For the traditions he discusses are more than patterns of intellectual inquiry:

> In each of them intellectual enquiry was or is a part of the elaboration of a mode of social and moral life of which the intellectual enquiry itself was an integral part, and in each of them the forms of this life were embodied with greater or less degrees of imperfection in social and political institutions which also draw their life from other sources. (p. 349)[4]

He also seems to assume that the non-intellectual aspects of a tradition are essential to its role in the defense of claims about practical reason and justice:

> The conclusion to which the argument so far has led is not only that it is out of the debates, conflicts, and enquiry of socially embodied, historically contingent traditions that contentions regarding practical rationality and justice are advanced, modified, abandoned, or replaced, but that there is no other way to engage in the formulation, elaboration, rational justification, and criticism of accounts of practical rationality and justice except within some one particular tradition in conversation, cooperation, and conflict with those who inhabit the same tradition. (p. 350)

Here he clearly seems to claim that a purely intellectual movement could not play the role that he ascribes to a socially embodied tradition.

[4] On social embodiment, cf. also pp. 389f.

What follows from this about my example of the Presocratics? MacIntyre might mean either of two claims: (1) Such a case is not empirically possible; there are no purely intellectual movements of the sort that I attempted to describe, and I have simply neglected facts about the Presocratics that make them part of a genuine tradition. (2) Such movements are empirically quite possible; they are just not what he means by 'tradition'.

We may be tempted to exaggerate the plausibility of the first answer, if we assume a less precise conception of social embodiment than MacIntyre intends. For some non-intellectual conditions clearly affect the growth and survival of inquiries even into the most abstract questions of mathematics, physics, or logic. These inquiries will not have much historical continuity or significance unless inquirers have access to the relevant material resources, leisure, education, and so on; and it is highly likely that the social environment that provides these will also tend to affect the conduct of research, the sorts of questions that are asked, the sorts of inquiries that are feasible, and the dissemination of their results. If this is what MacIntyre means in saying that traditions must be socially embodied, then his claim is not terribly controversial.

The passage recently quoted, however, makes it clear that this is not all that MacIntyre means by social embodiment. For he thinks that social embodiment, as well as the purely intellectual aspect of a tradition, plays an essential role in justification. This justifying role for social embodiment clearly expresses a more controversial claim than the one I mentioned in the previous paragraph. If one insists on this justifying role, then one cannot accept the second answer I suggested above. For MacIntyre cannot recognize purely intellectual movements that have some apparently viable pattern of argument and justification that is independent of their social embodiment. He must therefore defend the first answer. His claim that rational inquiry depends on tradition and tradition depends on social embodiment actually implies a controversial claim about justification.

III. SOCIAL EMBODIMENT

Why does MacIntyre believe that the non-intellectual aspects of social embodiment play an essential justifying role? He suggests a reason in a comment on the relation between a theory and its social context:

> Forms of social institution, organization, and practice are always to great [sic] or lesser degree socially embodied theories, and, as such, more or less rational according to the standards of that type of rationality which is presupposed by tradition-constituted enquiry. (p. 390)

The initial rationality of institutions and practices gives philosophical theory somewhere to start. Perhaps MacIntyre means that a philosophical theory that tried to begin from no social reality, and set out to defend its theories from first principles with no social embodiment, would have no satisfactory starting point. For we might always accuse philosophers of arbitrariness in their choice of these 'disembodied' first principles, and we could repeat the same accusation about any further disembodied principles that might be adduced in support of these principles. This charge of arbitrariness is answered (one might think) if one begins from socially embodied institutions and practices; for we have some reason to try to understand them, and if they are a going concern, they have some internal rationality that it is worth our while to try to articulate.

If this is MacIntyre's view, how far is the social embodiment of a theory meant to circumscribe its content? Must a good theory, for instance, always presuppose the fundamental rationality of the basic social practices in which it is embodied? It is hard to see how this can be avoided, if social embodiment is to play the role I have suggested. Clearly, philosophical theory might be a source of criticism and reform, if we discover that the beliefs underlying one institution are in conflict with the beliefs underlying a more fundamental institution in the same society. But if we discover that the moral principles that seem plausible to us condemn the basic institutions of our society, must we not, on MacIntyre's view of tradition, conclude that we have simply made a mistake in our efforts to articulate the principles underlying the social reality that we began from? If the philosophical principles we find cannot be justified by their role in articulating the beliefs embodied in social reality, then MacIntyre seems to be committed to charging them with the arbitrariness that is supposed to be avoided by appeal to social embodiment.

A further question about social embodiment arises when we have to choose between two theories. Some opponents of Socrates, Plato, and Aristotle defended the democratic assumptions and institutions that the Socratic tradition rejected.[5] If they could do this, does it not follow, on MacIntyre's view, that their theories were correct, and that the theories in the Socratic tradition were wrong, if the socially embodied tradition plays some essential role in the justification of theories? If we agree with MacIntyre on the issue about justification, we seem to impose a different test on theories from the one we normally think we impose in asking whether one theory is more defensible, or closer to the truth, than another.

MacIntyre might reply by arguing that if a social institution or practice turns out to be open to devastating philosophical criticism, it is thereby shown not to be fundamental for the society it belongs to; perhaps what is fundamental is not to be determined simply by the relation of an institution to other institutions, but by the society's fundamental moral beliefs. But if MacIntyre were willing to argue in this way, it would be less clear why we should insist that philosophical theories must be socially embodied in the first place – for if philosophical argument could by itself deserve our acceptance despite its rejection of all the aspects of its social embodiment, then why should we agree that social embodiment plays an essential role in justification?

MacIntyre's claims, then, imply a significant restriction on the rational justifiability of fundamental philosophical criticism; the more fundamental the criticism, the more confident we can be, according to his view, that it is unjustified. Since this is a significant restriction, implying the rejection of some forms of criticism that we might take to be both possible and important, we ought to see why MacIntyre thinks such restrictions are justified.

[5] MacIntyre mentions these opponents (p. 392). He does not discuss them at length in his main discussion of Greek political theory (chs. 3–5). See below, Section VI.

IV. TRADITION AND JUSTIFICATION

Any argument or attempted justification that succeeds in persuading an interlocutor has to begin from something that the interlocutor accepts; and it is (in many cases, at least) a contingent fact about particular interlocutors that they do or do not agree on some assumptions from which we can persuade them. If, then, the assumptions accepted by interlocutors depend on the traditions they belong to, successful persuasive argument depends on tradition. But it by no means follows that justification depends on tradition. For what I have just said is quite consistent with the further claim that p is a good argument for q, and justifies belief in q, whether or not it persuades someone in a particular tradition. This further claim implies that p is not simply a good argument within this tradition, but a good argument without qualification, and that what makes it a good argument is not simply the fact that it counts as good within the tradition, but a fact about the relation between the argument and its actual subject matter.

This is a relatively simple-minded view that we might think especially appropriate for arguments in mathematics, logic, and natural science. We think that the proofs, derivations, and arguments can be shown to be the right ones for that subject matter, not simply the right ones for inquirers in that tradition. To say they are the right principles because they are the right ones for inquirers in that tradition is to get things the wrong way round; for – we think in a simple-minded way – a particular tradition of inquiry is the right one for inquiry into this subject matter precisely because it has the appropriate, truth-revealing methods, not the other way round.

The scientific and mathematical examples suggest that we ought to distinguish two claims:

(i) These are good arguments, and their goodness consists not in their counting as good within a tradition, but in their adequacy to their subject matter.
(ii) You can see that they are good arguments whether or not you are within a given tradition.

If we don't know anything about quantum physics or about proof theory, we will hardly know whether a given argument in one of these disciplines is a good one or not. If a 'neutral and universal' point of view is one in which we set aside all the mathematical and physical beliefs that distinguish contemporary physicists and mathematicians from Aristotle, then it is a fairly unpromising point of view from which to defend arguments in quantum physics.

It is important, then, if we are not to caricature the position that MacIntyre rejects, to separate the claim about the epistemological status of particular arguments from claims about how you can show that they have that status. For convenience (and without, I hope, begging any questions), I will call claim (i) the 'absolutist' claim and claim (ii) the 'neutralist' claim.

Now I take MacIntyre to be rejecting both the neutralist and the absolutist claim, and to reject them in favor of what I will call a 'contextualist' conception of justification, according to which the context provided by a preexisting tradition determines whether or not an argument is a good one. I take him to mean the strong contextualist claim, that the tradition determines whether the argument *is* good, and not simply the weaker claim that the tradition determines whether particular people *think* it is good.

I cannot find any place where he definitely distinguishes the stronger from the weaker claim.[6] But he seems to affirm the strong contextualist claim against absolutism. In describing the situation of someone who does not already accept a particular tradition he says:

> Such a person is confronted by the claims of each of the traditions which we have considered as well as by those of other traditions. How is it rational to respond to them? The initial answer is: that will depend upon who you are and how you understand yourself. This is not the kind of answer which we have been educated to expect in philosophy, but that is because our education in and about philosophy has by and large presupposed what is in fact not true, that (1) there are standards of rationality, adequate for the evaluation of rival answers to such questions, (2) equally available, at least in principle, to all persons, whatever tradition they may happen to find themselves in and whether or not they inhabit any tradition. (p. 393, reference numbers added.)

Taken one way, MacIntyre's answer ('that will depend . . .') is uncontroversial (and hence it *is* 'the kind of answer which we have been educated to expect in philosophy'). For what it is subjectively rational for me to believe and do depends on what I already believe and want; any argument that persuades me must start from where I am. But if this were all MacIntyre meant, he could not reasonably claim that it is not what we have been educated to expect in philosophy, and it would be quite compatible with (1) and (2), which he rejects. Since he rejects (1) and (2), he must intend his answer to imply that nothing outside a particular tradition determines what it is *in fact* rational (whether or not we realize it) to believe and do. Hence he must reject absolutism. If this is what he means, then he is right (I hope) to say that his answer is not what we have been educated to expect in philosophy, but I do not see a good case for re-education.

In trying to understand MacIntyre's claim, I have introduced a distinction between what is subjectively rational for a particular person and what is in fact rational (or, let us say, 'objectively rational'); I would find it hard to state MacIntyre's position clearly without some distinction along these lines. To avoid misunderstanding, I should make it clear that if we say S fails to conform to objective standards of rationality, it does not follow that S is open to criticism for behaving irrationally. If S is a Roman Stoic, say, and has been persuaded by the Stoic defense of divination, then (we may concede) S is not to be blamed for using divination to predict the future. Nonetheless, we can recognize grounds for saying that divination is not in fact a rational method to follow in predicting the future, and that therefore S is not following an objectively rational method. To avoid trivializing his claim about rationality, MacIntyre needs to recognize some sort of

[6] The book badly needs, but unfortunately lacks, an index of topics.

rationality that is distinct from subjective rationality (or 'what is rational by S's lights'); once we see this, we see (as I will try to explain below) that his claims about rationality face some objections.

In the passage I quoted above, MacIntyre rejects absolutism. He may also intend to be stating and rejecting neutralism. But he does not clearly succeed in doing this. For (2) need not commit us to neutralism, if 'at least in principle' is suitably interpreted. In one sense of 'in principle' quantum physics is available in principle to Aristotle, insofar as it is not logically impossible that if he dropped in for a visit now, he could eventually be taught quantum physics. An absolutist is not committed to any stronger sort of availability in principle than this. If MacIntyre rejects this weak sort of availability in principle, then he rejects the absolutist position.

Another remark on liberalism also suggests the rejection of absolutism. In commenting on the failure of liberalism to find a universally accepted neutral standpoint, he infers:

> That liberalism fails in this respect, therefore, provides the strongest reason that we can actually have for asserting that there is no such neutral ground, that there is no place for appeals to a practical-rationality-as-such or a justice-as-such to which all rational persons would by their very rationality be compelled to give their allegiance. There is instead only the practical-rationality-of-this-or-that-tradition and the justice-of-this-or-that-tradition. (p. 346)

The mere rejection of neutralism would not support MacIntyre's strong ontological claim (in the last sentence quoted) that there is no such thing as justice-as-such and so on. For simple rejection of neutralism leaves open the option of believing in the existence of justice-as-such, and believing that a true (or more approximately true) account of it is given by one tradition rather than another. But since MacIntyre means to deny that there is any such thing as justice-as-such, he must reject the option I just described, and hence must reject absolutism as well as neutralism.

· In describing the absolutist position as 'simple-minded', I mean only that it is a common and intuitive way of thinking about the relation of theories and arguments to reality – and it is found to be quite intuitive in the different traditions that MacIntyre discusses.[7] I do not mean that it is free of philosophical difficulties; perhaps it can actually be shown to be incoherent. And in distinguishing absolutism from neutralism, I do not mean that it is necessarily wrong to attack absolutism by attacking neutralism; for we might be able to show both that absolutism must appeal to the truth of neutralism and that such an appeal undermines absolutism. If we could show that, it would be so much the worse for absolutism.

Still, it is unwarranted to take arguments against neutralism to be arguments against absolutism unless we have previously argued that absolutism requires

---

[7] Some of his discussion of truth, facts, and correspondence is relevant here; pp. 356ff. See also his discussion of Aquinas, pp. 169–71.

neutralism; and it is unwarranted to assume that other philosophers reject absolutism, if we show only that they reject neutralism, and do not show that they think absolutism requires neutralism.

I will try to show later, in discussing Aristotle, that MacIntyre fails to notice the gap between neutralism and absolutism, and that his failure undermines one of the major contrasts that he wants to draw between different conceptions of practical reason. At the moment I will simply remark that he offers no clear argument against absolutism, though he is committed to the rejection of it. To show how serious this problem is, I would like to explore a difficulty that arises from applying his views about justification to his own argument.

V. THE RATIONALITY OF TRADITIONS

My questions about MacIntyre are examples of a familiar sort of question about someone who takes his view. He wants to deny standards of rationality that are independent of traditions; but on the other hand, he wants to say that traditions may develop more or less rationally, and that we should pay special attention to those that develop rationally. It is not clear to me how he can make the second, and perfectly reasonable, claim without some modification of the first claim.

MacIntyre offers a contextualist, tradition-based account of the justification of first principles. Since his own argument is about first principles, the contextualist account presumably applies to it as well, and it is intended to be convincing only within the context provided by a tradition. What tradition is this?

At the end of the book MacIntyre suggests that the Thomist synthesis of the Aristotelian and Augustinian traditions is less vulnerable to attack than the other three traditions are (p. 402). Perhaps, then, we ought to take MacIntyre to be an adherent of this tradition, and ought to understand his contextualist account of justification, and his criticism of other traditions, as a product of this tradition. If MacIntyre's claim about the superiority of the Thomist tradition were offered from some putative point of view outside any tradition, it would commit the neutralist error that he normally attacks. Hence, he ought in consistency to mean only that, from the point of view of the Thomist tradition, the Thomist tradition is superior to others. From this it evidently does not follow that from the point of view of other traditions the Thomist point of view is superior.

Still, the Thomist criticism of other traditions may make adherents of these other traditions aware of incoherences in them. In MacIntyre's view, the Scottish tradition could not successfully, even to its own satisfaction, stand up to Hume's subversive criticism, and the liberal tradition cannot, even to its own satisfaction, cope with the criticisms that MacIntyre offers of its first principles. MacIntyre allows enough communication and mutual understanding between traditions so that, in the appropriate circumstances, criticisms expressed within one tradition may seem cogent within another.

If MacIntyre has stated the situation accurately, how should we react to it? No doubt it will make Thomists think they are right to accept the Thomist tradition over others. Will it make the adherents of other traditions think the Thomist tradition is superior to theirs? Presumably that depends on why the Thomist tradition is so immune to refutation. The reason might be that Thomists are unusually dogmatic in accepting bizarre but consistent first principles; from their perspective they cannot see the cogency of objections that, in the view of other traditions, are fatal to the Thomist position. If this is true, then the fact that it is difficult to convince Thomists that they are wrong is not necessarily a point in their favor, from the point of view of non-Thomists.

MacIntyre quite legitimately replies that this is not the right way to describe the Thomist tradition. Traditions are capable of being rational. A tradition may develop a theory of rational inquiry to explain the critical activity that gradually becomes self-conscious (p. 359); and it may take a rational attitude towards 'epistemological crises' and ways to overcome them (p. 361–64). A rational form of tradition-based inquiry is not so dogmatically and blindly committed to its first principles that it commits itself in advance to the rejection of all fundamental criticisms; indeed, it may find itself having to admit that the answers given by some other tradition are superior to its own (p. 365). If, then, a rational tradition compares itself with others and prefers itself, this result may be significant; it cannot be dismissed as a foregone conclusion.

It is quite correct to point out that a tradition may include these principles and methods of rational inquiry, and that if a tradition follows them, we may justifiably have more confidence in the conclusions it reaches than we would have if its methods of inquiry protected its basic beliefs from falsification at any cost. But though this is correct, I am not sure from what point of view MacIntyre is entitled to say it. For he insists that 'there is no set of independent standards of rational justification by appeal to which the issues between contending traditions can be decided' (p. 351);[8] and hence we presumably can approve of rational development of a tradition only if we are taking the point of view of a tradition. But this does not seem to be MacIntyre's attitude to the rationality of a tradition. He offers it as a reply to the relativist (p. 354) who wants to replace claims about truth and rationality with claims about truth and rationality relative to a tradition.

Now MacIntyre has one reasonable reply in mind. Even if we reject rationality-as-such, we need not be confined to rationality-relative-to-a-tradition to a degree that precludes communication between traditions. For perhaps the adherents of tradition T_1 will find that tradition T_2 does better (from the point of view of T_1) in answering questions that arise within T_1, and, to this extent, adherents of T_1 have reason (relative to T_1) for taking T_2 seriously.

Does this reply, however, undermine relativism? The possibility of communication allows traditions to change in response to one another. But why should we suppose (as an absolutist does) that it is possible for T_1 to come closer to the truth by learning from T_2? We can suppose this only if we suppose (i) that there are standards that a tradition conforms to insofar as it approaches the truth, and (ii) it is possible that T_2 meets these standards better than T_1 met them before T_1 was modified in the light of T_2. What makes them the right standards and conditions

---

[8] MacIntyre adds that competing traditions share some standards; he mentions a shared acceptance of logic (p. 351). But he insists that "that upon which they agree is insufficient to resolve those disagreements [viz., about first principles]" (p. 351).

cannot be the fact that they are endorsed by T_1, or the fact that they are endorsed by T_2; they must be the right standards and conditions because of objective facts independent of traditions. And, in saying this, we have reintroduced justice-as-such and rationality-as-such (whatever we say about our prospects or resources for access to them).

To sharpen the issue I have tried to raise here, I would need to be more careful to distinguish metaphysical from epistemological questions, to avoid any tendency to confuse claims about truth with claims about justification. I am not sure, however, what MacIntyre's position would look like if it were formulated with more explicit attention to these distinctions; I hope I have at least raised a relevant issue. While I cannot claim to be certain about MacIntyre's intended conclusion, or about the exact form of his argument for it, it seems to me that he is committed to the rejection of absolutism, and therefore (against his expressed intention) to acceptance of some form of relativism. His account of the rationality of traditions, therefore, seems both to be necessary for his reply to relativism and to be inconsistent with his general view of the role of tradition in justification. For he seems to assert that traditions can be compared with each other to see if they develop rationally and respond rationally to challenges; and he seems to think that traditions that develop and respond rationally are preferable on those grounds. We may suppose that these claims are made from within, say, the Thomist tradition; but if we do not suppose that we have reasons for believing that this tradition corresponds to standards of rational development that are independent of it, then I do not see how we can claim to answer a relativist.[9]

A special difficulty seems to arise for MacIntyre insofar as he regards himself as an adherent of one tradition in particular, for it is not clear to me that the Thomist-Aristotelian tradition embodies the attitude to rationality that he advocates. Certainly Aristotelians and Thomists argue within a tradition of inquiry, but they think they discover principles that should be accepted on grounds that exist independently of any tradition. They think that their tradition is the right one, and the results it reaches are to be taken seriously, precisely because they think they discover such principles; they do not think the correctness of the principles consists in the fact that they are the outcome of this tradition of inquiry.[10] MacIntyre refers to this issue insofar as he notices that Aquinas does not reduce the concept of truth to the concept of warranted assertibility (pp. 169f.). But I do not think he sufficiently recognizes the Thomist-Aristotelian reasons for preferring one method or conclusion over another. Aristotle and Aquinas believe firmly in such things as justice-as-such and rationality-as-such; indeed, that is exactly the sort of thing they hope to give an account of in a successful philosophical inquiry.

---

[9] Perhaps MacIntyre believes that these facts about the rationality of traditions are indeed independent of any particular tradition, and that they give us some basis for choosing between traditions, but believes nonetheless that they are insufficient to vindicate one (or even a few) of the conflicting conceptions of rationality and justice against others. This question does not allow an easy answer, but I do not think MacIntyre's arguments settle the question.

[10] Aristotle's conception of inquiry as a progress from what is known 'to us' to what is known 'by nature' implies that the proper terminus of inquiry is fixed by external reality itself (signaled in 'by nature'), not by its relation to our inquiry.

MacIntyre's denial of such things is a basic disagreement with the tradition that he claims to accept.

If, then, MacIntyre disagrees with Aristotle and Aquinas, from what point of view does he disagree with them? Either he speaks from within some other tradition, or he speaks from outside the point of view of any tradition. In the first case, his view conflicts with his preference for the Thomist-Aristotelian tradition. In the second case, he adopts a point of view that, on his own account, ought not to be available.

MacIntyre means to anticipate and to answer some objections of the sort that I have raised. He wants both to reject absolutism and to allow for rational comparison of different traditions. I do not think he has explained how he can legitimately do both.

VI. ARISTOTLE ON JUSTICE

MacIntyre rests his case about the tradition-based character of beliefs about justice and rationality not only on the relatively *a priori* arguments I have been examining but also on discussions of particular philosophers. These discussions need to be convincing independently of MacIntyre's *a priori* thesis about justification and tradition; for if we accepted the *a priori* thesis, but found shared presuppositions about justice and rationality among otherwise different traditions, we would have found an area of overlap between these different traditions. MacIntyre's *a priori* argument tells us that if we find radical disagreements between traditions, these radical disagreements will not be soluble. But it does not tell us what questions will arouse radical disagreements; to find these, we need to look at the historical evidence.

In my view, MacIntyre's historical claims are wrong often enough to cast serious doubt on his main argument. In saying this, I do not mean to take a narrowly positivist view about the study of the history of philosophy – as though all issues of interpretation could be settled on purely empirical, non-philosophical grounds. I am not trying to confront MacIntyre with the assured results agreed on by all competent scholars. I want to suggest that on some issues where MacIntyre thinks he sees different traditions disagreeing radically in the way predicted by his theory, a reasonable historical case can be made against him. Here, I raise only a few illustrative objections to MacIntyre's historical picture. I begin with Aristotle and the Greek tradition, and add a few remarks on the liberal tradition.[11]

In conformity with his views about tradition, MacIntyre prefaces his account of Aristotle with an account of Greek, especially Athenian, moral and political views that form the appropriate background to the theories of Plato and Aristotle. He traces some issues about justice back to a conflict that he sees in post-Homeric Greek societies between 'goods of excellence' and 'goods of effectiveness'. The goods of effectiveness are those that are effective in the pursuit of 'external rewards'

---

[11] I therefore forgo any discussion of Hutcheson, Hume, and the Scottish tradition. Some aspects of MacIntyre's treatment of this tradition are helpfully discussed by Julia Annas (in a review forthcoming in *Philosophy and Public Affairs*), who also raises further important questions about MacIntyre's whole conception of a tradition.

that people might pursue independently of any commitment to excellent performance – riches, power, status, prestige (p. 32). The goods of excellence are those that define excellent performance of some activity independently of its actual success in gaining external rewards.[12] MacIntyre remarks correctly that the presuppositions of the morality and society depicted by Homer conceal many possibilities of conflict between these two sorts of goods, and that the possibility of conflict comes out clearly in post-Homeric society.[13]

The conflict between these two types of goods influences, in MacIntyre's view, people's conception of justice. From the point of view of effectiveness, justice consists in "what is required by the reciprocity of effective cooperation" (p. 37); it can be represented as (whether or not it actually is) the outcome of a bargain for mutual advantage. The point of this cooperation, then, is instrumental; one values the cooperation for its consequential advantages, not because one values cooperation for itself. From the point of view of excellence, however, justice is "what is due to excellence" (37).

Neither conception of justice, however, captures the beliefs about justice that underlie Greek democracy. Some Greek theorists accept the instrumental conception of justice that MacIntyre describes. It is put forward by Glaucon and Adeimantus in *Republic* ii, rejected by Aristotle (in *Politics* iii 9), and later accepted by Epicurus (whose account of justice is not mentioned by MacIntyre).[14] But we have no reason to suppose that either this conception or MacIntyre's other conception is especially characteristic of democrats.

It was characteristic of Athenian democracy to demand 'equal laws' (*isonomia*) for rich and poor,[15] and 'equal speaking' (*isegoria*) in political contexts. The Syracusean democratic leader Athenagoras defends democracy (according to a speech in Thucydides) as just, not simply as effective or as a reward of merit.[16] It is easy to connect these claims about justice with the belief that some equal rights belong to a citizen as such. If that is so, then not all aspects of justice are exhausted

---

[12] MacIntyre exaggerates the extent to which the distinction is clear in Homer. He says: "by 'more excellent' we do not *mean* 'victorious'; 'more excellent, but defeated' is not a contradiction, as Hector recognized when, having affirmed his own preeminence as a warrior, he nonetheless foresees his own defeat (*Iliad* VI, 440–465)" (pp. 27–28). The example of Hector does not seem to me to support the distinction MacIntyre draws between being superior and being victorious. Admittedly, Hector does not expect to be victorious over everyone – he thinks he will lose to Achilles. He does not claim that he has more *aretê* than everyone else; he recognizes that he is inferior in *aretê* to Achilles. An example of even more radical dependence of *aretê* on external circumstances is provided by the remark that Zeus takes away the half of a man's *aretê* on the day he becomes a slave (*Odyssey* 17.320–23)

[13] MacIntyre might have usefully mentioned some of the poems of Theognis (despite the disputed date of the corpus as a whole). In saying that "those who used to be *kakoi* are now *agathoi* (57–58) because people of nonaristocratic birth can now expect to achieve wealth or political office, Theognis vividly displays the dissolution of some Homeric assumptions – for he finds himself constrained to call *agathoi* people whom he clearly detests.

[14] See *Republic* 358e–359b, *Politics* 1280a25–b23 (perhaps not discussing exactly the same position), Diogenes Laertius x 150–51.

[15] The exact type of equality implied in demands for *isonomia* is a matter for dispute. For discussion, see Gregory Vlastos, "Isonomia politikê," in *Platonic Studies*, 2nd ed. (Princeton: Princeton University Press, 1981), ch. 8.

[16] Thucydides vi 38–39. Since Thucydides makes Athenagoras appear foolish and short-sighted, and indeed (in Thucydides's jaundiced view) a typical democratic leader, it is suitable that he should be provided with some typical democratic sentiments.

by considerations of reward for merit. On the other hand, while one might try to defend democratic equality by appeal to instrumentally effective cooperation, we have no reason to suppose that Greek democrats supposed that such a defense was necessary to vindicate their belief. Some beliefs about equality underlie democratic institutions and practices, but no evidence suggests that democrats accepted either of MacIntyre's conceptions of justice as a necessary or appropriate support for beliefs about equality.

The importance of equality in a prevalent Greek conception of justice is clear from Plato and Aristotle.[17] Their testimony is all the more useful because equality does not fit smoothly into their conceptions of justice. Both of them try to loosen the connection between justice and (what they call) 'numerical' equality in favor of 'proportional' equality (leaving room for numerical inequality). Without going into this aspect of their views, I think it is fair to say that they implicitly recognize that they have an uphill struggle against the tendency to connect justice with equality. Since this is a rather striking example of Plato's and Aristotle's treatment of their political tradition, it would be worth the attention of someone with MacIntyre's concerns. One might get the impression from MacIntyre that the tradition more or less assumed that a conception of justice would involve either concern for effectiveness or concern for rewarding merit, but I think this impression would be historically false and liable to distort our expectations about Aristotle.

I emphasize desert and merit because it plays a very large role in MacIntyre's argument to show that there is some fundamental difference between the Aristotelian conception of justice and the conception characteristic of other traditions – a difference fundamental enough to justify us in speaking of 'different justices'. In describing the difference he says: "So Hume and Rawls agree in excluding application for any Aristotelian concept of desert in framing rules of justice, while they disagree with each other on whether a certain type of equality is required by justice" (351).[18] Now the mere fact of some concern with desert is not enough to show that a theorist speaks out of a wholly different tradition, for evidently modern philosophers often have quite a bit to say about merit and desert also.[19] It must be the particular role played by desert in Aristotle's conception that marks his conception of justice as one of a number of justices. What is this particular role?

Unfortunately, MacIntyre's account of Aristotle's actual discussion of justice is not very detailed. To get a fair picture of the role of desert, we need to see its place in Aristotle's total theory. He divides justice into general justice, which is the whole of virtue as it relates to other people, and special justice, which is the branch of

[17] E.g., *Ethica Nicomachea* 1129a32–b1.

[18] I think this claim about Rawls rests partly on a misunderstanding that I will not discuss further.

[19] Two fairly random examples: W.D. Ross, *The Right and the Good* (Oxford: Clarendon Press, 1930), pp. 26f. (who rather exaggerates the role of merit in justice), and James Griffin, *Well-Being* (Oxford: Clarendon Press, 1986), ch. 12. In my remarks, I fail to distinguish steadily between merit and desert; since MacIntyre does not seem to distinguish them either, I hope no confusion results from the over-simplification.

general justice concerned with avoidance of 'overreaching'.[20] And the concern of general justice is 'the things producing and maintaining happiness and its parts for the political community'.[21] Insofar as general justice is concerned with this, it is concerned with the common interest; insofar as special justice is subordinate to general justice, it must also aim at the common interest. The different types of special justice preserve equality and seek to prevent overreaching, with the aim of promoting the common interest. Only one of the divisions of special justice involves differential reward for merit; this is distributive justice. Corrective and commercial justice proceed on grounds distinct from any concern to reward the parties involved for their comparative merits.[22] One might speak in general terms of desert in all these cases, but in corrective justice we are concerned with infliction of the deserved penalty, insofar as it is proportionate to the offense, and in commercial justice we are concerned with achieving the right sort of reciprocity in transactions. To say that one party 'deserves' a certain treatment in these cases is to say that it is suitable for him, but not that his virtue or past services make it a fitting reward.

Even this brief summary of the main divisions of justice, as Aristotle conceives it, suggests to me that MacIntyre considerably exaggerates the role of rewarding merit. Even in the division of justice that is concerned with rewarding merit – distributive justice – Aristotle's concern is subordinate to his concern with the common good of the community. He begins from the assumed connection between justice and equality, and remarks that while we can agree that special justice involves the preservation of equality and the avoidance of overreaching, there is no universal agreement about the sort of equality that should be preserved.[23] Aristotle thinks the dispute is to be resolved by deciding what sort of community the city is, and what sort of end it aims at.[24] He argues that it aims at 'fine actions', rather than mere survival or commercial exchange or mutual defense, and infers that distribution should accord with different people's contribution to these fine actions.[25] Questions can certainly be raised about the plausibility of several steps in Aristotle's argument, but the argument he offers is intelligible. His concern with

[20] MacIntyre adds a point about the translation of *pleonexia* (which I have rendered here by 'overreaching'), objecting to Hobbes's explanation of it as 'a desire of more than their share' (p. 111). MacIntyre thinks the sort of acquisitiveness discussed in *Pol.* i 9 (he cites 1257b41) is an example of *pleonexia*, even though it involves simply trying to get more than you previously had, not getting more than someone else has. He takes the failure of translators to notice that Aristotle condemns acquisitiveness as *pleonexia* to be a sign of their inability to recognize that he does not think acquisitiveness in itself is good and necessary.

I do not see that MacIntyre has proved his case. Sometimes there is room for doubt about whether *pleonektein* implies simply having more than (or getting the better of) someone else, or also implies having more than one ought to in relation to someone else. (See, e.g., E.M. Cope, *Aristotle's Rhetoric* (Cambridge: Cambridge University Press, 1877), vol. 1, p. 67, vol. 2, p. 170, and *Introduction to Aristotle's Rhetoric* (London: Macmillan, 1867), p. 273.) But as far as I can see, it always implies comparison and competition with someone else (not simply with oneself). Though Aristotle rejects the acquisitiveness discussed in *Pol.* i 9, he does not call it *pleonexia*; MacIntyre gives no reason, and I cannot see any reason, for believing that Aristotle intends i 9 as a discussion of *pleonexia*. MacIntyre cites no example of *pleonexia* with the sense he attributes to it. On this point, then, I think Hobbes's linguistic and historical judgment is sound, as far as concerns Aristotle at least.

[21] *EN* 1129a17–19.
[22] *EN* 1132a2–6.
[23] *Pol.* 1280a11–25.
[24] *Pol.* 1280a25–40.
[25] *Pol.* 1281a1–8.

distributive justice and with rewarding merit is subordinate to his concern with achieving the common good of the community; to this extent, his disagreement with other accounts of justice is not so radical as to make it appropriate to speak of different justices.

In this particular case, then, MacIntyre's claim about a fundamental difference between conceptions of justice belonging to different traditions does not rest on plausible historical argument. Once we trace Aristotle's theory back to its principles, it turns out to rest on claims and assumptions that are quite intelligible within other traditions. We need not deny that there are quite striking differences in the conclusions that Aristotle reaches, but we can trace these differences back to disagreements about, for instance, the sorts of goods that are the proper concern of the political community.

VII. ARISTOTLE ON PRACTICAL REASON

To contrast Aristotle's conception of practical rationality with 'the standpoint of modernity', MacIntyre focuses on Aristotle's rejection of neutralism. On the modern account:

> the individual human being confronts an alternative set of ways of life from a standpoint external to them all. Such an individual has as yet *ex hypothesi* no commitments, and the multifarious and conflicting desires which individuals develop provide in themselves no grounds for choosing which of such desires to develop and be guided by and which to inhibit and frustrate. From Aristotle's point of view such an individual has been deprived of the possibility of rational evaluation and rational choice. (p. 133)

Aristotle offers an alternative to the neutralist point of view, insofar as he thinks the right sort of upbringing and the right sorts of commitments are necessary for practical rationality. Only within the commitments provided by the political community can questions about practical rationality be asked and answered.

MacIntyre explains his claim by offering an analogy with scientific inquiry:

> From a standpoint outside that of any established scientific community, on the basis of data uncharacterized in terms of any established theory, there are and can be no sufficiently good reasons to suppose in respect of any particular subject matter of inquiry, let alone in respect of nature as such, that there is one true fundamental explanatory theory. (p. 134)

For practical rationality, in Aristotle's view, the political community plays the role that MacIntyre here attributes to the scientific community.

This description of scientific inquiry suggests that MacIntyre means to reject (as I suggested earlier) both neutralism and absolutism, and to claim that Aristotle rejects both positions. When he claims that from the external standpoint there are no good reasons for believing in one true explanatory theory, he might mean the relatively modest claim that if we know nothing about natural science we will be in a poor position to *see* any reasons for believing it or its presuppositions. This modest claim implies the rejection of neutralism. But when he says there *are* and *can be* no good reasons outside a scientific community, he seems to imply the stronger claim that conflicts with absolutism. For absolutists might readily agree that we cannot see the good reasons for believing in an explanatory theory if we lack the training that would make us members of a scientific community, but they will insist that there are good reasons for believing this, and that the point of scientific training is to lead us to see the good reasons that in fact there are.

If MacIntyre intends to reject absolutism here, then he goes beyond anything he has found in Aristotle on practical rationality. Aristotle certainly thinks moral training is necessary if we are to see all the reasons for acting one way rather than another.[26] But it does not follow that only the well-trained and virtuous person has reasons, or that only for such a person are there reasons, to do the virtuous action. On the contrary, vicious people are mistaken precisely because they fail to do what there are good reasons for them to do.[27]

MacIntyre is justified, then, in claiming that Aristotle rejects neutralism. But he does not show that Aristotle also rejects absolutism. To infer the falsity of absolutism from the falsity of neutralism we need to accept some unwarranted (for all MacIntyre has shown) assumptions; while MacIntyre himself accepts them, he gives no good reasons for attributing them to Aristotle.

It is not clear what MacIntyre thinks Aristotle believes about the connection between virtue and practical rationality, but he attributes a more restrictive view to Aristotle than Aristotle appears to hold. Aristotle thinks virtue and rationality are closely connected, insofar as all and only virtuous people see, and act on, all the good reasons there are for them to act in a particular way; to this extent, they are more rational than vicious, incontinent, or continent people. It is equally important, however, to notice the degree of rationality that Aristotle ascribes to vicious and to incontinent people. By misinterpreting Aristotle on these points, MacIntyre exaggerates the contrast between Aristotelian and modern conceptions of practical rationality.

First, he underestimates the degree of rationality that Aristotle attributes to the incontinent agent. MacIntyre's mistake on this point is reflected in his claims about the nature and extent of *prohairesis* in Aristotle. He rejects 'choice' and 'decision' as renderings of this term (without offering one of his own), on the ground that they "have as much application to the selection of actions by the *akratic* as they do to that by the virtuous and the vicious, while *prohairesis* is restricted by Aristotle to the latter (*EN* 1111b14–15 and 1139a33–35)" (p. 136).[28] This is not correct. In the first passage cited by MacIntyre, Aristotle says that the incontinent does not act on

---

[26] Prolonged training and experience is more necessary in the moral than in the scientific case; see *EN* 1142a10–20. But something analogous is needed in the scientific case too, to avoid *apaideusia*.

[27] Aristotle summarizes some of these reasons in *EN* ix 4.

[28] This argument actually raises another issue about translation. MacIntyre remarks that Aristotle uses *prohairesis* in a 'semitechnical' way; 'semi-' indicates the fact that the term is not Aristotle's invention, but belongs to ordinary Greek. If Aristotle's readers would think he was imposing unintuitively restrictive conditions on *prohairesis*, that suggests that a relatively ordinary English term such as 'choice' or 'decision' might not do too badly in conveying the impression that Aristotle's term might make on his original readers or hearers.

his *prohairesis*, not that he makes no *prohairesis*.[29] In fact, Aristotle claims that incontinent people make the right *prohairesis*;[30] unlike virtuous, vicious, and continent people, they fail to act on the *prohairesis* they form.[31] The aspect of practical rationality that belongs to *prohairesis* is present in incontinent people.

This aspect of Aristotle's view undeniably complicates his account of incontinence. Some of the complications matter for MacIntyre's claims about the distinctive features of Aristotle's view of practical rationality. MacIntyre defends the view that the conclusion of a practical syllogism is an action; agents act immediately on affirming the premises of the syllogism.[32] "This portrayal of the rational agent as acting immediately and necessarily upon affirming his reasons for action is once again very much at odds with our characteristically modern way of envisaging a rational agent" (p. 140). Unfortunately for MacIntyre's case, the view he wants to contrast with the modern view is not Aristotle's. Since incontinent people make the right *prohairesis*, something must intervene between their *prohairesis* and their doing the wrong action; if the making of a *prohairesis* is drawing the conclusion of a practical syllogism, the conclusion of a practical syllogism cannot be the action that is required by the premisses. I do not think this difficulty is insoluble, since I do not think Aristotle regards the conclusion as the action in any case.[33]

Some of the less plausible elements in MacIntyre's account of Aristotle on practical reason and incontinence turn out to be important for the contrast he wants to draw between an Aristotelian and a 'modern' view of practical reason. According to the modern view, an agent

> may rehearse the good reasons which he or she has for taking a particular course of action and then at the very least may hesitate without at all ceasing to be rational. The thought may cross his or her mind that there may be some other good to be pursued or that the promptings of some other desire should be listened to. Or the person may just not feel like acting in the way dictated by good reasons. . . . No set of practical reasons, however compelling, need, on this dominant modern view, be treated as conclusive. (p. 140)

The features that MacIntyre ascribes to the modern view seem to me either to be present in the Aristotelian view as well or not to be features of any dominant

---

[29] Aristotle says only *epithumôn men prattei, prohairoumenos d'ou*. But 'act on' is justified by the parallel with the continent person, who *anapalin prohairoumenos men <prattei>, epithumôn d'ou*. Since continent people clearly have disordered appetites, Aristotle's point must be that they do not have an appetite for the action they actually do; hence, he will intend the corresponding point for incontinents.

[30] *EN* 1148a4–11, 1152a15–17.

[31] *EN* 1150b29–31.

[32] MacIntyre remarks that Aristotle does not use the expression 'the practical syllogism' (p. 129). It is not clear that this fact is significant; for though he does not use the phrase in the singular, he does speak of 'practical syllogisms' (*hoi sullogismoi tôn praktôn*, 1144a31–2), and evidently thinks of practical reasoning as having premises and conclusions (1143b2, 1147a27), and hence as having some of the structure of a syllogism.

[33] I believe 1147a27–8 is inconsistent with the view that the conclusion is the action. The aorist participle *sumperanthen* implies that the conclusion has been drawn before the action. On this question, see further David Charles, *Aristotle's Philosophy of Action* (London: Duckworth, 1984), pp. 117–24, esp. p. 119n.

modern view. Aristotle also leaves room for agents to reconsider whether they have actually taken everything relevant into account; failure to deliberate carefully is a sign of rashness.[34] As for someone who just does not feel like acting on reasons recognized to be as good and compelling as you like, I do not know what more it would take to show that such a person is irrational. It is a common modern view that incontinence is a form of practical irrationality, but such a view would be unintelligible if MacIntyre were right about the content of the prevalent modern view.[35] The contrasts that MacIntyre alleges here are spurious.

So far I have questioned MacIntyre's view that the incontinent person lacks *prohairesis*. Sometimes, however, he also misinterprets Aristotle's account of the vicious person, and in doing so seems to introduce an inconsistency into his own view of Aristotle. In the passage I quoted earlier (p. 63) MacIntyre correctly takes Aristotle to allow *prohairesis* both to virtuous and to vicious people. But then it is surprising that he draws this contrast between the virtuous person and other people:

> Without the virtues the desires cannot be informed by reason, cannot be transformed into and be effective as desires for whatever reason prescribes. The very existence of *boulêsis,* rational wish, as practically effective depends on the possession of the virtues. (p. 137)

I agree that there must be some sense in which MacIntyre's first sentence is true; otherwise, there would be no basis for Aristotle's evident belief that the virtuous person is in some way more rational than the vicious. But the second sentence does not give an acceptable sense in which the first sentence might be true. For a *prohairesis*, as Aristotle conceives it, essentially involves *boulêsis*;[36] and since (as MacIntyre agrees) vicious people have a *prohairesis*, they must also have a *boulêsis*. Hence a *boulêsis* cannot require the virtues.

If this is correct, then MacIntyre himself has given us reason to believe that Aristotle attributes a considerable degree of practical rationality to the vicious person. Even MacIntyre's own account of *prohairesis* shows why he must be wrong to deny rational wish to the vicious person, and his account of incontinence itself considerably underestimates the rationality of the incontinent person.

Some of the main points in MacIntyre's case, therefore, turn out to rest on dubious exegetical claims. He has given us no good reason to believe in a sharp and radical contrast between the Aristotelian and the modern view of practical rationality. In saying this, I evidently do not mean that Aristotle agrees with everything that Hume, for instance, says about practical reason. I mean only that there is no good reason for believing in a contrast so sharp that only MacIntyre's theory of tradition will explain it.

---

[34] *EN* 1150b19–28.

[35] Hume may imply that incontinent preferences are not contrary to reason (*Treatise* ii 3.3), but it would be a considerable exaggeration to identify his view with the dominant modern view.

[36] See 1113b3–5, 1142b18–20. For different views about the nature of *boulêsis*, see G.E.M. Anscombe, "Thought and action in Aristotle," in *Collected Papers* (Oxford: Blackwell, 1981), vol. 1, pp. 66–77; Charles, *Aristotle's Philosophy of Action*, 151–55. Though Charles and Anscombe disagree on some important issues, neither agrees with MacIntyre's claim that only the virtuous person can have a *boulêsis*.

These points of Aristotelian exegesis are also relevant for one of the important contrasts that MacIntyre sees in the transition from Aristotle to Aquinas. MacIntyre argues that Augustine's views on the will mark a radical difference from Aristotle's views on reason and action (p. 156), and that the Augustinian influence causes Aquinas to reinterpret and transform Aristotle's views on *prohairesis* (p. 190f.). I am quite doubtful about the innovation attributed to Augustine, but I will not go any further into that issue here; I will concentrate on the claim that Aquinas "does not so much render *prohairesis* into Latin as offer instead an alternative concept" (p. 191). MacIntyre's reason is this:

> For Aristotle the person whose conclusions as to what means to adopt do not spring from that person's character is someone as yet morally uneducated, or at least not fully educated, open to *akratic* impulse; as such that person has not yet entered into the maturity of moral enquiry. Aquinas, by contrast, sees every human being as held responsible from a relatively early age for his or her choices even before character is adequately formed; even before character is adequately formed I am to make those choices which will lead toward an adequate formation of character. Even an immature rationality is adequate to that task. (p. 191)

The contrast that MacIntyre draws here rests on the assumption that Aristotle thinks that (i) *prohairesis* is impossible without a fully developed character, and that (ii) people are not responsible for their actions until they have a fully developed character. I have already challenged the first claim about Aristotle, and I see no foundation for the second claim. MacIntyre's view implies that Aristotle denies responsibility to incontinents, but Aristotle thinks incontinent people act voluntarily,[37] and that incontinence is blameworthy.[38] He does not restrict the range of responsible agents in the way he would have to if MacIntyre's contrast with Aquinas were justifiable. On this point also, then, MacIntyre's claims about the differences between traditions are exaggerated.

VIII. THE LIBERAL TRADITION

At this point, I would like to pass quickly from the earlier to the later stages of MacIntyre's story, and comment briefly on some of his claims about the liberal tradition. In the previous section, I argued that some of the differences that MacIntyre claims to see between Aristotle and later thought are in fact the products of errors about Aristotle. I believe that something analogous is true about his treatment of the liberal outlook, and that the stark contrast that he presents is partly the result of misinterpretation.

His treatment of 'the liberal self' (i.e., of the conception of the self that is characteristic of the liberal tradition) is basically Hobbesian:

> So it is important for all areas of human life and not only for explicitly political and economic transactions that there should be acceptable rules

[37] *EN* 1152a16–17.
[38] *EN* 1146a3–4, 1148b2–9.

of bargaining. And what each individual and each group has to hope for from these rules is that they should be such as to enable that individual or that group to be as effective as possible in implementing his, her, or their preferences. (p. 337)

Let us, for present purposes, accept this as an accurate statement of how Hobbesian individuals conceive themselves, and of the problem that they set out to solve through a social contract.[39] MacIntyre intends it to apply also to a contemporary liberal such as Rawls. And it is easy to see why he thinks it applies to Rawls: Rawls's account of the reasoning in the Original Position is full of references to game theory, strategy, and bargaining between mutually disinterested agents who are rational only in a narrow economic sense and who are allowed access only to a very thin theory of the good.

This presentation of the liberal self seems to me to overlook an important aspect of Rawls, and in doing so to overlook an important outlook that belongs as much as the Hobbesian outlook does to the liberal tradition. MacIntyre refers rather briefly to Kant (e.g., pp. 11, 175f., 334) and still more briefly to the conceptions of the self that he has inspired. One such conception is the one that MacIntyre seems to regard as characteristic of Kant, appealing to a self characterized by universality and impersonality (p. 334). It is striking that when Rawls claims to develop a Kantian line of thought, he explicitly rejects this view of what is most significant about Kant.[40] Rawls takes the central Kantian claim to involve autonomy; moral principles are chosen by agents who want to express themselves as free and equal selves.[41] Though the Original Position incorporates strategies of bargaining and so on, its point is not to show that moral principles are the rational outcome of such thinking; its aim is to capture the principles that would adequately capture the aspirations of rational agents who want to express themselves as free and equal selves.

It would be foolish to pretend that these claims about rational self-expression are easy to explain or defend. But they are evidently not peculiar to Kant and Rawls. Both acknowledge a debt to Rousseau, and the same debt is evident in the various interpretations of rational self-expression offered by Humboldt, Mill, Green, Bradley, and Marx. These ideas of the self and human nature seem quite close (as Rousseau and Kant believe) to Aristotelian and Stoic views.

This point illustrates a more general question about MacIntyre's use of evidence. I remarked earlier that he tends to homogenize the Greek tradition; the conclusion of my remarks about Kant and Rawls is that he homogenizes the liberal tradition as well. If we focus exclusively on one aspect of one tradition, and then focus on the

---

[39] I doubt if it is exclusively modern. It is also (as I remarked above in commenting on the Greek tradition) a plausible account of how Epicurean individuals see the problem of justice.

[40] See John Rawls, *A Theory of Justice* (Cambridge: Harvard University Press, 1971), p. 251: "It is a mistake, I believe, to emphasize the place of generality and universality in Kant's ethics. . . . It is impossible to construct a moral theory on so slender a basis, and therefore to limit the discussion of Kant's doctrine to these notions is to reduce it to triviality."

[41] See Rawls, *Theory of Justice*, p. 255. The Kantian aspects of Rawls have been discussed often enough for MacIntyre's silence about them to be surprising.

antithetical aspect of another tradition, it is easy to conclude that the two traditions are sharply opposed. If we attend to the different aspects of each tradition or historical period, the differences may seem less sharp, and the common elements more impressive.

CONCLUSION

MacIntyre has not proved, as far as I can see, the claim that is implicit in the title of his book. Neither historical nor philosophical arguments support the claim that traditions of inquiry play the extensive role that MacIntyre assigns to them in setting the terms of the debate about justice and rationality.

For these reasons I do not see that MacIntyre has formulated a clear or defensible version of a historicist view of the history of ethics. He expresses a historicist attitude in his claim that there is no one justice, and no one rationality, that different philosophers have described more or less accurately. I certainly am not suggesting that I have proved that he is wrong in his claim, but I hope I have explained why his arguments do not provide strong grounds for accepting it.[42]

Philosophy, Cornell University

[42] I have benefited from comments by Nicholas Sturgeon, several contributors to this volume, and especially Eric Snider. I am grateful to Alasdair MacIntyre for his helpful comments on a draft of this paper. His comments allowed me to correct some misunderstandings of his position, but he should certainly not be taken to agree with the account of his views that I offer here.

ETHICS AND STOCHASTIC PROCESSES*

By Russell Hardin

Introduction

There is some irony, and perhaps a bit of gallows humor, in opening a paper in this volume with the claim that "applied ethics" is a misnomer. Yet that claim is true in the following sense. What we need for most of the issues that have sparked the contemporary resurgence of moral and political theory is not the application of ethics as we know it, but the revamping of ethics to make it relevant to the issues we face. It is in our concern with major policy programs that ethics and political philosophy are most commonly rejoined to become a unified enquiry after a nearly complete separation through most of this century. Yet, ethical theories may be shaken to their foundations by our effort to apply them to policy problems. I do not propose to revamp ethics here, but only to show that much ethical theory cannot readily be applied to major policy problems.

There are at least three important characteristics of major policy issues in general that may give traditional moral theories difficulties. First, such issues can generally be handled only by institutional intervention; they commonly cannot be resolved through uncoordinated individual action. Theories formulated at the individual level must therefore be recast to handle institutional actions and possibilities. Second, major policy issues typically have complicating strategic interactions between individuals at their bases. Third, they are inherently stochastic in the important sense that they affect large numbers with more or less determinable (or merely guessable) probabilities. C. H. Waddington calls such issues instances of "the problem of the ethics of stochastic processes."[1]

Elsewhere I have addressed implications of the first two of these problems for utilitarianism,[2] and I will not consider them independently here. Instead, I will focus on the third issue, the stochastic nature of major policy problems. The three classes of problems are not entirely separable, however, because large-scale stochastic problems generally require institutional resolution and the institutional

* I wish to thank Thomas Christiano, Ed Curley, William H. Kruskal, Ellen Frankel Paul, and many participants in this volume, in a colloquium at the University of Maryland, and in my informal workshop on contemporary moral and political theory at the University of Chicago for constructive comments on an earlier draft of this paper. I also wish to thank the Chicago Council on Foreign Relations and especially Arthur Cyr for provoking my initial work on this topic. If the paper has any felicities or merits, these may be taken as evidence that stochastic processes can be beneficial.

[1] C.H. Waddington, *The Ethical Animal* (Chicago: University of Chicago Press, 1967; first published 1960), p. 17. The term "stochastic processes" is somewhat loosely used here. It originates from a Greek root meaning "proceeding by guesswork" or, literally, "skillful in aiming."

[2] Russell Hardin, *Morality within the Limits of Reason* (Chicago: University of Chicago Press, 1988).

structure for dealing with such a problem may also depend on the nature of the individual strategic interactions at the base of the problem. For example, if we wish to overcome a disease, such as smallpox in the past or AIDS today, we may best be able to do that by affecting the interactions that contribute to its spread.

Virtually all stochastic problems that provoke major public policy action may involve external effects, both from the behavior being regulated and from the regulation itself. Hence, discussion of risk or probabilities pure and simple, as in individual gambling decisions, misses something at the core of stochastic policy issues. For large-scale stochastic problems it is often inescapably true that the policies will similarly be stochastic. There will be harms as well as benefits resulting from *any* policies that deal with them. Moreover, in some meaningful sense, those harmed may not be those benefited. These characteristics will fit many policies that moral theorists of all stripes are likely to find acceptable, even morally mandatory.

My purpose here is not to establish definitive claims for the rightness or wrongness of particular policy prescriptions, but only to establish the form that such assessments must take. Such assessments depend on a combination of social scientific and ethical understandings of the nature of the problems we face and of the plausible resolutions of them. Throughout, I will discuss a problem – vaccination against a major disease – that should not be very controversial, either in the realm of morals or the social sciences. Just because it is not likely to be morally controversial, it will be very useful in exemplifying the nature of stochastic policy problems. Many policy issues are importantly similar to the vaccination example.

Even from this brief account of the nature of stochastic policy problems, it may already appear that the difficulties of dealing with them will be more acute for nonconsequentialist moral theories than for some consequentialist theories. This appearance does not deceive, as even a sketch of several nonconsequentialist classes of moral theory suggests. For example, virtue theories are largely inadequate to the task of handling major policy problems without the addition of a large element of consequentialist concern. Virtue theories often put ends and means in a functionalist relationship, so that, to specify what is a virtue, we must first say what is the end that we wish the virtuous to achieve. Consent and contract theories might in principle be able to handle stochastic problems, but they can do so only at a rationalist level of hypothetical consent – even at that level, moral theorists seem unable to reach consensus. Theories that are based on respect for persons or the rights of persons are arguably far more interesting for the evaluation of policies. But they are acutely afflicted with problems of stochastic processes, and it is to such theories that most of the discussion here will be addressed.

I. THE STOCHASTIC NATURE OF POLICY ISSUES

To see the peculiarly stochastic characteristics of the complex policy problems we often face, consider a relatively simple problem: vaccination against some disease (say, smallpox before it was finally eradicated in 1977). Suppose the facts are roughly these. We vaccinate millions, almost the entire population. If we vaccinated no one, perhaps ten percent of these people would contract serious cases of smallpox. Many of these would die, many would be permanently, even hideously, scarred, perhaps most would be at worst slightly scarred but also beneficially inoculated against further attack from smallpox. When we vaccinate almost everyone, a very small number of those vaccinated suffer serious cases of smallpox from the vaccination itself, a few of these die, and a few are badly scarred. There is virtually no question that fewer are harmed by vaccinating than by not vaccinating the population. But it is eminently plausible to suppose that many of those who suffer from the vaccination would not have suffered from the disease if we had not vaccinated. Have we done them harm for which we should be held responsible when we vaccinate?

Perhaps it matters what the rest of the story is. It could be that, *ex ante*, everyone has voted for vaccination and that all have voluntarily presented themselves for it. But, *ex post*, many of these people must reckon that the vaccination was a mistake for them. If we all voluntarily gambled on the benefits of vaccination, no one might seem to be responsible for the losses of those few who lost the gamble. Alternatively, it could be that we have required vaccination in order to overcome the natural tendency of many people to want to free-ride on the effects of the vaccination of others. They can free-ride if enough people are vaccinated, because then even the unvaccinated may be relatively secure against infection. Now the losers on the vaccination gamble may seem to have a justified complaint that, in a sense, they were made to suffer in part in order that others might benefit.[3] In the world of actual policies, this is commonly the problem we face: there is no prospect of universal consent, so that some will have their wishes overridden or will even be coerced.

Many vaccination programs have been coercive. The current vaccine of "choice" for polio in the United States since 1962 is the Sabin live vaccine. The alternative to it is the Salk killed vaccine. From the live vaccine, some of those vaccinated contract serious cases of paralytic polio (five to ten cases a year currently in the United States, or one case per 560,000 first doses of the vaccine).[4] From the killed vaccine, no one contracts polio. There are disputes over the effectiveness of the two vaccines, so that one might finally conclude that running the risk of contracting polio from the live Sabin vaccine is offset by the reduced risk of the failure of the vaccine to protect one from naturally contracting polio in the wild, or one might conclude the converse. But there is an additional argument that is used in defense of the Sabin vaccine, which is that that vaccine, because it is live, may lead to the secondary protection – "herd immunity" – of the unvaccinated by giving them mild doses of the disease from contact with recently vaccinated children.[5] Hence, if we do not directly reach everyone with our vaccination program, we may reach more people with the live than with the killed vaccine. This argument clearly relies on directly using some people to protect other people. It is not given as a public rationale to the parent whose child faces the risks of the Sabin vaccine. One suspects that many parents would, if given a choice, choose the killed Salk vaccine for their children.

[3] See Marjorie Sun, "The Vexing Problems of Vaccine Compensation," *Science*, vol. 227 (March 1, 1985), pp. 1012–14.

[4] Leslie Roberts, "Change in Polio Strategy?", *Science*, vol. 240 (May 27, 1988), p. 1145.

[5] *ibid.*

To make the stochastic quality of the issue clearer, consider some actual data on smallpox vaccination. In Massachusetts in 1721, Zabdiel Boylston used live pox to inoculate 247 people, his son and friends, against smallpox. Six died (one in 41). Boylston was reviled. In a subsequent epidemic, the remaining 241 of his vaccinees survived, while one in seven of the rest of the population died.[6] Inoculation, even in Boylston's crude form, seems to have posed the lesser *ex ante* risk. (Of course, he was performing an experiment in a state of such ignorance that he could not have known how good the odds were.) If nothing but chance controlled which of Boylston's vaccinees died of smallpox and which would have died from the later epidemic, then most or all of those who died in the inoculation would have survived had they not been vaccinated, while thirty to forty others in the group would have died.

In recent times, the odds in favor of vaccination against smallpox had become radically better for those who were at much risk of getting smallpox. For populations in which vaccination was widely prevalent, such as the United States, the risks from vaccination may still finally have become greater than the risks from not being vaccinated because one was more likely to contract the disease from an initial vaccination than from exposure in the wild while not vaccinated. For diseases that have vectors other than human carriers, the odds may not finally tilt so strongly against vaccination for an individual in an otherwise well-inoculated population.[7]

Other issues that are similarly stochastic are policies on the building of highways and various safety devices for them, policies on permitting various levels of air traffic, policies creating long holiday weekends, policies for testing new products (perhaps especially chemical products), policies on the generation of energy, and, of course, policies on testing nuclear weapons. Less obviously, another stochastic problem (in large part) is the policy of nuclear deterrence. Even the policy of raising the level of education might be associated with a rise in the suicide rate, as Philippa Foot supposes.[8] For the smallpox vaccination, we might be quite confident of just what the odds are, as we may also be for variant policies on highway driving speed, variant levels of taxation on cigarettes or alcohol, and many other policies. For nuclear deterrence, we can do little more than guess what would be the likely casualty levels of maintaining or abandoning the deterrence policy. For many stochastic problems, we can perform tests; for others we cannot. For many, we can observe statistical regularities at some micro-level over a long period of time (as in our knowledge of various effects on highway traffic fatalities); for others, we can observe them only at a macro-level at which the learning comes too late to have a beneficial effect on policy (as in nuclear deterrence policy or policies on various contributions to the greenhouse effect, which itself might even turn out to be beneficial).

[6] Daniel E. Koshland, Jr., "Benefits, Risks, Vaccines, and the Courts," *Science*, vol. 227 (March 15, 1985), p. 1289; *Encyclopedia Britannica* 15th ed., s.v. "Boylston, Zabdiel."

[7] For example, vaccination against diphtheria, pertussis, and tetanus (DPT) may cause 50 cases of permanent brain damage among 3.5 million children vaccinated. But in populations that have elected to drop such vaccination, as Japan and the United Kingdom did during the 1970s, death rates were reportedly worse. See Sun, p. 1012.

[8] Phillippa Foot, "The Problem of Abortion and the Doctrine of the Double Effect," in *Virtues and Vices* (Berkeley: University of California Press, 1978), pp. 19–32, esp. p. 19.

But all of these issues have in common their stochastic quality. One might say, "It's wrong for people to die in traffic accidents." But if asked to unpack such a claim, one must grant that its meaning at the policy level can only be that we should suffer certain costs to reduce the incidence of traffic accidents. It cannot imply an absolute injunction. Similarly, in the vaccination case we simply have no choice but to vaccinate or not to vaccinate, even though our vaccine may bring immediate harms. We cannot wait for a perfectly safe vaccine without seeing a high incidence of smallpox in the meantime. In every case, the policy decision is one between different evils, as in fewer versus more deaths. Waddington supposes that such stochastic problems are the common product of technological innovations. Since we often want the benefits of such innovations, we might have a public policy of indemnifying or especially caring for those who turn out to be the losers from our interventions, although in the United States we traditionally have not done this. The losers on the highways, in vaccination programs, in the airlanes, and in many other contexts have often borne their own losses, sometimes through *ex ante* insurance or implicit self-insurance, even though it would seem to be meaningful to say that they have paid to some extent in order to relieve others of various burdens.

In all of these stochastic problems, arguments for and against various policies are often essentially utilitarian. Fewer people will suffer if we vaccinate than if we do not vaccinate. Arguments against deliberate interventions that directly require certain behaviors by people, however, often take the form of a defense of libertarian rights. The individual has a right to refuse to be vaccinated, to refuse to wear seatbelts or safety helmets. Such arguments virtually never arise in certain contexts, such as air safety, in which my refusal to follow some safety rule may have clear external effects on the safety of others.

The vaccine case has one uniquely interesting quality that distinguishes it from many of these cases. In it, *ex ante*, or before the policy is implemented, everyone is in the same position. That is to say, the *ex ante* costs and the *ex ante* benefits are the same for all. Moreover, the costs are borne almost entirely internally by the affected group. These characteristics are virtually in the nature of the problem. There are minor costs of time and money that may be borne unequally, but these are trivial in comparison to the other costs and benefits. Only free-riders on the vaccination of others benefit from significantly unequal costs. The costs of reducing highway traffic fatalities need not be borne entirely internally by the affected group, and the costs and the expected benefits may not be at all equally distributed *ex ante*. The costs and benefits may be approximately fitted – for example, through carefully designed user fees – to the affected group, but in principle they need not be. Many other major stochastic policy problems are more nearly like the highway traffic problem in this respect than like the vaccination problem. Resolutions of these problems do not naturally entail particular forms of cost-sharing.

Virtually all policies on large-scale stochastic problems require the imposition of risks on someone. Suppose that a large fraction of our population refused to seek vaccination against smallpox (or polio, or AIDS, or whatever) on the claim that they would rather take their chances with nature than with the vaccine, even if nature's dice seem to be more heavily loaded against them. If eradication of the disease depends on eliminating it from human carriers, as eradication of smallpox did and as eradication of AIDS might, leaving this fraction out of our net might mean the continuation of the disease through this generation rather than its final eradication. If we force vaccination on these objectors, as we commonly have done in the case of school children, we force a particular stochastic risk on them in the cause of reducing overall risks.

The form that risks might take can vary enormously for policies on various stochastic problems. For the vaccination policy, the stochastic form of the risk is that it would be distributed across a small fraction of the affected people with virtual certainty: that is, it would imply a high cost for a small number of unidentified people. In stark comparison, for the policy of nuclear deterrence, the risk is supposed by strong supporters of deterrence to be a small likelihood of an extraordinarily large cost. For the vaccination policy, we might be quite confident of and in agreement on the numbers who would be affected by alternative policies. For the deterrence policy, we might have only vague guesses about relative numbers affected *ex ante* and we might substantially disagree on these guesses. Indeed, guesses in print disagree wildly. Such differences in the form and confidence levels of the risks may be very important differences, but they do not have immediately evident moral significance.

Typical of both the vaccination and the nuclear deterrence policies is that they are inherently consequentialist in their rationales. It seems unlikely that we can give a compelling nonconsequentialist rationale for imposing vaccination on objectors. The consequentialist rationale is one of trading off risks to the well-being of some against risks to the well-being of others. For example, in the vaccination case, we accept immediate harm to a few in return for reducing harm in the long run to very many. In some nonconsequentialist theories, such as theories of rights or of respect for persons, the basic moral principles concern what harms we may inflict on persons. It would typically be wrong on such a theory to kill certain people in order to secure the survival of others, even very many others. But surely, even on such a theory, it cannot be wrong for me to undertake any action whatever that might entail the risk, however slight, of harm or death to another. Last night, I drove my car to a restaurant merely for the sake of a pleasing dinner for my family. In doing that trivial thing, I plausibly risked killing someone in an accident. Even though it would have been wrong for me to kill someone in order to give my family a pleasant dinner, it seems incredible to suppose that it was wrong to drive us to dinner at the very slight risk of killing someone. This is, in essence, an individual-level analog of large-scale stochastic policies.

One might have an immediate intuition that it would be wrong to risk doing what it would be wrong to do deliberately. But such an intuition cannot withstand scrutiny. Individual risks of doing harm to others in order to benefit oneself are inherent in living, and the harms to others that one risks are typically harms one could not do deliberately without the justification of offsetting benefits. Of course, this is true not only at the individual level but also at the level of social policy. For example, to have a criminal justice system imposes the risk of convicting innocents. We may attempt to reduce that risk, but we cannot eliminate it entirely if we have a practical justice system. Despite that risk, we will want such a system, and will think it more just to have such a system with its particular injustices than not to have one at all.

"If these ideas are right," Judith Jarvis Thomson says of a similar account of individual actions for minor gain that put others at slight risk of great harm, "– and it really does seem that they are – then risk-imposition does generate an independent problem for moral theory. For there is a further question that then arises, beyond the question what harms we may or may not cause in what circumstances, namely, the question what risks of what harms we may or may not impose in what circumstances."[9]

Thomson's point here, that risk-imposition is a special problem for moral theory, is compelling for a moral theory that focuses on act-kinds,[10] as it is for many theories that focus on the rightness of kinds of actions, such as lying, truth-telling, killing, or letting die. Her point is not compelling for a theory that focuses on consequences. In a consequentialist theory, the risk of a particular harm may simply carry less weight than the harm itself – it hardly poses an "independent problem." In a theory of the rightness of act-kinds, however, we must include the probabilities of various outcomes from the acts of various kinds in the definition of the act-kinds if relevant risks are to count. If we do that, the theory begins to smack of consequentialism. If it is characteristic of the theory not to be consequentialist but to value something about acts or persons other than their consequences, this move is apt to seem demoralizing. For such a theory, risk-imposition may be not only a special but also a pernicious problem.[11]

II. Stochastic Implementation

It is characteristic of stochastic problems of large scale that policies to deal with them are implemented by large, complex organizations, indeed, typically by a complex array of such organizations, that, themselves, behave stochastically. Hence, in understanding how they are implemented, we must understand how relevant institutions can work and are likely to work. This means, inherently, that in deciding what the policies should be we must similarly understand what are the possibilities for implementation. This is merely an instance of the moral philosopher's dictum that 'ought' implies 'can'. If I cannot possibly do something, say, rescue you from a shark, then it is wrong to say that I ought to, and it would be wrong to hold me responsible for "failing" to. For example, when the World Health Organization (WHO) set about the task of eradicating smallpox from the world through its Intensified Smallpox Eradication Program in 1967, it was essentially enabled to think of that goal as a policy goal by the fact that many nations had already effectively blocked the entry of smallpox into their populations. Hence,

[9] Judith Jarvis Thomson, "Imposing Risks," in *Rights, Restitution, and Risk* (Cambridge: Harvard University Press, 1986), pp. 173–91, at p. 185.

[10] *ibid.*, p. 183.

[11] For this and other reasons, especially the problem of strategic interaction in producing good results, basing moral theory on some notion of a "kind" of action verges on incoherence. See Hardin, *Morality within the Limits of Reason*, pp. 68–70.

WHO could target the few populations in which smallpox was residual and in which it may still have resulted in two million deaths each year.[12]

Even then, WHO could only do this as well as it was permitted by its organizational capacities for gaining relevant information on the whereabouts of smallpox, capacities that mainly turned on the capacities of certain impoverished nations to discover such information about their own populations. In the United States, a new smallpox case would most likely have become known to national health authorities almost instantly through well-organized channels for reporting. The reporting system is backed by strong sanctions and positive incentives, by communication systems that make such reporting easy and effective, and by a long and well-established tradition of reporting. Such systems were not available to WHO in Ethiopia, Somalia, West Africa, Brazil, and Bangladesh. Its task was simultaneously to vaccinate in all communities in which smallpox was known to be endemic, and to try to develop a reporting system that would alert it to additional communities it must vaccinate. To be confident it had succeeded in eradicating the disease (by isolating the last infected person in the world until that person was no longer contagious while also vaccinating everyone in that person's near vicinity), it eventually had to develop a nearly complete reporting or discovery system to be sure that all communities everywhere were free of smallpox. Making a mistake of omission might have meant a devastating epidemic. An alternative to its policy might have been to try to vaccinate far more people than necessary in an effort simply to be complete. The policy of "case-finding and ring vaccination," or isolation of any affected person and vaccination targeted to those who were especially likely to be exposed, was, if it could be made to work, the more beneficial and less harmful policy, because it would avoid needless exposure to the vaccine for those who were otherwise unlikely to be exposed to the disease.

Suppose we (at WHO) have decided how to go about eradicating smallpox. We are, to some degree, in the position of Zabdiel Boylston. We will cause harm to some who would have escaped it otherwise, but we will have reduced the overall incidence of harm from smallpox. When we now inoculate a particular person in the Sahel or in Bangladesh, it would be odd to suppose we were responsible only for what happens to that person as a result. We cannot divide the vaccination policy into a right and a wrong part, the part that benefits most people and the part that harms a few. These "parts" are one and inseparable. The good is produced at the cost of the harm. *Our responsibility is for the overall policy, given that we understand how it is to be implemented, not merely for isolated results of the implementation of it.* If we send fifty vaccinators into the field and one of these has a smallpox death result from her vaccinations, we would not wish to say she was responsible for that death and that the other vaccinators were responsible only for the protections that they successfully gave to their vaccinees. It would be utterly silly to say that our unfortunate vaccinator acted immorally in her one wayward case. We who adopted

---

[12] Frank Fenner, "Smallpox, 'the most dreadful scourge of the human species': Its global spread and recent eradication – Part 2," *Medical Journal of Australia*, vol. 141 (December 8 and 22, 1984), pp. 841–46, esp. p. 843.

the policy are essentially responsible for its overall result, including the one death and the presumed thousands of those protected who would otherwise have died.

This is the essential structure of the form of implementation of policies on major stochastic problems, and of the form of moral responsibility for their results. I think it reasonable to say that there is no moral responsibility for the occasional harm from vaccination if the risk of that harm is justified by the great overall benefit from it. Indeed, I think it reasonable to say that we may legally coerce people to accept vaccination in some circumstances. For example, in the United States, children are required to get certain vaccinations before they are allowed to attend school – but they are also required to attend school. Alternatively, we might wish to suppose, as many parents of American children harmed by DPT vaccination have supposed,[13] that we are responsible for the harm to the occasional unfortunate victim of our vaccination. (I think it more reasonable to suppose that we should make it part of our vaccination policy, whose purpose is to enhance the general welfare, to compensate the losers from that policy in some degree – just because this addition to our policy further enhances the general welfare both *ex ante* and *ex post*.)

A utilitarian naturally would argue that the harms are a tradeoff that we suffer in order to avoid even greater harms and that they, while still harms, are not subject to moral criticism if the overall tradeoff is justified. Proponents of many other moral theories strongly object to such tradeoffs *between people* in many contexts and might similarly object to them in this context. They argue, for example, that individuals or individual rights are inviolable in that, in some sense, they cannot be sacrificed merely in order to make others better off. Sometimes, such theorists allow tradeoffs of harms to avoid greater harms. Without such a caveat, an in-principle objection to any tradeoffs between individuals is apt to strike almost everyone except arcane moral theorists as odd or even perverse, since it would inherently put us in a moral quandary in the face of many, perhaps all, stochastic policy problems. In the world of major policies, we must assume that, whatever moral principles we otherwise follow, such tradeoffs are permissible at least in principle in many cases when lesser likelihood of harm to some is traded for greater likelihood of harm for others. Such tradeoffs are the central rationale for many policies. To refuse such tradeoffs in principle is to say that even a policy of vaccination with known vaccines, all of which occasionally cause harmful, even deadly side-effects, is impermissible – no matter how beneficial those vaccines might be on balance.

III. Tradeoffs in Stochastic Policy Problems

In the early effort by Zabdiel Boylston to inoculate his son and friends against smallpox, it is plausible that the losers from his actions were people who would have been losers from the smallpox epidemic shortly afterwards. But each individual, *ex ante*, seems to have stood to gain from the risk of being vaccinated. Eventually times changed for smallpox vaccination. The strategic structure of benefits and risks, figured *ex ante*, for an individual in a population facing the prospect of vaccination or disease can become approximately that of the Prisoner's Dilemma once enough

---

[13] Sun, p. 1013.

other people have become inoculated. If the vaccination program genuinely works to reduce the likelihood that smallpox can get established at all in the population, then, at some point, the risk to the additional person of being inoculated is greater than the risk to that person of not being inoculated. Yet it may still be true that the benefit (figured in *ex ante* likely cases of smallpox) to the whole population from the additional person's inoculation is greater than the net risk to that person. Of course, if our program is intended to eradicate the disease altogether, the overall value of the additional persons inoculation may seem especially great. I am the additional person; I do not wish to have my welfare put at risk for the sake of enhancing the welfare of others. What can you say to me to justify forcing the vaccination upon me? A utilitarian need have no difficulty saying that what matters here is that the net benefits far outweigh the costs, even though the costs are borne by me and the benefits mostly by others.

It is commonly supposed that one very important class of moral theories, associated with the theory of Kant, rules out the kind of strategic, consequentialist rationale that the utilitarian uses here. Kant himself, for example, asserts that it is wrong to lie no matter what the supposed consequences of the lie. It is only the purity of the moral action of lying or telling the truth that matters. To make his view incontrovertibly clear, he asserts that one should not even lie to an intended murderer who wants to know if his intended victim is in one's house. Even though it might mean the intended victim's immediate death, Kant supposes that one should truthfully answer that the victim is in the house. Even for a Protestant Prussian of Kant's time, that seems to be an unduly formalistic view. He was challenged in his view by Benjamin Constant, who argued that a moral injunction here clearly turned on how immoral the circumstances are that one faces. Kant replied at length in print, concluding with what may be one of the clearest deontological, anti-consequentialist arguments ever framed:

> ... we must not understand [the issue as one of] the danger of *doing harm* (accidentally), but of *doing wrong* and this would happen if the duty of veracity, which is quite unconditional, and constitutes the supreme condition of justice in utterances, were made conditional and subordinate to other considerations; and, although by a certain lie I in fact do no wrong to any person [such as the intending murderer], yet I infringe the principle of justice in regard to all indispensably necessary statements *generally* (I do wrong formally, though not materially); *and this is much worse than to commit an injustice to any individual*. ...[14]

There are two remarkable aspects of Kant's view that should be mentioned. First, one may note that almost no one other than Kant thinks his radical principle about lying follows from his larger moral theory. Indeed, W.I. Matson, a sympathetic critic who defends Kant's larger moral theory against Kant's odd

---

[14] Immanuel Kant, "On a Supposed Right to Tell Lies from Benevolent Motives," ed. and trans. Thomas Kingsmill Abbott, *Kant's* Critique of Practical Reason *and other works on the Theory of Ethics* (London: Longman's, 1909, 6th edition; German original first published 1797), pp. 361–65, at p. 365, final emphasis added.

judgment in this instance, thinks the "repellent fanaticism" of this passage merely shows that Kant lived too long as a philosopher.[15] Second, one should note that the issue here is far more general in its import than the realm of lying, and in this respect the lesson to be drawn is relevant to Kant's larger theory. The more general issue is the relation between actions that are relatively narrowly-defined and the consequences that result from them. It is characteristic of *strategic* actions that their character and definition is typically supposed to follow from their likely results or, more commonly, their likely range of potential results. I do x in order to achieve c. It is almost impossible to formulate many policy statements without formulating them in terms of their intended consequences. To formulate them exclusively in terms of the actions permissible under them would ordinarily be quite cumbersome, or even irrelevant.

Of course, a deontological moral theory that focused exclusively on kinds of actions, rather than on the results of actions, need not moralize everything, so that many actions, as such, might be neither required nor prohibited by a particular theory, while many others, such as lying, might be rigidly governed by the theory. One cannot make much sense of a moral injunction to vaccinate or not to vaccinate someone without tying it to the actual *ex ante* assessment of the effects it is supposed to have.[16] Hence, one cannot have a sensible principle on vaccination in the way one might have a general principle on lying as somehow right or wrong independently of its likely consequences. Of course, this conclusion is quite general in its import: it applies not only to vaccination but also to a vast class of large-scale stochastic policy problems.

Moral theories that persuasively proscribe such act-kinds as murder, lying, and so forth cannot transparently be applied to such act-kinds as those that put some at risk of great harm for the sake of slight or even great benefit for others. Hence, they cannot transparently apply to many policy issues. Indeed, they cannot even transparently apply to the act-kinds that fill quotidian life. Such stochastic choice issues are at the core of public policy and applied ethics as well as practical personal life. If they pose an independent problem for a moral theory, then that theory must master this problem before it can speak confidently to us on such issues.

It may be that any sensible policy on vaccination is ultimately utilitarian. One whose moral theory is based on act-kinds need not disagree with utilitarian prescriptions in such a policy issue. Such a theorist could concede vaccination prescriptions to utilitarian considerations and, with utilitarians, conclude that the act-kind of vaccinating someone is made right or wrong by its general fit with the

---

[15] W.I. Matson, "Kant As Casuist," ed. Robert Paul Wolff, *Kant: A Collection of Critical Essays* (Garden City: Doubleday Anchor, 1967), pp. 331–36, at p. 336. Matson says further, "Surely no one will undertake to defend Kant's conclusion. Hence, if that conclusion really follows from his theory, then that theory is convicted of absurdity or worse. . . ." According to student notes of his university lectures, a younger Kant held less consistent, more humane views on lying under duress. See Immanuel Kant, *Lectures on Ethics*, trans. Louis Infield (New York: Harper, 1963), pp. 226–29.

[16] One might try to bring the problem of vaccination under Kant's principle of benevolence. That principle is not conceived to address stochastic problems such as those in which the ostensibly benevolent action may benefit some but harm others, but rather to address essentially determinate problems such as those in which one's benevolent action has a clear and *de facto* sure benefit for a particular person or persons.

policy. But then the distinctive character of that person's theory may have no role in the moral evaluation of policies on vaccination and many other stochastic problems. This would be a hard lesson. But perhaps it is such lessons that we should expect from the resurgence in moral and political theory that has been stimulated in large part in recent decades by concern with major policy issues. If the young movement of "applied ethics" is successful, it will bring new understandings of ethics and not merely moral prescriptions for policy.

Political Science and Philosophy, University of Chicago

MORAL INDIVIDUALISM: AGENT-RELATIVITY AND DEONTIC RESTRAINTS*

By Eric Mack

Introduction

My goal in this essay is to say something helpful about the philosophical foundations of deontic restraints, i.e., moral restraints on actions that are, roughly speaking, grounded in the wrongful character of the actions themselves and not merely in the disvalue of their results. An account of deontic restraints will be formulated and offered against the backdrop of three related, but broader, contrasts or puzzles within moral theory. The plausibility of this account of deontic restraints (and of the conception of moral rights which are correlative to these restraints) rests in part on how well this account resolves the puzzles or illuminates the contrasts which make up this theoretical backdrop.

The first and broadest part of the backdrop is the tense relationship between the theory of the good and the theory of the right. There is a strong impetus to assert the existence of deontic restraints (and correlative rights) that (at least sometimes) stand athwart and deny moral permissibility to actions that promote the individual or social good. At the same time, we do not want these restraints and rights to be free-floating moral phenomena unattached to considerations of value and disvalue, discoverable only by some special deontic intuition. Yet when we try to attach restraints or rights to considerations of value and disvalue, their independence is threatened and, with that, their capacity to exercise a moral veto over the promotion of the good.[1] The account of deontic restrictions I attempt to present depicts a connection between these moral constraints and a certain concept of the good that does not reduce restraints and rights to the status of instruments, either direct or indirect, for the promotion of the values identified by that theory of the good.

The second part of the backdrop against which my account appears is the two-sided character of the standard barrage of criticisms directed at consequen-

* Work on this essay was recently supported by a grant from the Murphy Institute of Political Economy at Tulane University and less recently supported by a grant from the Earhart Foundation. I wish to thank the editor of *Social Philosophy and Policy* for her helpful comments and Mary Sirridge for her listening and advice.

[1] Cf. Thomas ScanIon, "Rights, Goals and Fairness," ed. S. Hampshire, *Public and Private Morality* (Cambridge: Cambridge University Press, 1978), p. 93.

> In attacking utilitarianism one is inclined to appeal to individual rights, which mere considerations of social utility cannot justify us in overriding. But rights themselves need to be justified somehow, and how other than by appeal to the human interests their recognition promotes and protects?

tialism.[2] On one side is the *integrity objection* – the objection that the demands placed upon individuals by consequentialism are incompatible with individuals' developing coherently-integrated lives through genuine commitment to their respective and particular life projects. This objection focuses on the purported damage that an agent must do *to himself* as an integrated self if he is to be disposed to accede to the external demands of consequentialism. The *integrity objection* is naturally formulated in the idiom of value and disvalue. Its prognosis is that the global impartiality of consequentialism is blind to the local value and significance that resides in the pursuit and realization of personal projects, commitments, and aspirations.

On the other side of the two-sided barrage is the *justice objection* – the objection that consequentialism sanctions (indeed, mandates) unjust impositions of sacrifices upon individuals for the sake of the general good. This objection focuses on the damage (indeed, the wrongful damage) which threatens an agent at the hands of *other agents* when those other agents march under the banner of consequentialism. This sort of criticism appeals to the theory of the right, i.e., principles of justice or rights that deontically bar at least certain fruitful impositions. The conception of moral individualism that I advance provides a particular, sustaining interpretation of each of these objections – one which invokes what I describe as the value pole and the deontic pole of moral individualism.

The third, related part of the backdrop consists of puzzles about the correct elucidation of moral individualism. I have in mind questions about whether affirmations of the separateness or separate importance of persons' lives are to be construed as claims within the theory of the good or as deontic claims, as well as related questions about why, if these claims are most naturally and immediately construed as claims about value, they should so often be invoked as a basis for persons having *rights* or otherwise being protected by principles of justice. I maintain that the more immediately accessible facet of moral individualism is its value facet, and that this consists in the agent-relativity of value, i.e., in the relativity of all value and value-based reasons for action to the particular agents for whom these values and reasons exist. But this facet of moral individualism is complemented by a deontic facet – indeed, *calls for* such a complementary facet – which consists in the familiar negative basic rights of political individualism. The disposition to think that rights have been undergirded when the existence of an "overall social good" is denied, or when the importance of each person's separate existence is asserted, is not entirely mistaken.[3] It is correct insofar as the agent-relativity of value expressed in these claims signals part of a rational response to the importance of our separate existence; the other, interdependent, part of it is a

---

[2] On the integrity and justice objections, see Samuel Scheffler, *The Rejection of Consequentialism* (Oxford: Clarendon Press, 1982), and below. Consequentialism is construed very broadly to encompass any doctrine that assigns impersonal rankings to alternative worlds and prescribes actions (or, alternatively, rules, virtues, etc.) entirely on the basis of their tendency (or expected tendency) to produce more highly ranked worlds. The ranking of worlds need not be a matter of aggregating their constituent values. Nor is there any restriction on what counts as valuable and disvaluable, e.g., one isn't restricted just to ranking pleasures and pains.

[3] Cf. Robert Nozick, *Anarchy, State and Utopia* (New York: Basic Books, 1974), p. 33.

recognition that others are not morally available means for the pursuit of one's agent-relative value. The pole of agent-relativity represents the core of moral individualism's theory of the good, and it is the component of moral individualism that sustains the *integrity objection*. The pole of protective side-constraints represents the core of moral individualism's theory of the right, and it is the component that sustains the *justice objection*.

The case for the existence of such deontic restraints does not rest on the value (agent-neutral or agent-relative) that is promoted or protected by agents' abiding by them, but rather on two features of the acknowledgment of such restraints. First, the acknowledgment itself is a rational response to the existence of other bearers of (agent-relative) reasons for action. Second, it provides a fitting interpersonal complement to the otherwise disruptive recognition of the agent-relativity of value. Restraints and rights are, then, connected to a theory of the good without assuming the status of instruments for the promotion or protection of the specific values endorsed on the basis of that theory.

The argument of this essay proceeds through a series of interlocking sub-arguments, not all of which lock as securely as I would like. In Section I, I begin by defending the *coherence* of a system of agent-relative values within which value is essentially value for this or that specific agent who stands in some particular relationship to the valuable state and who, through that relationship, has reason for promoting that state. In Section II, I assert the *existence* of such values and argue that they are the only sort of values we have reason to assert. In Section III, I maintain that the rejection of agent-neutral values does not imply the subjectivity of values, i.e., their dependence upon our existing affections. Moreover, I argue for the objectivity of agent-relative values. Section IV contains a critical examination of contentions by Samuel Scheffler and Thomas Nagel[4] about the relationship of agent-relativity and deontic restraints. In particular, I challenge Scheffler's rejection of deontic restrictions, but I find Nagel's defense of them to be inadequate. In Section V, I sketch a positive account of deontic restraints as the complementary pole to the agent-relativity of value in a bipolar expression of moral individualism.

I. The Coherence of the Agent-Relativity of Values

In this section, I distinguish between agent-relative and agent-neutral conceptions of rankings, values, and reasons for action. The standard objections to the coherence of a system of agent-relative values are surveyed and rejected. I do this through a critical analysis of G.E. Moore's classic arguments against the coherence of one agent-relative theory, viz., ethical egoism.

Considerations of value are essentially tied to rankings of alternative states of the world. A given state of affairs, e.g., the occurrence of this pleasure, that success, or so-and-so's performance, is valuable if and only if it is a basis for ranking a world with that state of affairs higher than an otherwise identical world that lacks that state of affairs. The ranking of world W_1 over world W_2, in turn, provides a reason (a reason of value) to promote W_1 rather than W_2. Values, rankings, and reasons of

---

[4] Thomas Nagel, *The View from Nowhere* (Oxford: Oxford University Press, 1986).

value can be construed in either an agent-relative or an agent-neutral fashion. A state of affairs S_1 is valuable relative to an agent A_1 if and only if S_1's distinctive presence in W_1 is a basis for A_1 ranking W_1 over W_2, even though S_1 may not be a basis for any other agent ranking W_1 over W_2. Indeed, the *absence* of S_1 may be valuable relative to agent A_2, and this absence in W_2 may be a basis for A_2's ranking W_2 over W_1. The rankings of these worlds would be agent-relative; W_1 is preferred to W_2 relative to A_1 and W_2 is preferred to W_1 relative to A_2. The prospect of S_1 or the associated ranking of W_1 over W_2 provides A_1 with a reason for promoting W_1. But this reason is agent-relative. Its existence, reflective as it is of value and ranking relative to A_1, tells us nothing about whether A_2 has any reason to promote W_1. Indeed, it is perfectly consistent with A_1 having reason, all values considered,[5] to promote W_1 that A_2 has reason, all values considered, to promote what is incompatible with W_1 and hence to thwart A_1's doing what he has, all values considered, reason to do. Values, rankings, and reasons are agent-relative if their descriptions include essential references to an agent who has that value, prefers that ranking, or has that reason.[6]

A state of affairs S_2 has agent-neutral value if and only if its presence in W_2 is a basis for each agent to rank W_2 over an otherwise identical W_1 which lacks S_2. If S_2 is agent-neutrally valuable, W_2 is better than W_1 *full stop*. This goes beyond W_2 being better relative to agent A_1, better relative to A_2, ... better relative to A_n. In the latter case, A_1's reason for promoting S_2 remains its value for A_1; A_2's reason remains its value for A_2, etc. Even W_2's being better for everyone does not make it agent-neutrally better. If S_2 is impersonally better than S_1, each agent in position to promote S_2 has a reason of value to do so. W_2 is the world in which the agent or the set of agents who can most effectively produce S_2 do so. Thus, W_2 is, of the alternatives under consideration, The World That Ought To Be Promoted, The World That Ought To Exist. It is the world which is best from an angelic perspective and is free of all partiality. If W_2 has this exalted status, it calls upon each agent to contribute to its promotion, all values considered – though, for some individuals, that promotion will consist simply in acceding to the actions of the most effective producers of W_2.[7] A value, ranking, or reason is agent-neutral if its description does not include an essential reference to a person who has that value, prefers that ranking, or has that reason.

There is a substantial tradition of objections to the very idea of the agent-relativity of values or, at least, to the coherence of affirming agent-relative values for agents who may find their respective values to be in competition. The specific target of these objections has been ethical egoism, which paradigmatically

<hr>

[5] That is to say, all things considered except for possible side constraint, deontic reasons for or against the action.

[6] Cf. *The View from Nowhere*, pp. 152-53.

[7] If alternative worlds can be ranked impersonally, any competing personal ranking of those worlds will have the status of an idiosyncratic departure from rational evaluation, and thus will have no rational force for determining how that idiosyncratic agent should act. Nor, it seems, could a competing personal ranking which simply stands alongside a valid impersonal ranking warrant an agent-centered prerogative of the sort proposed by Scheffler (one that would block the inference from W_2 being What Ought To Exist to the idiosyncratic agent's obligation to promote W_2).

maintains the agent-relativity of all value.[8] These objections deserve a brief consideration – and dismissal.

The first of three recurring and related objections is that the goodness of any state of affairs must be agent-neutral. Thus, in a well-known passage, G.E. Moore argued:

> What, then, is meant by 'my own good'? In what sense can a thing be good *for me*? It is obvious, if we reflect, that the only thing which can belong to me, which can be mine, is something which is good; and not the fact that it is good. When, therefore, I talk of anything I get as 'my own good', I must mean either that the thing I get is good, or that my possessing it is good. In both cases it is only the thing or the possession of it which is *mine*, and not the *goodness* of that thing or that possession.[9]

The core of Moore's argument seems to be the claim that the only intelligible function of the "for me" in the assertion that "S_1 is good for me" is to indicate that I am the person in possession of (or subject to) S_1. The "for me" locates the good (or its ownership). The "for me" indicates S_1's actual or potential receptacle, but it is incidental to S_1 being good. The goodness of S_1 is not a function of its location, of its standing in the relation to me of being possessed, enjoyed, desired, etc., by me. This, I take it, is also what Moore means by the claim that ".. it is only the thing or the possession of it which is *mine*, and not the *goodness* of that thing or that possession."

If there is any force at all to Moore's argument, it is a product of Moore's mischaracterization of the ethical egoist's position. Moore's language suggests that the egoist believes in a type of axiological Midas effect through which, by being touched by my possession, by being mine, S_1 acquires value. But according to the egoist, S_1's being "mine" signifies its standing to me in some further and more substantive relation, (e.g., its fulfilling my preference, its satisfying my desire, its being constitutive of my self-realization), in virtue of which *I* have reason to promote S_1. S_1's fulfilling, satisfying, or realizing *my* preference, desire, or self is what provides me with reason to produce S_1. Since the occurrence of S_1 need not also fulfill the preference, etc., of agent A_1, it need not provide A_1 with any reason for action whatsoever.

The second common argument for the incoherence of affirming agent-relative values for agents whose values may come into competition is that this affirmation implies that each agent's values are the supreme values. Thus, e.g., Moore goes on to argue that:

> If, therefore, it is true of any single man's 'interest' or 'happiness' that it ought to be his sole ultimate end, this can only mean that man's 'interest'

---

[8] For a survey and critique of these objections, see Jesse Kalin, "In Defense of Egoism," ed. David Gauthier, *Morality and Rational Self-Interest* (Englewood-Cliffs: Prentice-Hall, 1970), pp. 64–87, "Two Types of Moral Reasoning: Egoism as A Moral Theory," *Canadian Journal of Philosophy* (November 1975), pp. 323–56, and Eric Mack, "Egoism and Rights," *The Personalist* (Winter 1973), pp. 5–33, "Campbell's Refutation of Egoism," *Canadian Journal of Philosophy* (November 1974), pp. 659–63.

[9] G.E. Moore, *Principia Ethica* (Cambridge: Cambridge University Press, 1960), p. 98. In Nagel's language, Moore is denying that the reference to the person who "possesses" the good is essential to its description.

or 'happiness' is *the sole good, the* Universal Good, and the only thing that anybody ought to aim at. What Egoism holds, therefore, is that *each* man's happiness is the sole good – that a number of different things are *each* of them the only good thing there is – an absolute contradiction![10]

But, clearly, no inference of the sort Moore expresses is justified. What egoism holds is that each man's happiness (or whatever) is *his* sole ultimate good – that there are as many distinct ultimate goods as there are persons, each being the ultimate good for the person whose happiness (or whatever) it is. Only if the first objection to the relativizing of the good to individual agents were correct (which it is not) would the damning inference of the sort Moore expresses be justified.

The third common argument against ethical egoism as an instance of the agent-relativity of value turns on the demand for the compossibility of all the actions that agents ought, all values considered, to perform. It is held to be a sign of irrationality for an ethical system to require both that A_1 do X and that A_2 do Y in some actual or even merely possible situations such that the performance of both X and Y cannot occur. An ethical system should tell people What Ought To Be Done. But in such situations ethical egoism can be charged either with failing to indicate What Ought To Be Done – should it be X or should it be Y? – or with prescribing the impossible. The latter charge will bear the weight of the argument if it is maintained that every rational ethical system must include the principle that if X ought to be done and Y ought to be done, then X-and-Y ought to be done.

The demand for the compossibility of all value-justified actions reflects the belief that there is some principle for ranking alternative worlds which picks out the best available world *full stop,* and that the promotion of that best world determines how each agent should act. As soldiers in pursuit of a common cause, whatever it is that A_1 and A_2 should respectively do, those actions must be compossible. Both specific charges illicitly presuppose the agent-neutrality of values. With respect to the former charge, egoism does fail to indicate What Ought To Be Done; insofar as this phrase implies transcendence of the perspective of particular agents, the ethical egoist (as our representative agent-relativist) denies its valid application. When, all agent-relative values considered, A_1 ought to do X and, all agent-relative values considered, A_2 ought to do Y, and X and Y are not compossible, the agent-relativist is ... well, neutral *qua* moral theorist between X and Y. He does not pretend to wield a morality which pronounces on whose interests or happiness should be sacrificed to whom. With respect to the latter charge, if it were true that X Ought To Be Done and that Y Ought To Be Done, then presumably it would follow that X-and-Y Ought To Be Done – done by agents enrolled in the collective whose common cause requires X and requires Y. But the ethical egoist, as agent-relativist, only affirms prescriptions of the form "A_1 ought to do X" and denies inferences from such claims to ones of the form "X Ought To Be Done (by A_1)."[11]

[10] Moore, *Principia Ethica*, p. 99.
[11] See especially Kalin, "Two Kinds of Moral Reasoning," pp. 340–44.

II. The Exclusive Existence of Agent-Relative Values

I have argued extensively for the coherence of affirming agent-relative values but only incidentally for the existence of such values. In this section, I assert the existence of agent-relative values more emphatically and argue that only such values exist, i.e., that agent-neutral values do not exist. If people ever have reasons for action, the satisfaction of their own desires, the realization of their own purposes (or commitments, or capacities), must be among those reasons.[12] The objects of such reason-based actions are values, albeit each relative to the agent whose satisfaction, realization, etc., it will be. The acceptance of the agent-relativity of at least some values seems required if one agrees that "the distinction between any one individual and any other is real and fundamental" so that, according to Sidgwick,

> 'I' am concerned with the quality of my existence as an individual in a sense, fundamentally important, in which I am not concerned with the quality of the experience of other individuals: and this being so, I do not see how it can be proved that this distinction is not to be taken as fundamental in determining the ultimate end of rational action for the individual.[13]

The existence of agent-relative values is, I take it, the presumption embodied in the conception of rationality in economics and decision theory. Some things are reasons for action: in order for something to provide me with a reason for action, it must enter into my utility-function. Yet its so providing me with a reason for action, its being a value (for me) implies nothing at all about its providing others with reasons for action. Indeed, the presumption of economic rationality is that *all* value is agent-relative. As is often noted, the modesty of this conception of rationality makes it an attractive minimalist starting place for moral theory.

Perhaps the most basic reason – and therefore the most difficult of explication – for believing that the good is always the good for (i.e., the good relative to) this or that particular agent is that this proposition renders the good (and/or the reason-providing capacity of the good) less mysterious than on agent-neutralist conceptions of it. One way of exhibiting the mysteriousness of agent-neutral value is to highlight how similar belief in such value is to belief in "agent-external" value. At least most of what is puzzling about agent-external value also is true of agent-neutral value. After briefly focusing on the mysteriousness of the agent-neutrality of values, I consider and reject three particular arguments for the agent-neutrality of some values that appear in Thomas Nagel's *The View from Nowhere*.

[12] Does anyone ever *deny* that people have reasons for action? At points in *The View from Nowhere*, Nagel suggests that such a denial comes in the form of maintaining that the normative realm is illusory, that there are beings moved by motives of various sorts, and this is all (pp. 140–41). On such an eliminative view, the intense pain that I would undergo were I to rest my hand on a hot stove explains my keeping my hand off it. But it does not indicate that I am rational in doing so. Nagel holds, in contrast, that "I have a reason, and not just an inclination, to refrain from putting my hand on a hot stove. (p. 157) Nagel contrasts "the purely psychological, antirealist account," (p. 145) which he labels "Humean subjectivism," (p. 142) with "normative realism" (p. 139). Yet the latter seems to go beyond a simple denial of Humean subjectivism; normative realism also denies that our reasons for action are limited to "our preexisting motives."

[13] Henry Sidgwick, *The Methods of Ethics* (Chicago: University of Chicago Press, 1962), p. 498.

Agent-external value is value that would exist even were no agent ever to exist and, hence, were no agent ever to encounter, or relate to, the valuable object or property in any way.[14] Nagel believes that "the objectifying tendency produces a strong impulse to believe that there are" external values. Yet Nagel himself seems to think that belief in such values can be plausible only if it

> avoids the implausible consequence that they retain their practical importance even if no one will *ever* be able to respond to them. (So that if all sentient life is destroyed, it will still be a good thing if the Frick Collection survives.)[15]

Yet, as far as I can see, being good even if no one will ever be able to respond to that goodness is the central necessary feature of any external good. The question is what, if anything, distinguishes such externality of value from neutrality of value? I want to argue that if a value is not conceived of as agent-relative, it must be conceived of as agent-external. Thus the sponsor of agent-neutrality has to choose between the enemy of agent-relativity and the oddity of agent-externality.

One might imagine a sponsor of agent-neutral value proposing that a necessary condition of any X having agent-neutral value is that *someone*, *sometime* and *somewhere*, stand in some relation to X of the sort through which advocates of agent-relativity think value arises. Given this necessary condition, for any X which qualifies as having agent-neutral value, it will not be the case that the X would have that agent-neutral value even were no agent ever to exist, etc. In this way, the sponsor of agent-neutral values may seem to distance himself from sponsorship of agent-external values. But what justifies the imposition of this necessary condition? We might have here merely a stipulation that a putative value will not be labeled an agent-neutral value unless *someone*, *sometime* and *somewhere*, stands in some R relation to it. But such a stipulation leaves open the question of whether that value would exist – would exist as an external value – even were the condition for its being labeled a neutral value not satisfied. It leaves open the possibility that the value which the sponsor of agent-neutral values wants us to affirm (and to label as agent-neutral) is agent-external.

We can be sure that the value we are affirming (under the label of agent-neutral) is not agent-external only if it is *in virtue of* X's standing in relation R to *someone*, *sometime* and *somewhere*, that X's value arises. The imposition of the *someone/somewhere* condition on X's having value will be *justified* if it is thought that it is (at least in part) through the satisfaction of this condition that X has its value. But if this is

[14] To deny the existence of external values is not to deny the existence of "external reasons" as that term has recently been used by Bernard Williams. An external reason is a reason which, when possessed, need not motivate the agent possessing that reason. External values of the sort debunked here would provide agents with external reasons. But an agent might have an external reason, e.g., his (recognition of his) objective need for X, which was not indicative of such an external value. It looks like the reasons we have purely in virtue of deontic restraints are external reasons in Williams's sense. Cf. Bernard Williams, "Internal and External Reasons," ed. R. Harrison, *Rational Action: Studies in Philosophy and Social Science* (Cambridge: Cambridge University Press, 1979), pp. 17–28.

[15] *The View from Nowhere*, p. 153. The survival of the Frick Collection might, of course, fulfill the posthumous interests of various agents and, in this way, be a good thing. But this would not support the collection's external value.

the way X's value is conceived, then it appears that X's value is agent-relative – in particular, relative to the agent who stands in relation R to X. For how, in turn, could the satisfaction of the *someone/somewhere* condition give rise to X's value? The only way I can imagine is that the value arises *in and through* some particular *someone*'s particular relation to X. And if X's value arises *in and through* this particular relation to agent A – by being, e.g., the object of A's desire or need or ambition – then it is A who can directly and especially be said to have reason to promote X. That is to say, X's value will be relative to A.

We can summarize the present argument as follows: the satisfaction of the *someone/somewhere* condition with respect to X either is not essential to X's value or it is essential to X's value. If it is not essential to X's value, then X's value (if it exists at all) will be agent-external value. If it is essential to X's value, then that value will be agent-relative. So the theorist who seeks to avoid the agent-relativity of all values will have to affirm the agent-*externality* of some of them. This conclusion should be of no surprise in light of Nagel's own characterization of external value as "value which is not reducible to [its] value *for* anyone."[16] For, if a value is not external in this sense, the value *will* be "reducible" to its value for someone, i.e., it will be agent-relative.[17]

Some of these same points, and others, can be made more concretely by examining Nagel's own specific example of an agent-neutral (dis)value: the purportedly agent-neutral badness of pain. Nagel begins with the claim that

> primitive pleasures and pains provide at least agent-relative reasons for pursuit and avoidance – reasons that can be affirmed from an objective standpoint [i.e., reasons that "can be recognized" ... from outside] and that do not merely describe the actual motivation of the agent.[18]

But does pain provide, in addition, an agent-neutral reason for its avoidance? Although he is fully aware of the difficulty of constructing arguments for this conclusion, Nagel does offer three somewhat discrete arguments.[19] The first we

---

[16] *ibid.*

[17] Moreover, it does not seem that X's external (and, hence, fully intrinsic and self-contained) goodness as such would provide reasons for action among such agents as might appear on the scene. Property G (or whatever it is that purports to be intrinsically good) will provide such agents as appear with reasons for action only insofar as the realization of G in some way fulfills or is constitutive of their desires, projects, or selves. But, in that case, the agents' respective reasons for action will correspond to the agent-relative value of diverse realizations of G and not to the supposed external goodness of G. Even were it to exist, the intrinsic good would be too dissociated from the life of flesh- and purpose-bound agents to provide those agents with reasons for action.

This conclusion may be too quick. Perhaps the perception (veridical or not) of the Form of the Good could itself motivate an agent. In such a case, it would be putting the cart before the horse to say that the agent's reason for action corresponds to the agent-relative value of his participation in the Good. Of course, the agent will not be acting with reason unless his perception of the Good is veridical.

[18] *The View from Nowhere*, p. 158. In the uncut version of what appears within the brackets, Nagel (p. 150) speaks more portentously of reasons that "can be recognized and *accepted* from the outside."

[19] *ibid.* Nagel claims to have already argued that "the *possibility* of assigning agent-neutral value to pleasure and pain should be admitted." (p. 160) But this, I think, is mistaken. He seems to be referring to arguments made in a section labelled "Antirealism" (pp. 143–49). Yet in this section Nagel's target seems to be "disbelief in the reality of values and reasons," and this can clearly be rejected without embracing even the possibility of agent-neutral values and reasons. The situation is further complicated by Nagel's characterizations of "realism" (p. 139), which suggest that realism takes one step or more beyond reason-acknowledging doctrines such as "the position that each person has reason to do what will satisfy his desires or preferences" (p. 149).

may label "the dissociation argument"; the second, "the concern by/for others argument"; and the third, "the impersonal hatefulness argument."

Dissociation occurs, according to Nagel, if I do not assign agent-neutral badness to my pain. My objective self would become dissociated from my subjective self because the latter would see that my suffering should stop while the former, as objective spectator, could only and would only acknowledge that EM, the observee, has reason to want it to stop.[20] My subjective self is, as my four-year-old daughter would say, "really really" against this suffering; but my objective self is ... well, objective, disinterested. If only agent-relative badness is assigned to my pain, only the agent whose pain it is can take a substantive, contentful stand against pain. If only agent-relative badness is assigned to my pain, the only judgment that the objective self can make is that this person, EM, whom the objective spectator is observing, has reason to negate the suffering. My objective self is, then, as distant from my subjective self as other reason-acknowledging agents are.

If I had an objective self, if I were in part an objective self of the sort Nagel is imagining, then I *might* be concerned about being dissociated from my subjective self.[21] On the other hand, the dominant strand within the dualist tradition looks with great favor upon dissociation. What's the point of having two selves unless the objective, rational, depersonalized, and disembodied self can free itself from, rise above, and *view with detachment* the concerns of the subjective and particularistic self? To assert both the existence of two selves (or two parts or aspects of the self) and a structure for value which allows those two selves to live in harmony may be a matter of wanting both to have and to eat one's metaphysical cake. Furthermore, while in itself belief in the agent-neutral badness of EM's suffering will tend to align and associate my objective self with my subjective self, belief in the agent-neutral badness of *others'* suffering will have the opposite effect. The agent-relative badness of suffering tells me (or my subjective self) to focus on the reduction of my suffering, while the agent-neutral badness of suffering at large tells me (or my objective self) to focus on the reduction of suffering at large. In almost all circumstances, one of these practices will have to be sacrificed to the other. If I am disposed to respond to the impersonal values affirmed by my objective self, I will usually have to suppress the counsel of my subjective self. The result may not be Nagelian dissociation of my objective and subjective selves. The result may only (!) be the loss of an integrated (subjective) self. It is this fear which underlies the integrity objection.

[20] The relevant couple of sentences in Nagel, *ibid.* p. 160, read:

> The dissociation here is a split attitude toward my own suffering. As objective spectator, I acknowledge that TN has a reason to want it to stop, but I see no reason why it should stop. My evaluation [i.e., the evaluation of the 'objective spectator'?] is entirely confined within the framework of a judgment about what it is rational *for this person* to want.

[21] Perhaps the reason that Nagel thinks that this intra-personal dissociation is worrisome is that, although my objective self acknowledges that EM has reason to end his suffering, the inability of my objective self to *share* this reason suggests that its existence is an illusion, i.e., it suggests the Humean subjectivism according to which there are motives, but not reasons. This suggestion runs counter to Nagel's recognition that even agent-relative reasons count as real reasons. Nevertheless, Nagel does continue to flirt with his earlier view that the only real reasons are agent-neutral ones. Cf. the next passage from Nagel in the text.

The second argument, "concern by/for others," suggests that plausible accounts of others being moved by our suffering and our being moved by others' suffering invoke the agent-neutral badness of suffering. Nagel argues that

> If . . . we limit ourselves to relative reasons, [the sufferer] will have to say that though he has reason to want an analgesic, there is no reason for him to have one, or for anyone else who happens to be around to give him one.[22]

This is partially correct; but mostly misleading. Clearly, if the badness of suffering is agent-relative, the sufferer cannot say that there is an agent-neutral reason for him to have the analgesic. But that is not to deny the existence (or "objectivity") of an agent-relative reason for him to have it. Nor is it to deny the existence of agent-relative reasons had by some of those who happen to be around him to provide him with an analgesic. A blissful cessation of my screams, or even my feeling better, may be among the states of affairs that are good for some or all of these agents. Nagel asks us to imagine a fellow sufferer who

> professes to hope we both will be given morphine, but I [the first-person, agent-relativist sufferer] fail to understand this. I understand why he has reason to want morphine for himself, but what reason does he have to want *me* to get some? Does my groaning bother him?[23]

That may be it. My groaning may be drowning out the answers on Hollywood Squares. Or it may be that my groaning bothers him because my being in pain, in a way that is vivid and present to him, bothers him. Because I am near to him and he is a person of normal sympathies, his sympathy extends to me and he is discomforted by my suffering. So he has reason to want it to stop – a reason which does not extend to the suffering of those whom, perhaps simply because of their distance from him, his sympathies do not embrace.

But implicit in Nagel's final rhetorical question is another, more difficult question. Does the fellow patient's reason for wanting my suffering to cease rest merely on his tastes and distastes, e.g., merely on his distaste for my groaning or on his distaste for my suffering? Nagel, as a "normative realist," wants to hold about reasons for action that "we have to discover them instead of deriving them from our preexisting motives."[24] For such a realist, the suggestion of the rhetorical question is that it is the badness of suffering that makes the preference for its disappearance rational, not the preference for its disappearance that makes the suffering bad. It is this "real" or "objective" badness of my suffering that underlies my fellow patient's discomfort at my groaning. This suggested answer leads to an affirmation of the agent-neutrality of the fellow patient's reasons given a further, implicit premise, viz., that values which are "real" or "objective," so that the rationality of tastes, desires, preferences, etc., depend on their fit with "real" or "objective" values, must

---

[22] *ibid.*, p. 160.
[23] *ibid.*
[24] *ibid.*, p. 139.

be agent-neutral values. But this further premise is clearly contentious and is one which I reject in the next section.

One further point needs to be made about the reasons that others might have for relieving my suffering. Even the total absence of *value-based* reasons for others to alleviate my suffering hardly entails the absence of *all* reasons; my doctor may have a duty to do so whether he likes it or not, whether it advances his values or not. To say that all values are agent-relative and that, therefore, all value-based reasons for action are agent-relative, is not to deny the existence of other sorts of reasons for or against action; in particular, it is not to deny the existence of deontic constraints on people's behavior.

Nagel's third argument, "impersonal hatefulness," urges us to see a component of our rejection of pain as occurring on an impersonal plane where objective self confronts agent-neutral value:

> the pain, though it comes attached to a person and his individual perspective, is just as clearly hateful to the objective self as to the subjective individual. The pain can be detached in thought from the fact that it is mine without losing any of its dreadfulness. It has, so to speak, a life of its own.[25]

One response to this passage runs as follows: I understand, of course, that pain which is not my pain can be as dreadful to the sufferer as my pain is dreadful to me. I understand what it is like to be subject to such dreadful stuff. But except for those rare individuals who achieve or succumb to an extraordinary identification with others (and who, therefore, can say, "Their pain is my pain"), the discovery that an impending pain will be suffered by another and not oneself does radically reduce its perceived dreadfulness.

Yet this focus on perceived dreadfulness, i.e., on the way that a prospective pain is frightening, misses the real force of this passage. The force lies in the simple idea that pain is dreadful. It is dreadful in itself so that the *correct* response to prospective pain is dread; pain is the sort of thing that a rational person wants not to exist. This is the claim of the normative realist with respect to pain. But is this force well-directed? Does it specifically point to the agent-neutral badness of pain? One can agree that the dreadfulness of pain has "a life of its own" – so that anyone facing the prospect of pain has a reason to avoid it whatever his attitude toward pain – without agreeing that the "real" or "objective" awfulness of pain gives everyone reason to want a specific prospective pain not to exist. In recognizing the dreadfulness of the pain faced by another, I do more than understand his motivation in avoiding it; I also see that he ought to want to escape it. But as a mere objective spectator, I do not, thereby, have reason to prevent his pain.

However, other passages within Nagel's "impersonal hatefulness" argument seem designed to block the idea that the awfulness of pain may yet sustain only agent-relative reasons. This is how we may read the argument that:

> The [sufferer's] desire to be rid of pain has only the pain as its object. . . .
> [I]f I lacked or lost the conception of myself as distinct from other possible

25 *ibid.*, p. 160.

or actual persons, I could still apprehend the badness of pain, immediately.... [T]he fact that it is mine – the concept of myself – doesn't come into my perception of the badness of my pain.[26]

We seem to have come full circle to a version of Moore's original claim that whether or not the pain is mine is incidental to its badness. It may be that the pain I desire to get rid of happens to be mine, but I do not apprehend its badness as mine.

It is true that I do not have to *register* the pain as mine in order to apprehend its badness. I don't have to say to myself, "This is the pain that *I* am undergoing," before I can recognize that it merits elimination. I simply indict pain as I immediately experience it. But the pain that I indict is the pain that is immediate to me, which is to say, my pain. "The immediate attitude of the subject" of the pain is simply that this current condition should cease. The subject does not, within that immediate indictment, address the issue of who has reason to eliminate this suffering. But if it is his suffering that he indicts, and if he recognizes that others in parallel fashion indict the suffering immediate to them, the natural conclusion is that each has reason, assuming mutual disinterest, to eliminate his own suffering.[27]

Thus, two bases have been offered against the existence of agent-neutral values: (1) belief in agent-neutral values commits one to belief in agent-external values, and (2) three positive arguments for the existence of agent-neutral values are deeply flawed. Sections I and II together constitute a case against agent-neutral value and against arguments for interpersonal principles that are based upon impersonal consequentialist rankings of alternative worlds.

III. THE OBJECTIVITY OF AGENT-RELATIVE VALUES

In this section, I seek to clarify what is and, especially, what is not implied by the agent-relativity of all values. I am especially concerned to distinguish between the agent-relativity of value and the subjectivity of value. The primary motivation here is to insulate the case for the agent-relativity of values from arguments against the subjectivity of values. The secondary motivation is, simply, to acknowledge the objectivity of (agent-relative) values. The tertiary motivation is a *suspicion* – which remains unexamined in this essay – that the argument of Section V – to the effect that rationality requires a practical recognition of others as bearers of value-based reasons for action – works better if the values that provide people with these reasons are objective and not themselves merely reflective of people's affections.

The agent-relativity of all values does not imply hedonism, egotism, or subjectivism. Agent-relativity does not imply hedonism because it does not restrict the good to states of pleasure or felt satisfaction. Nor does agent-relativity represent a commitment to egotism. The egotist believes that states of affairs are important and valuable in virtue of their connection with his special self. By being within his unique existence, this experience, this trial or triumph, this exercise of skill or power is especially worthy of esteem. The egotist and whatever he identifies with

---

[26] *ibid.*, p. 161.

[27] Moreover, it is implausible to imagine, as Nagel does, that an agent who lacked or lost the conception of himself would form the sophisticated judgment, "*This experience* ought not to go on, *whoever* is having it." *ibid.*, p. 161.

become, in his eyes, *the* center of the universe. It is generalized egotism, not the agent-relativity of value, that is subject to Moore's charge of absurdity. It is, however, a further matter to indicate the relation between agent-relativity and ethical egoism. The fact that recent discussions of the agent-relativity of value were prefigured in defenses of the coherence of ethical egoism does not justify the identification of agent-relative and egoistic value. But this relationship is another matter that cannot be pursued within the confines of the present essay. Instead we turn to the relation between agent-relativism and subjectivism.

Here "subjectivism" designates the view that "values are the products of our affections," and is classically represented by Hobbes's claim, "But whatsoever is the object of any mans Appetite or Desire; that is it, which he for his part calleth *Good* : And the object of his Hate, and Aversion, *Evill* . . ."[28] Value comes into existence by being conferred upon otherwise valueless states of affairs, and it is conferred by our preferences or desires or commitments. Subjectivism in this sense contrasts with objectivism, the view that affections can, at least sometimes, be evaluated as rational or not depending upon whether their objects are worthy of our affections. Against subjectivism, objectivism asserts (for Nagel, under the label, "normative realism") that "there are reasons for action, that we have to discover them instead of deriving them from our preexisting motives."[29]

Subjectivism, it seems, does not require that the good and the bad be restricted to types of experience. As David Gauthier points out:

> It might be thought that subjectivism implies that only what is itself subjective – only a state of sentient experience – could possess intrinsic value. But subjectivism concerns the ground of value, not its object. There is no restriction on the nature of those states of affairs that may be objects of preference, and so that may be valued.[30]

Nor is subjectivism automatically tied to the agent-relativism of value. It might be thought that, by being the object of someone's desire, a state of affairs has agent-neutral value conferred upon it. This seems to be the idea that links J.S. Mill's subjectivism with his agent-neutralism when he makes his notorious inference from each person's happiness being a good (for that person) in virtue of being desired (by that person) to the general happiness being what all persons should aim at.[31] Moreover, subjectivism can take cultural or societal forms, according to which value is conferred by cultural or societal preferences and provides reasons neutrally across members of that culture or society. Still, putting aside such organic subjectivism, there are plausible links between subjectivism and agent-relativism.

---

[28] David Gauthier, *Morals by Agreement* (Oxford: Clarendon Press, 1986), p. 47. The Hobbes passage is quoted by Gauthier on p. 51.

[29] Of course, the assumption here as elsewhere throughout this paper is that we are talking about ultimate values and fundamental preferences: values that are not simply instrumental for the production of other values, and preferences that are not merely responsive to perceived instrumental value.

[30] *ibid.*, p. 47. It would probably be better for Gauthier to speak of "final" or "ultimate" value than of "intrinsic" value

[31] J.S. Mill, *Utilitarianism* (Indianapolis: Bobbs-Merrill, 1957), pp. 44–45.

Subjectivism is a natural expression of the more general agent-relativist idea that what is valuable is valuable *in and through* its relation to agents. Subjectivism specifies affective relations as those in (and through) which states of affairs have value. And the idea that value exists as the bestowal of affection, in turn, supports the non-neutrality of value. Paradoxically, this support reflects some hesitancy about the idea that preference or desire can confer value. Given this hesitancy – more on which shortly – one is apt to think that while my desire for S_1 may have the power to confer value on S_1, it is difficult to see that power as sufficient to bestow an impersonal value upon S_1 that would call on others for its promotion. The value that my desire confers, the reason that my preference generates, seems at most to extend to the person whose desire or preference is at work.

I propose to argue that subjectivism is mistaken. Since I have already asserted the agent-relativity of all values, I must deny that the objectivity of values implies their agent-neutrality. Indeed, this denial has already occurred in the course of criticizing certain of Nagel's arguments against the agent-relativity of the badness of pain. Nagel's forceful claim was that the awfulness of pain is such that a rational person should want to avoid it: that the reason comes from the pain and not one's attitude toward it. But the force here proceeds from and requires only the objectivity of the badness of suffering, not the agent-neutrality of suffering.[32] In any case, the first task at hand is the rejection of subjectivism.

The (non-perverse) subjectivist and the objectivist agree that pleasure and other forms of felt satisfaction are good while pain and other forms of felt dissatisfaction are bad. But is pleasure good in virtue of the attitude of its subject? Do we perhaps each undergo various pleasures for a while, decide or otherwise come to form a preference for pleasure, and thereupon *make* pleasure a good thing and *give* ourselves reason to pursue it? The case for objectivism rests on the implausibility of affirmative answers to these and like questions. There is, of course, almost always some felt satisfaction in the perception that one's preferred state has come to pass (and, almost always, some further felt satisfaction in the perception that one *has attained* one's preferred state). Desiring S_1 can set the stage for the felt satisfaction of S_1 obtaining (and for the felt satisfaction of one's attaining a preferred state). In particular, preferring the pleasure may bestow on an agent the possibility of self-congratulatory satisfactions upon the occurrence of that pleasurable state and, thereby, the possibility of the good of those satisfactions. But none of this indicates that the agent's preference for the pleasure is what makes the pleasure good, nor does his preference for the pleasure make good the felt satisfactions which attend the pleasure's appearance. If one has reason to do what promotes one's pleasure and other felt satisfactions, it seems that this reason proceeds from the enjoyableness of

[32] The identification of the subjectivist/objectivist distinction with the relativist/neutralist distinction is very strong throughout Nagel. When he proceeds to argue for the agent-relative (i.e., "personal") status of certain values (e.g., *success* as a pianist or as a mountain-climber), Nagel's argument is that the value of these states of affairs are (merely) conferred upon them by the agents who are in pursuit of them. The implicit premise is that *the* alternative to agent-neutrality is subjectivity. This identification of the two distinctions also pervades Lomasky's *Persons, Rights and the Moral Community* (Oxford: Oxford University Press, 1987), especially ch. 9. Gauthier clearly rejects this identification, although he sees a natural association between subjectivism and relativism on the one hand and objectivism and neutralism on the other. Cf. *Morals by Agreement*, pp. 46–59.

pleasure, from its being an experience *worth having*, and not from one's forming (or having a primordial) preference for pleasure.

Parallel arguments can be offered if we concern ourselves not with a pervasive preference for pleasure homogeneously conceived, but rather with much more particular appetites, the objects of those appetites being specific experiential states. Consider, e.g., Loren Lomasky's example of an appetite for a kosher dill pickle.[33] What reason could one have for indulging such a desire? One unlikely possibility is that the *act* of ingesting a kosher dill pickle, in contrast to the taste-experience of its consumption, is itself a worthy enterprise. We shall shortly have to consider whether the worthiness of states of affairs and activities (in contrast to experiences) is susceptible to a subjectivist account. But here we are concerned with the value of the experience of eating the kosher dill. Does the existence of the desire provide a reason to favor the occurrence of the experience? Lomasky points out that a person subject to such an appetite can sometimes choose between satisfying that appetite and extinguishing it. If the existence of an appetite itself provides a reason to indulge it, then in such a case it would follow that the agent would be more rational to satisfy the appetite than to extinguish it. However, on the basis of those specified facts, it would not follow that the agent has more reason to satisfy the appetite than to extinguish it. What has been omitted from the specified facts is that the satisfaction of the appetite will *satisfy*; it will bring pleasure or some other form of felt satisfaction to the agent. It is satisfaction in the second sense, viz., the felt satisfaction of the agent, rather than in the first sense, viz., the coming into existence of the object of the affection, that provides the agent with reason for his action. It is the worthiness of the felt satisfaction, not the agent's affection for the satisfying state, that makes the agent's choice to satisfy his appetite rational.

Of course, the subjectivist is not committed to the objects of our preferences and, hence, is not committed to our values being limited to experiential states. An agent may desire an independent life, a successful career as a computer programmer, ownership of a complete set of braided-hair half-cent coins, true friendship, or growing the largest tomato in East Baton Rouge parish. And the occurrence of each of these conditions may be good for the agent; each may contribute to his well-being. Some of these desires are fairly readily represented as artificial appetites. An agent notices that appetites provide vehicles for the attainment of felt satisfactions, and so he searches for possible appetites – like the desire to grow the largest tomato in the parish – that he can cultivate. Having conjured up that desire, a field of purposively enjoyable activity and, perhaps, triumph becomes available to him. Nevertheless, even in a case of this sort, part of what is good for the agent is not merely the felt experience of growing the titanic tomato or the felt satisfaction accompanying that experience, but also actually having grown the prize fruit.[34]

---

[33] *Persons, Rights and the Moral Community*, p. 231. The argument in this and the next several paragraphs and, especially, the idea of a choice between satisfying and extinguishing desires, draws on Lomasky, pp. 229–37. See also Lomasky's unpublished "Rational Choice, Rational Choosers."

[34] What he cares about is growing a tomato that correctly is judged to be prizewinning. Were he to discover that the prize had been awarded by mistake, the afterglow would be lost. But why? The revelation of the mistake would not show that he had not achieved the felt experience of growing the prize tomato and the felt satisfaction of winning. Cf., of course, Nozick's experience machine discussion, *Anarchy, State, and Utopia*, pp. 42–45.

Moreover, even in a case of this sort, it is hard to picture the agent creating the artificial appetite out of a pure appetitive and normative vacuum. The creation of the appetite must draw on some combination of existing desires (e.g., for mucking around with shovels and hoes) and normative judgments (e.g., that it is good to learn how to grow tomatoes or, more broadly, that it is good to exercise one's talents and engage in productive activity).

The more we move away from preferences that can be thought of as appetites, either natural or artificial, and toward those preferences that can be described as commitments, projects, or plans, the more prominent becomes the role of normative judgments. One does not simply find oneself with long-term projects around which one's life is built in the way that one finds oneself with a yen for a kosher dill. The motivational force for such a project does not come from a craving or a vivid anticipation of the feel of its completion. Rather, it comes at least in part from a sense that the project is *worthy* of being undertaken and *worthy* of accomplishment. A person organizes much of his life in pursuit of, e.g., the eradication of racism, the unification of the sciences, a knowledge of the real author of the Shakespearean plays, the production of wood carvings of each of the 1955 Brooklyn Dodgers, or the well-being of his children, only if he judges that one of these goals merits achievement. It is only such a normative conviction that will sustain the goal's capacity to give structure to the agent's life. And, again, the conviction is about the value of the states of affairs aimed at, not merely the value of the felt experience of those states or the felt satisfaction that may accompany that experience. As Lomasky puts it:

> One cannot take one's commitments to projects as merely psychological quirks, for as such they could not command one's reflective loyalties...
> [T]o value one's projects is to value that at which the projects aim. It is in this way that consideration of rational activity necessarily points beyond itself, to value in the world.[35]

A person may well be passionate in his pursuit of such goals, but such passions are at least in part the products of and the servants of his judgments.

It is essential to the objectivist position that judgments of value are not self-validating. Agents indicate their recognition that they may be mistaken in their judgments of value when they agonize over whether or not to incorporate specific projects into their lives. It is, fortunately, not part of the project of this essay to indicate which judgments of value are correct or why they are correct. Two claims are sufficient for the present objectivist case. First, when an agent takes himself to have reason to direct and contour his life for the sake of a long-term goal, he must ascribe value to that goal which he himself does not bestow on it. Second, if it is not an illusion that agents do sometimes actually have reason to direct and contour their lives for the sake of long-term goals, then agents must sometimes be correct in their ascription of non-bestowed value to those goals.

No knockdown argument has been given against the "Humean subjectivist" who, as Nagel characterizes him, believes in motives but not reasons. This Humean

---

[35] *Persons, Rights, and the Moral Community*, p. 232.

denies that one has reason to promote either the objects of one's appetites or the objects of one's long-term goals. The prospect of these objects moves one, but this behavior is no more a matter of acting *with reason* than is, e.g., movement toward the pleasurable on the part of some sentient but pre-rational being. I do not see how to *argue* against the part of this proposal that denies that their prospective pleasure provides agents with reason for action. Perhaps it is simply self-evident that a person who pursues pleasure because it's pleasurable and avoids pain because it's painful has reasons for his action. A bit more can be said against the Humean denial that any long-term non-appetitive goal provides one reason for its promotion, viz., one cannot believe this about one's own long-term goals. This is sufficient to meet Gauthier's challenge to the objectivist that he make a plausible case that "reference to objective value occurs in *the best explanation* we can provide for our actions and choices."[36]

But is it possible that in rejecting subjectivism one has reopened the door to value-neutralism? It may appear that the invocation against the subjectivist of the good of pleasure, of felt satisfaction, of talents exercised, of knowledge, of friendship, and so on, constitutes an appeal to agent-neutral values and, hence, a surrender of agent-relativity. This is what Gauthier envisions when he talks about the

> pressure against a conception [of value] both objective and relative. . . The seemingly relative goods of the several kinds [of perfections] are really facets of absolute good. The demands of objectivity thus force an apparently relative conception of value into an absolutist [i.e., agent-neutralist] mould.[37]

Gauthier plausibly anticipates that the anti-subjectivist who seeks to remain an agent-relativist will appeal to an account of value according to which the human good is the satisfaction or realization of human appetites, sentiments, capacities, and faculties. The greatest good in the case of any particular agent A_1 is something like the richest overall realization of A_1's desires and potentialities. Such a realization would be the object of his rational plan of life; the particulars of this plan of life would be pervasively colored by A_1's specific appetites, abilities, and circumstances. But then the rhetorical question may be asked: why does this fulfillment count as a good? The rhetorical implication is that the fulfillment counts as a good – assuming that it does – because it exemplifies some general good: e.g., pleasure, health, knowledge, or friendship; the goodness of that good does not exist in and through its relation to A_1 (as fulfillments of his desires or potentialities).[38] The fulfillment possessed by or located in A_1 is simply a "facet" of an agent-neutral good.

The fulfillment theory of human good *may* be the ground upon which a theorist seeking to combine objectivism with agent-relativity will naturally attempt to

---

[36] *Morals by Agreement*, p. 56.

[37] *ibid.*, p. 53.

[38] This sort of argument appears in John Finnis's *Natural Law and Natural Rights* (Oxford: Oxford University Press, 1980), chs. III and IV. Finnis clearly, albeit implicitly, takes "basic goods" to be agent-neutral.

build. Even if it is, no further explication or defense of that theory can be attempted here. But it is necessary for the argument of this essay to place barriers against the slide (or ascent?) anticipated by Gauthier, from objectivism to agent-neutrality. Consider a person whose life is significantly devoted to learning the true authorship of the Shakespearean plays. This goal is certainly pursued with a sense that a correct historical understanding of these works is important. The literary researcher thinks, "It's a good thing to know who wrote those plays," not "It's good to fulfill my epistemic capacities." It sounds as though the worthiness that the researcher responds to derives from the general, non-relative worthiness of knowledge; i.e., it is just a "facet" of the basic and agent-neutral good of knowledge. Nevertheless, if our researcher is not a fanatic, he will recognize that the worthiness possessed by his project does not as such call for others to support him in his endeavor. He will recognize that other agents may, without fault, be completely indifferent to this question of authorship (it may not at all engage their "desire to know"), and that these agents will have no reasons parallel to his own for pursuing this issue. Moreover, the nonidiosyncratic quality of our researcher's account of his reasons can be understood without appeal to their agent-neutrality. When the researcher asserts, "It's a good thing to know who wrote those plays," he is not merely citing his (agent-relative) reason for his endeavors. He is also pointing to a particular goal; its achievement, either directly or vicariously, may be valuable to others and he may be inviting them to share in it. In addition, he is conveying the character of his reason for action by citing as his goal an instance of a type of end; other instances of it characteristically provide other agents with reason for action. He is thereby placing his action in a broader explanatory pattern and is associating his action with other actions fitting this pattern which both he and his listeners may value.[39]

Finally, we should note that some reasons for action may resist agent-relative analysis, not because they correspond to agent-neutral values, but rather because they are deontic. Part of an agent's total reason for making the eradication of racism a guiding project of his life may be the injustice of racism and/or the injustice of his compliance with it. The agent's rational motivation need not be accounted for by the disvalue, either agent-relative or agent-neutral, of the existence of racism. In the next two sections of this essay, we turn to a consideration of deontic restraints and their connection to the agent-relativity of value or to the moral individualism that is partly manifested in the agent-relativity of value.

IV. How Not to Connect Agent-Relativity and Deontology

The agent-relativity of value is one of two commonly linked manifestations of the moral importance of individuals, of what Scheffler calls "agent-centredness." It is the aspect that supports and accounts for the integrity objection against

[39] Another possibility, not to be explored here, is that value is agent-neutral (or, at least, not agent-relative) while reasons of value for action remain agent-relative. Knowledge is good; knowledge as such is not an agent-relative value. But only those achievements of knowledge that realize the powers and/or aspirations of A_1 provide A_1 with reason to act. By loosening the link between value and reason, it may be possible to affirm the non-agent relative value of certain states of affairs without being committed to agents at large having reason to promote those states of affairs.

consequentialism. The other aspect of this moral individualism consists of restrictions on the types of treatment that one individual may inflict upon another – restrictions or moral side constraints that have the deontic coloration of standing athwart the promotion of value. There is a common theoretical hunch that, as characterized by Scheffler, "if there is a motivation for introducing any agent-centredness into a moral theory at all, then there is a motivation for introducing *both* agent-centred components."[40] I hope, eventually, to vindicate this hunch. But first it is necessary to deal both with Scheffler's debunking of this structural intuition and with Nagel's attempt to sustain deontic restrictions on the basis of agent-relativity (albeit not agent-relativity *of value*). In both cases, we learn something about where not to look for an illuminating connection between these components of moral individualism.

Scheffler's strategy toward denying that "agent-centred restrictions" ought to accompany "agent-centred prerogatives" emphasizes the "paradoxical" character of these moral side constraints – a feature that has been noted by, but presumably has not been sufficiently worrisome to, advocates of these constraints. Thus, Robert Nozick wonders:

> Isn't it *irrational* to accept a side constraint C, rather than a view that directs minimizing the violations of C? ...If nonviolation of C is so important, shouldn't that be the goal? How can concern for the nonviolation of C led to the refusal to violate C even when this would prevent other more extensive violations of C?[41]

How can we account for the wrong that A_1 does to P_1 when, with respect to P_1, A_1 violates constraint C, except by citing the disvalue of individuals undergoing violations of C or the effects of violations of C? But then, Scheffler repeatedly urges us, consider the case in which A_1 can prevent A_2 and A_3 from violating C with respect to P_2 and P_3 only by violating C with respect to P_1. Does not the very standard that, in the first case, led to the judgment that A_1 must not violate constraint C lead, in the second case, to the judgment that A_1 must violate C? If so, C is not a moral side constraint; rather, the nonviolation of C serves as a moral goal. Of course, the advocate of side constraints will want to deny that it is the *disvalue* of individuals undergoing violations of C that provides reasons for others to abstain from violating C. He will seek, as Nozick does, for some morally fertile property that establishes each individual as a bearer of rights. According to Scheffler, however, such attempts will not avoid his critique for long.

> For if one tries to think of agent-centred restrictions as a rational response to the possession of some feature by the victims of violations, then it is natural to suppose . . . that the feature in question must be one in virtue of which it is undesirable for persons to be victimized. And it is only a short step to the thought that the feature must be one in virtue of which violations are very bad things to have happen.[42]

[40] *The Rejection of Consequentialism*, p. 81.
[41] *Anarchy, State, and Utopia*, p. 30.
[42] *The Rejection of Cvnsequentialism*, pp. 100–101. The final section of this essay will cast doubt on this claim.

Hence, we return to the nonviolation of C as a goal.

For Scheffler, the more sensible route to the vindication of agent-centered restrictions is one that focuses, not on individuals as victims of the violation of such restrictions, but rather (may one say "paradoxically"?) on individuals as *subjects* of these restrictions. In effect, the hypothesis that Scheffler takes to be more worthy of exploration is that agent-centered restrictions do not represent a response to the justice objection; rather, along with agent-centered prerogatives, they represent a response to the integrity objection. Thus, Scheffler considers the following argument:

> Agent-centred restrictions ... serve to protect individuals from the demand that they organize their conduct in accordance with some canon of impersonal optimality. They prevent individuals from becoming slaves of the impersonal standpoint, and in so doing they serve to insulate the personal point of view against external demands.[43]

In fact, this is a pretty good argument ... *if* one interprets a restriction on A_1 as a constraint on what A_1 may to do to A_2 and sees it as responsive to a need of A_2 for protection against canons of impersonal optimality fired by A_1. But that is not Scheffler's interpretation. According to Scheffler, the agent-centered restrictions on A_1 contemplated in this argument require that A_1 give disproportionate weight to his personal values over against what is impersonally best. But such a requirement, Scheffler argues, would serve no purpose (toward maintaining an agent's integrity) beyond that already served by A_1's agent-centered prerogative. For that prerogative itself allows him to assign a proportionately greater weight to his personal interests, projects, commitments, etc, This permission already protects the individual against the disruptive effect of following impersonal value when there is great divergence between impersonal value and his personal values.

Scheffler also maintains that there is a downside to the addition of agent-centered restrictions, although here his argument is puzzling. He claims that belief in the usefulness of agent-centered restrictions (as he interprets them) depends upon a failure to recognize that individuals can identify with activities that promote the best overall states of affairs. But since individuals can identify with such activities, a restriction against promoting what is best overall would sometimes be an "arbitrary and unexplained constraint on the projects and activities of the individual."[44] Yet if an agent does identify with such activities and would undertake them from within his "own point of view," it is hard to see how a requirement that he give disproportionate weight to *this* point of view would bar him from those activities. Here it would have be better for Scheffler to argue that the agent-centered restrictions he has in mind would place a moral ban on agents engaging in supererogatory activities aimed at the impersonally best. But this correction will not undo the strangest aspect of Scheffler's discussion, viz., the idea that the source of deontic restraints on what A_1 may do (presumably, to *other agents*) is to be found, if anywhere, in the moral significance or standing of A_1. Scheffler's

43 *ibid.*, p. 94.
44 *ibid.*, p. 97.

search for a basis for deontic restrictions is immediately doomed by the direction in which he chooses to look. It remains, however, to see whether any alternative course avoids confrontation with paradox.

Nagel's intriguing account of deontic restrictions shares with Scheffler's the idea that constraints on what A_1 may do to A_2 must be understood from A_1's perspective. Yet it appeals neither to A_1's agent-relative values nor to related considerations touching on A's integrity. As he puts it, "the peculiarity of deontological reasons is that although they are agent-relative, they do not express the subjective autonomy of the agent at all. They are demands, not options."[45] These demands are a function both of the agent's perspective and the agent-neutral disvalue of what the prohibited actions would visit upon the victim. It is through the operation of the perspectives of agents on the evil that they intend that we are "far more responsible for what we do (or permit) than for consequences of action that we foresee and decide to accept but that do not form part of our aims (intermediate or final) . . ."[46]

Nagel invites us to consider a case in which only by painfully twisting the arm of an innocent child can one prevent a somewhat greater evil to one's stranded friends. Yet because the pain of the child would be intended while the greater harm that the friends will otherwise suffer would merely be foreseen, one ought not to twist the child's arm – even though "*things* will be better, what *happens* will be better . . ." if one were to twist that innocent's arm. The disproportionate weight one must give to the disvalue of what one would be intending (the child's pain) compared to the disvalue of what one merely would be foreseeing (the discomfort to one's stranded friends) reflects our status as agents with particularized perspectives.

> When I twist the child's arm intentionally I incorporate that evil into what I do: it is my deliberate creation and *the reasons stemming from it are magnified and lit up from my point of view*. They overshadow reasons stemming from greater evils that are more "faint" from this perspective, because they do not fall within the intensifying beam of my intentions even though they are consequences of what I do.[47]

It is not the agent-relative disvalue of the child's pain or of my causing the child's pain that, added to its agent-neutral disvalue, outweighs the disvalue of my friends' suffering. Rather, what makes the twisting wrong is that the magnified *agent-neutral* disvalue of the child's pain is greater than the disvalue of the friends' suffering. According to Nagel, what counts against the arm-twisting is the multiple of the agent-neutral disvalue of the child's pain that would exist within the perspective of (i.e., relative to) the agent who would intentionally bring about that pain. Presumably, intentions magnify the disvalue of their objects no matter *who* operates with such evilly oriented purposes – no matter how unaware one is of the multiplier effect of intention. Apparently the "perspective" within which the intended evil is intensified is not one which agents are free to adopt or reject. (It is not their "option," but whose "demand" is it?)

[45] *The View from Nowhere*, p. 181.
[46] *ibid.*, p. 180 .
[47] *ibid.* Emphasis added.

To a much greater extent than Nagel realizes, this account of deontic restrictions pays homage to the consequentialist model. One acknowledges that, absent the magnifying effect of one's intention, it would be better for the child to suffer and the friends to be spared. But in light of the magnifying effect, it would be better for the child to be spared and the friends to suffer. The morality of one's action is determined by this more subtle calculus of interests. This hardly fulfills Nagel's requirement that deontic constraints must "not themselves be understood as the expression of neutral values of any kind."[48] Rather than providing us with an explanation of the deontic wrongfulness of this agent's twisting of the child's arm, Nagel provides us with an account of the disvalue, relative to this agent, of the results of that action.

There are further problems with Nagel's agent-perspectivist account of deontic restrictions. Suppose that, despite the wrongness of doing so, I proceed toward intentionally twisting the child's arm. Presumably, since it would be deontically wrong for me to do this, it would be at least permissible (absent special complicating factors) for any other agent A_1 to prevent me from doing this.[49] But how, on Nagel's account, could A_1's interference be permissible? After all, as an objective self, A_1 sees that it would be better for the child to suffer and the friends to be spared than the reverse. If it would be permissible for A_1 to interfere, the reason must lie either in my magnification or in A_1's magnification. The first alternative will not serve because my perspectival magnification is what is supposed especially to give *me* reason not to twist the child's arm. And the Nagelian position surely is that, because of *my* magnification, *I* should not twist this child's arm even if that would prevent two other aspiring arm-twisters from doing their comparable deeds. Within their respective perspectives, the disvalue of their own prospective arm-twistings are magnified. But those magnifications remain perspectival, so that I count my arm-twisting magnified while I count theirs unmagnified. Similarly, when A_1 contemplates interfering with my arm-twisting, he should count the disvalue of the child's pain unmagnified. But then, rather than preventing my attack on the child, A_1 should look forward to it.

Perhaps, alternatively, it is in terms of A_1's magnification of the disvalue of the child's pain that the permissibility of A_1's intervention can be sustained. Nagel holds that deontic constraints apply both against intentionally doing harm and intentionally allowing it. So Nagel might argue that: (a) it must be permissible for A_1 to interfere because it is obligatory for A_1 to interfere, and (b) it is obligatory for A_1 to interfere because for A_1 not to interfere would be for A_1 intentionally to allow the child's pain. But this will not do. Even if, in this case, we grant that A_1 would be *intentionally* allowing the child's pain and that intentional allowing is equal in magnifying capacity to intentional producing, we get an unacceptably odd

---

[48] *ibid.*, p. 177. If I am right about the non-occurrence of agent-neutral values, Nagel's reliance on agent-neutral value is a further problem for his account of deontic restrictions.

[49] This assumes that philosophical pacifism is mistaken. Maybe it is not. But Nagel would probably be discomfited to discover that the defense of his account of deontic restraints depends upon philosophical pacifism – especially since it is the principle of double effect that is central to both his account of deontic constraints and many discussions of the legitimacy of defensive force, including Nagel's own discussion. See Thomas Nagel, "War and Massacre," *Philosophy and Public Affairs*, vol. 1, no. 1 (Winter 1972), pp. 123–44.

result. We get an account of the permissibility of A_1's interference with my deontically wrong action that in no way depends upon the wrongness of that action. On this odd account, A_1 may interfere with me because doing so enables A_1 to protect the child *against A_1's intentionally allowing the child's pain*! And there is a much more general problem that appears as soon as we shift away from the double-effect type of case. Suppose I simply aim at the child's pain; there is no further good that either I or A_1 might intend. And suppose that A_1 is simply indifferent to the child's pain. Or the small cost to A_1 of interference with my attack outweighs his slight concern for the child. Under such circumstances, A_1 can allow me to proceed against the child without A_1 intentionally allowing the child's pain. If he does not intentionally allow that pain, it is not magnified within his perspective and there is no reason for his interference with my attack to be permissible. But surely, if my attack on the child is deontically wrong, absent special complicating circumstances, it must be permissible for A_1 to interfere to prevent it.

One may even wonder whether, on Nagel's account, it is permissible for the *child* to prevent my attack. After all, the child too, as objective self, sees that it would be better that he undergo the pain than that my stranded friends suffer to a greater extent. What greater basis does the child have for interfering in my optimizing behavior? Nagel does assert that "there is also something to be said about the point of view of the victim."[50] Indeed, two things seem to be said. The first is a reminder that Nagel allows the existence of agent-relative values because the moral world is composed of individuals each of whose perspective "includes a strong subjective component." Due to his agent-relative values, the agent I am about to eviscerate in order to obtain the organs vital to saving the lives of five other persons need not accede to my actions as he would have to "on a purely agent-neutral consequentialist view." Yet this does not provide the target of my surgical intentions with anything like a deontic objection to my actions, and it provides each of the five other persons with their own agent-relative reasons of value to support my activity and suppress the victim's resistance to it.

The second thing said by Nagel about the point of view of the victim is that *as victim*, as the subject of the intended agent-neutral disvalue, he *also* gets to magnify that disvalue and to count that magnified disvalue in his evaluation of the action aimed at him. Why? After all, the intended victim is not intending that bad. Nagel's answer seems to be that, as the intended victim, the subject is entitled to draw upon the disvalue of what is aimed at *as it exists in magnified form within the perspective of the attacker*.

> The deontological constraint [that] permits a victim always to object to those who aim at his harm ... expresses the direct appeal to the point of view of the agent from the point of view of the person on whom he is acting. It operates through that relation.

We see here, I believe, a further indication of Nagel's account having turned deontic constraint on its head. The victim's basis for complaint derives from the

[50] *The View from Nowhere*, p. 183.

wrongfulness of what is done to him as gauged from within the perspective of the wrongdoing agent. Yet surely it should be that the wrongfulness of that agent's action derives from the wrong that it does to the victim. Nagel adds to the preceding remarks the claim that:

> The victim feels outrage when he is deliberately harmed even for the greater good of others, not simply because of the quantity of the harm but because of the assault on his value of having my actions guided by his evil.[51]

Indeed. But the victim is outraged about what is done to him, about the "assault on his value," and not about the fact that, within the magnifying perspective of the assailant, the act does more harm than it prevents. He would be just as outraged if the assault were carried out by God or some equally objective saint, who, viewing that act from nowhere, would not magnify the harm directly done. Nagel is correct to indicate that the victim's outrage is not to be explained in terms of the "quantity of the harm" done. But this is precisely the sort of explanation, albeit with a magnifying epicycle, to which Nagel appeals.

Finally, and also as a bridge to the next section's discussion of restraints and rights, we should note the implausibility of a general identification of deontic restraints with constraints, in the spirit of double effect, on intentionally producing (or allowing) bads. Consider any of the everyday deontic-like intuitions about the wrongness of one person subjecting another to a particular treatment, e.g., the wrongness of A_1 killing, maiming, or involuntarily confining A_2. The everyday intuition is that such actions violate some legitimate moral demand of A_2's against such treatment, some right of A_2's to his life, bodily integrity, or liberty. The intentional performance of such actions is especially to be condemned. But the addition of intention does not convert an activity that otherwise would have no deontic flaw into one that is deontically wrong. It is the fact that the activity is morally defective even in its nonintentional form that makes its intentional performance especially blameworthy. Even in their nonintentional forms, these activities may be resisted by their potential victims to an extent that cannot be given a satisfying consequentialist explanation – even if yet more extensive resistance may be justified against their intentional forms. And even in their nonintentional forms, the performance of such actions calls for compensation from the agent to the victim in ways that, also, cannot be given a sufficient consequentialist explanation.

V. RIGHTS AS COMPLEMENTS TO THE AGENT-RELATIVITY OF VALUE

It is now time to try positively to sustain the intellectual hunch noted, but rejected, by Scheffler that there is a natural link between (a) the agent-centeredness that appears as the agent-relativity of value and the agent-centeredness that appears as deontic side-constraints and (b) the moral individualism that is manifested in the integrity objection and the moral individualism that is manifested

[51] *ibid.*, p. 184.

in the justice objection. A characteristic statement of the association of these elements appears in Nozick's claim that:

> The moral side constraints upon what we may do, I claim, reflect the fact of our separate existences. They reflect the fact that no moral balancing act can take place among us; there is no moral outweighing of one of our lives by others so as to lead to a greater overall *social* good. There is no justified sacrifice of some of us for others. This root idea, namely, that there are different individuals with separate lives and so no one may be sacrificed for others, underlies the existence of moral side constraints....[52]

Unfortunately, this argument is hardly satisfying. It is one thing to deny the existence of impersonal value for the sake of which individuals should accept the imposition of sacrifices. It is quite another to show that A_1 wrongs A_2 when he pursues his projects over A_2's dead body. A_1 need not wave the banner of the agent-neutral "*social* good" as he proceeds against A_2; he may simply wave the banner of his agent-relative values.[53] This may not justify A_1's action *to A_2*. But it does not follow from such a lack of justification that A_2 enjoys a moral side constraint against A_1's proceeding. Furthermore, the agent-relative value for A_2 of A_1 not imposing sacrifices on A_2 will not provide a secure reason of the right sort for A_1 to avoid these impositions.

Let us return, however, to Scheffler's suggested argument for agent-centered restrictions – but, this time, with an understanding of them as constraints on A_1's treatment of A_2 that are "a rational response to the natural independence of [A_2's] personal point of view."[54] That argument ran as follows:

> Agent-centred restrictions ... serve to protect individuals from the demand that they organize their conduct in accordance with some canon of impersonal optimality. They prevent individuals from becoming slaves of the impersonal standpoint, and in so doing they serve to insulate the personal point of view against external demands.[55]

As we have seen, Scheffler's retort is that A_2 enjoys all the protection he needs against A_2's adoption of "some canon of impersonal optimality" in virtue of his permission to give disproportionate weight to his personal point of view. But A_2's "permission" involves no claim whatsoever against conduct by A_1. A_2's prerogative

---

[52] *Anarchy, State, and Utopia*, p. 33.

[53] Perhaps Nozick does want to say that, to vindicate his action, A_1 *must* appeal to an impersonal value that is advanced through A_2's loss and that such an appeal must always fail. See the comparable argument in Isaiah Berlin's "Two Concepts of Liberty."

> In the name of what can I ever be justified in forcing men to do what they have not willed or consented to? Only in the name of some value higher than themselves. But if, as Kant held, all values are made so by the free acts of men, and called values only so far as they are this, there is no value higher than the individual.

Note that the agent-relativity that Berlin invokes seems to be tied, in the name of Kant [!], to subjectivism. *Four Essays on Liberty* (Oxford: Oxford University Press, 1969), p. 137.

[54] *The Rejection of Consequentialism*, p. 94.

[55] *ibid*.

may leave him morally faultless when he chooses to develop his beachcombing potential instead of his enormously socially useful surgical aptitudes. But it provides him with no moral immunity against A_1's conscripting him into the National Medical Service. Indeed, A_2's "permission" to beachcomb is consistent with A_1 being obligated to impose surgical servitude on him. Within his own discussion, the failure of "permission" to have interpersonal force does not matter, because Scheffler is only concerned with whether an individual must choose *for himself* to forgo personal values in the impartial service of the impersonally best. But it matters very much if the presence of A_2's permission is supposed to satisfy A_2's need for protection against demands emanating not from his own adoption of impersonal morality but from other agents bent on interfering with A_2's choices.

Concern for A_2's secure capacity to lead an integrated life calls for moral restraints on A_1's treatment of him in two ways. It is important that A_2 not, in fact, be subjected to demands emanating from others such as A_1. For only then will A_2 be able securely to pursue his values, projects, and commitments. And it is important that A_2 be able to *condemn* actual or prospective impositions of these demands. For only then will he have a sense of being justified in his pursuit of his values, projects, and commitments. Also, we should note, these restrictions are actually needed, not against demands issued under the banner of impersonal value – the existence of such value has been rejected – but rather against the many different demands that each of many agents might press in the name of his agent-relative values. Moreover, there is nothing especially "agent-centered" about these restrictions. They do not reflect the agent-relative values or the particular perspective of the agent subject to them. They are responsive to the separateness of agents' respective rational plans of life and to the need for *some* rules of interpersonal force in a world of agent-relative value. But it is not the particular agent-relative value of A_2's chosen alternatives or projects – A_2's chosen alternative may be objectively bad for A_2 – that accounts for the restraints against others' intervention against A_2. Rather, it is the theoretical suitability of such restrictions to a world in which value is real, even objective, and therefore calls for recognition, but in which that recognition cannot take the form of acknowledging the impersonal weight of others' values, since all values are agent-relative. Thus, an improved rendition of Scheffler's argument would be:

> Deontic restrictions serve to protect individuals from demands by others that they organize their conduct in accordance with either some canon of impersonal optimality or the agent-relative values of others. These restrictions prevent individuals from becoming slaves to others' invocations of either the impersonal standpoint or their own personal standpoints, and in so doing these constraints serve to insulate the personal point of view from external demands and to ratify its significance.

It is crucial, of course, that the account of the moral side constraints that protect A_2 neither simply appeal to the agent-relative value for A_2 and/or A_1 nor the agent-neutral value of those constraints being respected. Fortunately, it does not. A survey of the elements of this account shows this.

The affirmation of the agent-relativity of value and the existence of moral side constraints are complementary rational responses to our "separate existences," to "the natural independence of the personal point of view." The former frees the individual from both his own and others' invocations of impersonal value. However, in each person being so freed, each becomes potentially subject to the permissible enslavement by others in the course of their pursuit of their agent-relative values. A rational response to our separate existences must include some element that stands athwart this permissible enslavement. That element cannot be any impersonal value, even the impersonal value of non-enslavement. For the initial and most straightforward portion of the rational response to our separate existences is the rejection of impersonal value. What rationally complements the agent-relativity of value, then, must be deontic restraint on how individuals may treat others in the pursuit of their respective goods.

The affirmation of the agent-relativity of values is the affirmation of *each* agent as the possessor of reasons for action oriented toward his respective values. Thus, this affirmation places each of us within a "world of reasons, including [one's] own, [that] does not exist only from [one's] own point of view." I join in Nagel's assertion that, in such circumstances, there must be "a practical analogue of the rejection of solipsism. . . ." [56] The theoretical recognition of other agents as inhabitants of a normative universe with an objective standing comparable to one's own must have some practical expression. Some difference in one's actions must be called for when one moves from the solipsistic conviction that the only real values in the universe are the values of one's unique self to belief in the equal existence of values-for-others. It would be bizarre for such an enormous shift in one's representation of the normative landscape – a shift from an egotistic subjectivism to the inclusion of others as possessors of objective reasons of value – to have no implications for one's views about how one ought to act. The agent-relativist asserts of each person that he is an end-in-himself in the sense that he has – the person who he is has – separate rational ends of his own. It would be incongruous to assert this and not to affirm that each person is an end-in-himself in the sense of not being a means morally available to others for the promotion of their ends. It would be incongruous to assert that each person occupies a distinct and independent moral position while allowing that these positions are morally open to invasion, i.e., to allow that these positions do not occupy any moral space. The sign of a non-psychopathic recognition of others' existence as beings with their own rational ends is a disposition not to treat others as natural resources available for one's use and exploitation.

But, once again, the practical recognition of others as equal co-inhabitants of the moral universe cannot take the form of an alteration in one's rational goals. The additional values one will have come to recognize are values relative to others which one needs in no way to share.[57] Indeed, one may recognize that the realization of certain of those values conflicts with one's own. Thus, the general form that

---

[56] *The View from Nowhere*, p. 140.

[57] Of course, the departure from solipsism will lead to the discovery or the formation of particular shared values with certain other individuals.

practical acknowledgment of the existence of one's co-inhabitants must take is constraint on the manner in which one pursues one's own goals. The practical analogue of the rejection of solipsism is not an alteration of one's ends, but rather a restriction on one's means of attaining them.

To define such restraints is to define what counts as violations of basic rights. I see this as a two-stage process consisting, first, of an identification of agents' basic rights understood as their rightful domains or jurisdictions and, second, of an identification of which incursions upon or losses of such rightful domains or jurisdictions count as violations of basic rights.[58] In identifying A_2's initial rightful domain, we are concerned with what mental and physical means, what resources for the pursuit of ends, are morally available for A_2's use and not for anyone else's use. The natural suggestion is that A_2 himself – the sum of his person, capacities, and energies – is the means for the pursuit of his ends to which A_2 has a unique claim.

For when we recognize that each person has his own separate and normatively rational purpose, we are not merely acknowledging that there exists a multiplicity of realizable agent-relative values, e.g., A_1-relative value, A_2-relative value, A_n-relative value. We are not merely affirming a multiplicity of dimensionless points from which the world is viewed and evaluated. The beings who have rational purposes of their own, who are the reason-bearing and value-pursuing beings, are constituted of integrations of mental and physical features and capacities. (And such an agent's good is something like the most complete feasible realization under his life circumstances of these elements of his personal constitution.) If one's genuine affirmation of others requires that one recognize rightful domains of others into which one's value pursuits may not intrude, then, in affirming each person as a being with his own rational ends, one must recognize each person as the unique claimant to his own personal constitution, i.e., recognize each person as having moral jurisdiction over the person he is.

It is this claim to jurisdiction over himself which offers A_2 protection against the demands which others may make in the name of their ends, as well as protection of his sense of the legitimacy of pursuing his own rational ends and of his resisting interferences with those pursuits (except such pursuits which themselves trespass on the persons, capacities, and energies of others). The entitlement of each to his own person involves no value claim on others; it does not provide others with neutral values which, if promoted, compete with their own relative values. Instead, it places others under deontic restraint. Respect for such restraints *may* require that an agent forgo the greatest possible promotion of his agent-relative values. When moral life exists between two quite different poles – the agent-relativity of value and moral side constraints – tensions between the reasons one must recognize will

---

[58] On the idea that basic rights are to be ascribed coherently by means of identifying persons' basic "titles" and not by seeking to identify what types of actions persons have rights to perform or have rights against the performance of, see Hillel Steiner, "The Structure of a Set of Compossible Rights," *Journal of Philosophy* (December 1977), pp. 767–75. On the two-stage process for identifying violations of rights, see Eric Mack, "Moral Rights and Causal Casuistry," ed. B. Brody, *Moral Theory and Moral Judgment in Medical Ethics* (Dordrecht: Kluver Academic Publishers, 1988), pp. 57–74.

be more than possible. That such tensions between different sorts of reasons exist cannot plausibly be denied, and moral theory that does not recognize them discredits itself. Unfortunately, how moral individualism addresses the tensions it recognizes must remain a topic for another occasion.

In addition to tensions between values and restraints, a given agent's respect for deontic restraints may require that a larger number of violations of these restraints be allowed to occur. It may require that A_1 forgo violating constraint with respect to P_1, even though only in this way will A_3 be prevented from violating constraint C with respect to P_2 and P_3.

Yet there is no paradox here. A world in which A_1 violates constraint C with respect to P_1 and thereby prevents A_3's violations of this constraint with respect to P_2 and P_3 is not impersonally better than the world in which A_3 wrongs P_2 and P_3. Typically, the former world will simply be better for P_2, better for P_3, and worse for P_1. There is no computation of agent-neutral disvalue that demands restraint by A_1 towards P_1 when P_2 and P_3 are not threatened by A_3, but which then demands that A_1 inflict C on P_1 when P_2 and P_3 are endangered by A_3. There is simply the deontic restraint on A_1, as on all other agents, not to subject other individuuals to C. Whether or not A_3 threatens P_2 and P_3, A_1 abides by this constraint by not subjecting P_1 to C.[59]

The rejection of agent-neutral value, then, also makes room for deontic restraints by helping to dissolve whatever air of paradox might seem to surround these restraints. But, I have argued here, an affirmation of these restraints, and of the moral rights correlative to them, does not rest simply on the value pole of moral individualism, viz., the agent-relativity of values. Rather, deontic restraints, the core of moral individualism's theory of the right, rest on a series of interlocking considerations. The first is the need for protective interpersonal principles created by the liberating effects of agent-relativity. The second is the impossibility of drawing general interpersonal principles from agent-neutralist evaluations. The third is the necessity (in light of the agent-relativity of value) for general interpersonal principles to take the form of restrictions on the means legitimately available to individuals for advancing their respective values. The fourth is the rationality of giving practical recognition to the reason-bearing cohabitants of one's normative universe. And the fifth is the set of ways in which the present account of deontic restraints resolves or illuminates the contrasts and puzzles that form the philosophical backdrop for this essay. It provides an interconnecting account of individualist theories of the good and the right and a unifying account of the integrity and justice objections. It accounts for the common theoretical hunch that

[59] One might try to recreate a paradox of deontic restraint by insisting that A_1's failure to prevent A_3 from inflicting C on P_2 and P_3 constitutes A_1's inflicting C on them. Thus, the absolutist aspirations of the deontologist would be defeated by the necessity for A_1 to choose between *his* fewer and more numerous violations of constraint C. But against such a view see "Moral Rights and Causal Casuistry," and Eric Mack, "Bad Samaritanism and the Causation of Harm," *Philosophy and Public Affairs*, vol. 9, no. 3 (Spring 1980), pp. 320–59. However, whatever the plausibility of ascribing the violation of the rights of P_2 and P_3 to A_1 on account of his failure to prevent A_3's infliction of C on them, this line of argument would not revive the "paradox" that Scheffler had in mind, viz., one that reveals the deontologist's inescapable reliance on the badness – in particular, the impersonal badness – of the results of the actions he seeks to proscribe.

the assertion of the agent-relativity of values does somehow connect with and support the affirmation of deontic restraints and, more broadly, explains the recurrent recourse, among defenders of political individualism, to skepticism about shared impersonal values. Nothing could be clearer than that the character and the manner of the interlocking of these considerations has not been sufficiently explicated. Nevertheless, perhaps enough has been said to lend credibility to the hypothesis that the agent-relativity of value and deontic restraints constitute two complementary poles within a rational response to individuals as separate, reason-possessing, and value-pursuing entities.

Philosophy, Tulane University

TWO-TIER MORAL CODES

By Holly M. Smith

A moral code consists of principles that assign moral status to individual actions – principles that evaluate acts as right or wrong, prohibited or obligatory, permissible or supererogatory. Many theorists have held that such principles must serve two distinct functions. On the one hand, they serve a *theoretical* function, insofar as they specify the characteristics in virtue of which acts possess their moral status. On the other hand, they serve a *practical* function, insofar as they provide an action-guide: a standard by reference to which a person can choose which acts to perform and which not. Although the theoretical and practical functions of moral principles are closely linked, it is not at all obvious that what enables a principle to fill one of these roles automatically equips it to fill the other. In this paper I shall briefly examine some of the reasons why a moral principle might fail to fill its practical role, i.e., be incapable of guiding decisions. I shall then sketch three common responses to this kind of failure, and examine in some detail the adequacy of one of the most popular of these responses.

I. PRACTICAL VIABILITY AND ITS BARRIERS

What is it for an agent to use a principle in making a decision? Let us begin by saying that an agent uses a principle as a guide for making a decision just in case the agent chooses an act out of a desire to conform to the principle, and a belief that the act does so conform. Thus, suppose Susan decides to signal a lane change because she desires to follow the highway code, and believes the highway code requires lane changes to be signaled. She has used this code to make her decision. We may say, then, that a principle is *usable* by an agent for making a decision, just in case the agent is able to use it in this sense.[1]

What barriers might there be to someone's using a principle to guide her decision? We can see at once that there could be several. For example, the principle itself may suffer from defects that prevent its practical use. A principle may be so vague that it sometimes leaves the moral status of actions indeterminate. Consider a principle which states that killing persons is wrong, but fails to clarify whether 'persons' includes early human fetuses or not. Then no one can use this principle in deciding whether or not to obtain an abortion, since she cannot tell whether or not abortions are prohibited. Obviously, this kind of vagueness in a principle not only prevents it from being used to make decisions, but also detracts from its adequacy as a theoretical account of right and wrong, since such a principle leaves the status

---

[1] See Holly Smith, "Making Moral Decisions," *Nous*, vol. 22 (1988), pp. 91–92, for further discussion of the kinds of usability.

of many acts indeterminate. Such a principle is flawed *both* as a theory *and* as a practical guide. Moreover, its defects as a practical guide seem to depend directly on its defects as a theoretical account of right and wrong. Clearly the appropriate response here (if any) is to revise the principle itself.

But there are many attractive moral principles having no such obvious defects *qua* theoretical accounts of right and wrong that agents are nevertheless unable to use in making decisions. In an important range of these cases it is natural to ascribe the flaw to the agent rather than to the principle, viewed as a theoretical account of right and wrong. But philosophers have often considered principles subject to such handicaps to be flawed *as action-guides*. What I have in mind here are cases where the agent suffers from one or more of a variety of *cognitive handicaps* that prevent him from making a decision by reference to the principle in question. We can distinguish, at least initially, four major types of cognitive handicaps.

(A) First, the agent may, by reason of his cognitive limitations, be unable to *understand* the principle in question: to grasp some of its crucial concepts (whether these are evaluative, formal, or empirical), or to comprehend the overall structure of the principle. For example, Donald Regan has recently proposed a principle entitled "Co-operative Utilitarianism" designed to enable consequentialist-spirited agents to achieve the best possible co-operative outcomes. Co-operative Utilitarianism is stated as follows:

> Each agent must hold himself ready to take part in co-operative effort. He must identify others who are willing and able to do their part . . . He must ascertain the behavior or dispositions to behave of the *non-co-operators* who have been identified thus far (that is, the agents who are *not* willing and able to do their part), and he must ascertain the best pattern of behavior for the co-operators in the circumstances. He must then decide whether anyone he currently regards as a co-operator has made any mistake so far. If any putative co-operator has made a mistake, then all who have made mistakes are eliminated from the class of putative co-operators, and the process of identifying the best behavior for the (reduced) class of co-operators is repeated. And so on, until it is discovered that no putative co-operator has made a mistake. At this point the inquiry shifts to the question of whether the putative co-operators are all terminating their investigations into each others' decision-making. If any putative co-operator is not terminating his investigation here but is going on to another round of checking on his fellow co-operators, then the agent in question goes on also, to be sure of catching any last minute errors the others might make. Only when the agent in question discovers that the putative co-operators are all stopping does he stop and do his part in the current best plan.[2]

A more detailed exposition of the process involved in applying CU occupies two pages. Regan himself admits that "CU is complicated"; my experience in

---

[2] Donald H. Regan, *Utilitarianism and Co-operation* (Oxford: Clarendon Press, 1980), pp. 165–66.

attempting to teach CU suggests that many average agents would not, and perhaps could not, understand Co-operative Utilitarianism. They could not infer what the principle required them to do. Such an agent is not *necessarily* prevented from using this principle in the sense I defined above. Perhaps he can form the desire to follow the principle when it is described in a way he can comprehend (e.g., he may form the desire to "follow Regan's new principle"). And he may come to believe on the advice of some trusted authority, such as his philosophy professor, that (e.g.) *voting for the Democratic candidate for governor* is required by the principle so conceived, even if he cannot work this out for himself.[3] But if no such authority comes to his assistance, he cannot use this principle to make any decisions. Most of the moral principles with which we are most familiar are stated in a manner lending itself to the comprehension of the average person. However, many of these may be quite beyond the cognitive capacities of mentally less well-endowed agents, who nonetheless face a variety of moral dilemmas. The fact that the most familiar moral principles can be understood by most of us may already reflect a perceived necessity to construct moral principles to fall at least within the range of normal cognitive grasp.

(B) The second kind of problem arises because an agent may not possess, or may not be able to acquire within the time allotted to her for making some decision, the *empirical information* necessary for deriving a prescription from the principle in question. For example, consider a government leader who wants to follow act-utilitarianism in deciding whether to agree to a certain disarmament treaty. Unfortunately, the leader is uncertain whether agreeing to the treaty would maximize the general happiness and so cannot assent to any empirical premise stating that one of her alternatives has the right-making characteristic specified by her moral principle. Hence she can deduce no prescription from that principle, and cannot use it in making her decision. This is true even if the decision-maker can assign definite probabilities to a given act's satisfying the principle. The government leader may think there is an eighty percent chance that agreeing to the treaty will maximize happiness, and so believe there is an eighty percent chance that agreeing to the treaty is prescribed by her principle. But this does not enable her to infer what the principle actually requires her to do. And since our definition of a moral principle's usability requires that the decision-maker be able to infer what that principle prescribes – not what it *may* prescribe, or what it *probably* prescribes – the leader is unable to use her principle in deciding what to do.[4]

(C) A third problem arises when an agent has sufficient empirical beliefs to deduce a prescription from her principle, but some of these beliefs are false, so that the derived prescription is (or would be) incorrect. For example, a juror may want to follow a deontological principle requiring adequate compensation for injured plaintiffs. The juror believes, falsely, that the plaintiff suffered damages to the extent of $100,000, but actually his damages amounted to $500,000. Hence the

---

[3] If the authority is reliable, the agent may even *know* that he ought to vote for the Democratic candidate.

[4] See Smith for an account of the adequacy of the most popular technique for surmounting this problem, namely supplementing moral principles with auxiliary decision-guides or "rules of thumb" designed to deliver prescriptions when agents possess probabilistic information at best.

juror's decision to vote for an award of $100,000 on the ground that this would provide adequate compensation does not in fact satisfy her deontological principle. Because I shall be referring to this problem frequently, let us label it the *Problem of Error.*

(D) A fourth problem arises when an agent possesses enough empirical information to calculate what act is prescribed by his principle, but he is intellectually unable (perhaps altogether, or perhaps just within the time available) to make the necessary calculations. For example, suppose the reaction process in a nuclear power plant starts to run out of control. The chief engineer must decide within 30 seconds whether to close down the reactor or to add extra coolant, and, if so, how much to add. Let us imagine that the engineer wants to make this decision by reference to act-utilitarianism, and that he actually has all the necessary information about the numerous consequences, and the corresponding values, of each option. However, he cannot calculate, in the available 30 seconds, which *set* of consequences has the highest overall value. This kind of case is one where the agent has the intellectual capacity to make the necessary calculations and merely lacks the necessary time. But it is clear that there are some possible (and perhaps otherwise very attractive) moral principles that ascribe rightness to an action as a function of a mathematically complex combination of characteristics that might exceed the computational ability of any human being to calculate – including human beings using powerful resources such as computers to extend their own computational abilities.

There are, then, at least four cognitive handicaps that could prevent human agents from utilizing a variety of moral principles in actual decision-making: incapacity to comprehend the principle, lack of sufficient information to apply it, erroneous empirical beliefs, and limited ability to make the requisite calculations. It is worth emphasizing that these problems may affect deontological principles as well as consequentialist ones. The difficulties I have described cut right across the consequentialism/deontologism distinction. These difficulties show that principles that might appear quite attractive as theoretical accounts of right and wrong may fail in many cases to be usable for decision-making. How are we to react to this failure?

II. Responses

The responses of moral theorists who have explicitly confronted this problem have tended to cluster into three different categories. I shall describe each kind of response briefly.

The first kind of response, which I shall call the *Replacement Response*, has been adopted by a wide variety of moral thinkers. According to these thinkers, the theoretical function of morality cannot be isolated from its practical or regulative function, in the sense that one test of a moral principle's theoretical correctness just *is* its practical usability. In David Lyons's words, these thinkers hold that moral principles must be designed to accommodate "the mistakes we make, the errors to which we are prone . . . our blockheadedness, ignorance, confusion, and stupidity."[5]

[5] David Lyons, *The Forms and Limits of Utilitarianism* (Oxford: Clarendon Press, 1965), p. 159.

Such Replacement Response theorists, on noting that the practical use of act-utilitarianism is hindered for most decisions by our lack of information about the future, have claimed that this fact provides good and sufficient reason to reject act-utilitarianism as a theoretical account of what makes acts right and wrong. Some such theorists have replaced it with a more readily usable deontological theory. Others have replaced it with "prospective" act-utilitarianism, which only requires the agent to determine which action would maximize expected utility, not which action would maximize actual utility. Others have adopted rule-utilitarianism for the same reason. Another example of the Replacement Response is provided by John Rawls, who argues that any acceptable principle of justice must be simple enough for everyone to understand, such that ascertaining which institutions satisfy the principle does not depend on information that is difficult to obtain.[6] To use a slogan, we might say that the Replacement Response attempts to narrow the gap between human decision-making capacities and the requirements of moral theory by *lowering* the theory to a level where fallible human beings can employ it.

The second kind of response, which I shall call the *Conserving Response*, claims that a moral principle's practical usability, or lack thereof, is no sign of its adequacy or inadequacy as a theoretical account of right and wrong. Conserving Response theorists tend to view moral principles on the model of scientific theories, and point out that we do not determine the truth or falsity of a scientific theory by ascertaining whether it would be easy or difficult to make predictions on the basis of that theory. Any difficulties we may experience in making predictions on the basis of a well-confirmed scientific theory should be seen as defects in *us*, not defects in the theory. Similarly, Conserving Response theorists say, if we are unable to use some normatively correct moral principle to guide our choices – because we lack sufficient empirical information, or are unable to perform the necessary calculations – that is a defect in us, not a defect in the theory. This kind of view is clearly expressed by Derek Parfit, who denies that a principle S is faulty because erroneous empirical beliefs prevent him from complying with S: "If this is the way in which S is self-defeating, this is no objection to S. S is self-defeating here only because of my incompetence in attempting to follow S. This is a fault, not in S, but in me."[7] To the extent that Conserving Response theorists are concerned with the practical use of moral principles, their slogan might be "Eliminate the gap between human decision-making capacities and the requirements of moral theory by *raising* human capacities to the level where human beings can employ the correct theory." Their advice to us is to improve ourselves by acquiring greater empirical information, increasing our ability to store information where it may be easily accessed, and employing computers to enhance our computational capacities. We should not tinker with the theory merely to disguise our own shortcomings.

[6] John Rawls, *A Theory of Justice* (Cambridge: Harvard University Press, 1971), p. 132, and "Construction and Objectivity," *The Journal of Philosophy*, vol. LXXVII (September 1980), p. 561.

[7] Derek Parfit, *Reasons and Persons* (Oxford: Clarendon Press, 1984), p. 5. Parfit applies his remarks to self-interest principles, not to patently moral principles.

The third response, which I shall call the *Moderate Response*, rejects both extremes, and claims that the best solution involves a two-pronged strategy. *First*, we are to determine which principle is the correct theoretical account of right and wrong without any reference to the practical usability of such a principle. *Second*, if that account proves impractical for making decisions, then we are to supplement it with appropriate second-level rules that are more readily applied in making decisions by human beings operating under normal constraints of information and computation. Perhaps the classic statement of the Moderate Response is found in John Stuart Mill, who used it to defend utilitarianism against the objection that "there is not time, previous to action, for calculating and weighing the effects of any line of conduct on the general happiness." Mill believed that *"whatever* we adopt as the fundamental principle of morality, we require subordinate principles to apply it by."[8] This response is a kind of halfway house between the two previous extremes, in the sense that, on the one hand, it denies that the content of the account of right and wrong must accommodate human cognitive limitations, but, on the other hand, it requires a moral theory to accommodate these limitations by *expanding* to include normatively appropriate decision-making rules as well as principles of right and wrong. Notice that the Moderate Response does not claim that we will be able to apply the correct principle of right and wrong *directly* to our decisions. Rather, the idea is that we will apply it *indirectly*, via direct application of the second-level rules to our acts. Thus, the demand that moral principles should be usable must be weakened to the demand that they should be usable at least in this indirect sense.[9]

III. RATIONALES FOR THE USABILITY CONDITION

Which of these responses to cognitive deficiencies in applying moral principles is correct? Clearly, the answer to this question will largely depend on one's rationale for believing that moral principles should be usable as practical decision-guides. Here I will briefly indicate four of the most salient reasons that have been used to support the idea that moral principles must be usable.

First, it may be argued that the very concept of morality requires that moral principles be usable for action-guiding purposes. Sometimes this is expressed as Prichard does, when he claims that ordinary thought holds that there can be no particular duty that is not recognized as such by the person obliged to do it.[10] Thus Prichard would hold that the juror has no duty to compensate the plaintiff with $500,000, since she is unaware this is her duty. Other moralists, of whom Hare might provide an example, hold that it is part of the meaning of moral terms, such as 'ought', that their function is to help guide choices. Clearly, to fulfill this role it is necessary that the principles governing the application of these terms be usable.

---

[8] John Stuart Mill, *Utilitarianism* (Indianapolis: The Bobbs-Merrill Company, Inc., 1957), pp. 30, 32. My emphasis. It is not wholly clear that Mill had in mind by "subordinate principles" precisely what I do here.

[9] Certain moral codes, such as utilitarianism, are often criticized on the ground that they demand too much of mere human beings by way of motivation: they require us to perform acts involving so much sacrifice of our own interests that no one could possibly be motivated to adhere to such principles. This is a criticism about the "strains of commitment." Notice that the same three responses that I have just outlined to problems of cognitive deficiency could also be proposed as responses to problems of motivational deficiency.

[10] H.A. Prichard, "Duty and Ignorance of Fact," in H.A. Prichard, *Moral Obligation and Duty and Interest* (London: Oxford University Press, 1968), pp. 18–39.

Still other moralists have held that "she ought to do A" implies "she can do A" in the sense "she would do A if she wanted to." This, in turn, implies that the agent *knows how* to perform the act in question. Moralities subject to this constraint could not be subject to some of the cognitive impediments to usability I have described.

A second justification offered in favor of usability has been stated most persuasively by Bernard Williams. He points out that there seems to be a special form of injustice created by moral principles which cannot be universally used. Suppose it turns out, for example, that certain moral principles cannot be used as widely by the dull or the poorly informed as by the highly intelligent and well-educated. Such a morality would violate the ideal that the successful moral life be available to *everyone*. Williams, who traces this ideal back to Kant, claims that it has the ultimate form of justice at its heart and embodies something basic to our ideas of morality.[11]

A third justification offered in favor of usability in moral principles holds that the function of a moral code is to enhance social welfare. Warnock speaks for many when he states that "the 'general object' of morality ... is to contribute to betterment – or non-deterioration – of the human predicament."[12] The usual idea here is that a moral code is to serve as a kind of informal analogue to a legal code, constraining behavior in ways that make every member of society better off. The connection between serving this function and being usable is thought to be roughly this: moral rules must be designed so that (a) they can be successfully followed, and (b) when they are successfully followed, they will increase social utility through actions that avoid violent conflict, enhance social cooperation, and so forth. Rules that cannot be followed cannot be guaranteed to lead to such desirable results, since the acts, and the consequences of those acts, resulting from misapplications of such rules are unpredictable or even pernicious.

Finally, a fourth justification for usability states that the function of morality is not to produce valuable social consequences, but rather to produce the best possible *pattern of actions* (where desirable actions are specified by the theoretical criterion provided by the morality). If certain actions are right, then it is a good thing if they are performed. Typically, but not always, moralists who take this line defend a deontological moral code. They argue that the ideal pattern of actions can only be achieved if the moral principles are usable without hitch or error by the individuals subject to them. Otherwise misapplications, or failures of application, will lead to morally inferior acts.

In this paper I shall take on a very limited task: what I shall examine is the extent to which a particular version of the Moderate Response constitutes a successful solution to the Problem of Error – the problem raised by the fact that decision-makers often have false empirical beliefs that would lead them to derive incorrect prescriptions from otherwise attractive moral principles. In considering which response is the best solution to the general problem of cognitive deficiency, I believe it is crucial to distinguish the various *kinds* of cognitive deficiencies that can hinder decision-making. Since a given response may provide a satisfactory solution

[11] Bernard Williams, "Moral Luck," in Bernard Williams, *Moral Luck* (Cambridge: Cambridge University Press, 1981), p. 21.
[12] C.J. Warnock, *The Object of Morality* (London: Methuen and Co., Ltd., 1971), p. 26.

to one kind of cognitive handicap but not to another, it is important not to be misled about the appropriateness of a response by conflating the various kinds of shortcomings it might be invoked to circumvent.

IV. TWO-TIER RESPONSES

As a response to the Problem of Error, the Moderate Response consists in advocating what I shall call a *two-tier system*. In this system, the first tier consists in principles that provide the correct theoretical account of right-making characteristics. Let us call the set of these principles M. The second tier consists in rules that are to be used for actual decision-making. Let us call these principles M*. Since people are often mistaken about the empirical nature of their prospective acts, they often err as to which acts are required by M, and so in attempting to follow M sometimes perform acts that it *pro*scribes. M*, on the other hand, is so constructed that agents who attempt to apply it will do what M itself prescribes. Two-tier systems of this sort are most familiar when the first tier is consequentialist and the second deontological. Sidgwick's view that commonsense morality ought to be used by most people in decision-making, even though utilitarianism is the correct account of right and wrong, is a salient example of this kind of proposal. However, any combination of deontological and consequentialist tiers is possible. For example, someone who believed the first tier should be deontological in character might recognize that the correct principles would be misapplied by many people, owing to their mistaken beliefs about the world. Such a theorist could advocate at the second level a set of principles less subject to erroneous application: these could either be simpler deontological principles or even simple consequentialist ones (referring only to easily ascertained effects of actions). Thus a deontologist might believe that in certain extreme circumstances, the use of torture by military officials is justified; but he might also believe that the likelihood of such officials' incorrectly believing themselves to be in these circumstances is so great that it would be better if they settled the issue of torture by reference to the simple rule "Never use torture."

For purposes of assessing the adequacy of the two-tier approach, one must begin by considering an *ideal* M* – i.e., one such that attempts to follow it would *always* lead the decision-maker to do what M prescribes.[13] There may seem little hope of

---

[13] Notice, however, that there seems no reason to demand that M* itself avoid the Problem of Error. That is, agents may make mistaken applications of M*, so long as their doing so does not lead them to violate M itself.

As Eric Mack pointed out in a discussion of this paper, there may be a difficult equilibrium problem in constructing coextensive pairs of M and M*, at least in cases where M is consequentialist. What concrete actions a consequentialist M requires depends on the specific historical context, which includes the nature of the moral code believed by the general population. Thus if the population believes code C, M may require agent S to perform act A (since it would lead C-believers to pursue certain courses of actions), while if the population believes code C', M may require agent S instead to perform act B (since it would lead C'-believers to pursue different courses of action than they would have had they believed in C). Thus to identify the relevant M*, we cannot simply start with M and ask what code would be coextensive with it; instead we have to start with M and a possible concrete historical context, including general belief in a given code, and ask whether that code is coextensive with M under those conditions. If not, we look at a different possible historical context and ask the parallel question, until finally we have found a matching pair. This may not be an easy task.

In this paper I am confining my attention to first-tier moral codes (i.e., candidates for M) that are *purely behavioral*: that is, they prescribe actions characterized solely in behavioral terms, not actions partly characterized in terms of the agent's beliefs, intentions, or other motivational states. Without this restriction it would be difficult or impossible to construct a coextensional M*, at least if that required the agent to have the same mental state as that required by M, as well as to perform the same bit of behavior required by M.

identifying such an M* for any M which we seriously believe might be an adequate theoretical account of moral rightness. However, I believe this pessimism is incorrect: ideal M*s can be identified. I will discuss how to do so later on. Given that there are ideal M*s, and hence ideal versions of the two-tier approach, we should focus on assessing them first, and only subsequently turn to an assessment of non-ideal versions of the two-tier strategy. Only in this way will we be able to see the advantages and disadvantages *intrinsic* to this kind of solution. We must beware of prematurely rejecting a solution because of difficulties or objections that arise only for non-ideal versions of the solution, the ones falling short of the objective: these difficulties may arise from the failure of the version to meet its objective, not from any inherent flaw in the strategy itself. Having assessed ideal versions, we may then turn to non-ideal versions. This paper, however, must confine itself to consideration of the ideal versions alone.

Two-tier solutions appear in various forms. The first major distinction among such forms concerns the extent of knowledge about the structure of the moral system permitted to the decision-maker who is to use the second-tier rules. One version, which we might call the *Enlightened Decision-Maker* version, allows this agent full awareness of the relation between M and M*. A second version, and the one I shall discuss here, keeps the agent in the dark about the status of M*. In this *Benighted Decision-Maker* version, the decision-maker falsely believes that M* is the correct theoretical account of rightness and wrongness, and never learns that the real role of M* is to secure conformity to M. On some variants of the Benighted Decision-Maker version, a coterie of enlightened persons retains knowledge of the true roles of M and M*. The elite itself uses M both for theoretical assessments and for decision-making purposes. Sidgwick labels such an arrangement an *Esoteric Morality*; it shall be the main focus of our discussion here.[14] On other variants, which Parfit calls *Self-Effacing*, even the enlightened see that it would be best if *they* no longer believed (and tried to follow) M, and so (perhaps by hypnosis) replace their belief in M with a belief in M* as the true theoretical account of rightness and wrongness. They then apply M* in their decision-making, and always wind up doing what M itself prescribes. No one remains who recognizes that M, not M*, is the correct theory about what makes actions right or wrong.[15]

Esoteric Morality solutions to the Problem of Error have had many detractors. Many of these detractors have viewed it as a solution required only by consequentialist, and particularly utilitarian, moralities, and therefore as constituting a disadvantage of such moralities as compared to others. As we have seen, it is a mistake to suppose that consequentialist moralities are the only ones vulnerable to the Problem of Error; consequently, it is a mistake to believe that consequentialist moralities are the only ones for which this problem might be remedied by the Esoteric Morality solution. If this solution is a poor solution, it should be avoided by any morality; and if a better solution cannot be found, then all moral systems are disadvantaged equally by the necessity of employing it. Let us

---

[14] Henry Sidgwick, *The Methods of Ethics*, 7th ed. (Chicago: The University of Chicago Press, 1962), pp. 489-90.
[15] Parfit, sec. 17.

begin our assessment of Esoteric Morality solutions by examining some of the standard objections that have been lodged against them. I shall argue that these objections have significantly less force than is commonly thought. I shall then argue that these solutions must be rejected for a wholly different type of reason.[16]

V. THE OBJECTION FROM MANIPULATION

Bernard Williams attacks the Esoteric Morality solution to systems with a utilitarian first tier. He envisions a society in which the secretly-utilitarian rulers encourage and maintain a non-utilitarian morality on the part of the general populace. This situation, he claims, would be inherently manipulative, because the rulers must be unresponsive to non-utilitarian demands made on them, and maintain their political position by means other than responsiveness to public demands. These means are likely to involve coercion or severe political restrictions.[17]

But Williams's complaint has little force against an ideal two-tier system. For the record, we should note that the secret utilitarian elite in an Esoteric Morality need not be the political rulers at all. They may have no particular power over the views or activities of others, but simply realize that the general populace produces more utility by following their nonutilitarian morality than they would by attempting to follow utilitarianism. The elite sit back and watch the situation with approval; but they may have no power to change it even if they wished to. Such an elite can hardly be charged with manipulation of the sort Williams describes.

But the more important point is that even a scenario in which the political rulers *do* form the utilitarian elite fails to be manipulative in Williams's sense. Williams claims that because of the difference in moral beliefs between the general populace and the rulers, the populace will demand that the government act in certain ways which the government must refuse to do. For example, the populace might demand, but the government resist, the setting of equitable (but non-utility-maximizing) taxes, the upholding of treaties (when violating them would better promote utility), or the punishment of criminals in a manner commensurate with

---

[16] In this paper I will focus primarily on the capacity of M* to secure the same pattern of action as M. Of course, on many views, M and M* would need to be compared on other grounds. For example, M* might be more costly overall to social welfare than M because it would be so difficult to teach; or M* might actually secure fewer right actions than M because even though people would be infallible in applying it, it would be far less capable of eliciting allegiance than M, and so produce less actual compliance. For the most part I shall leave these issues aside.

It is worth pointing out here, however, that a kind of two-tier morality (with a version of utilitarianism as the first tier, and a set of deontological rules as the second tier) has sometimes been proposed as a technique for avoiding *normative* objections to act-utilitarianism. Thus it is claimed that act-utilitarianism erroneously requires (for example) a sheriff to convict and punish an innocent person in order to avert race riots. This counter-intuitive result, it is said, can be averted by a system of rules prohibiting punishment of the innocent. Such a system allegedly could be justified on general utilitarian grounds, even though it would not prescribe every utility-maximizing individual act. This type of rationale for a two-tier system is not compatible with the kind of rationale I am exploring. The rationales explored in this paper assess a second-tier rule as better insofar as the acts it prescribes *match* those prescribed by the first-tier principle, while the normative-objection rationale only succeeds if the second-tier rules sometimes deliver prescriptions that *diverge from* those of the first-tier principle. I am grateful to Julia Annas for calling this point to my attention.

[17] Bernard Williams, "A Critique of Utilitarianism," in J.J.C. Smart and Bernard Williams, *Utilitarianism: For and Against* (Cambridge: Cambridge University Press, 1973), pp. 138–39.

the evil of their crimes (rather than in a manner calculated to maximize deterrence effect). But in the Esoteric Morality solution under consideration, the alternative morality M* to which the populace is committed is *coextensional* with the correct morality M (in this case, utilitarianism): all acts and policies required by the one are also required by the other. So, in general, the policies demanded by the populace will be the very same policies desired by the utilitarian elite.[18] There will be no more need in such a society for the government to resist its citizens' demands than is normally the case. No unusual engines of coercion will be necessary to ensure that the elite's policies are carried out. (Of course, insofar as utilitarianism requires certain forms of manipulation, both the governors and the populace will demand such coercion. But this is a straightforward consequence of utilitarianism as such, not a consequence of embedding utilitarianism within a two-tier system.) Manipulation in Williams's special sense is certainly not required by the presence of an ideal two-tier system: it only becomes necessary insofar as the system falls short of ideal correspondence between M and M*. Failure, not success, of the two-tier system gives rise to manipulation.

VI. Violating the Publicity Condition

We have seen that Esoteric Moralities will not, by themselves, lead to coercive political manipulation. When M and M* are coextensional, M does not require implementing governmental policies that contradict the will of the populace. The will of the populace and the will of the moral elite are the same. But it may be claimed that even ideal Esoteric Moralities will inevitably involve another evil, namely *deceit*. For the elite are required to conceal their own morality, and thus to violate what is now called, following John Rawls, the "Publicity Condition." The Publicity Condition, whose foremost advocate is Rawls, states that moral principles are invalid unless they can be publicly advocated without being self-defeating.[19] Rawls advocates the Publicity Condition on the following ground. He states that the principles of justice chosen by contractors in the Original Position are to serve as a public conception of justice: one which is acknowledged by all parties to a dispute, and which can be publicly appealed to by anyone in order to settle interpersonal conflicts within society. Thus the contractors in the Original Position will only choose principles in the understanding that they will be public knowledge.[20]

However, Rawls's assumption about the role of principles of justice does not provide a conclusive argument against an ideal Esoteric Morality. In a society with an ideal Esoteric Morality, the general populace *does* possess a common and publicized moral theory – namely M* – to which members of the general populace can appeal in order to resolve interpersonal disputes among themselves. Likewise

[18] More accurately, the two moralities are coextensional except for the cases in which it is the populace's *misapplication* of M* which would lead them to do or want what M requires. But in these cases what the populace mistakenly thinks required by their theory is what is actually required by the rulers' theory M, so there will be no conflict between the populace and the rulers on the moral character of the policies in questions.

[19] Rawls, *Theory of Justice*, p. 133. Rawls traces the history of the condition to Kant.

[20] *ibid.* See also the Dewey lectures (*Journal of Philosophy*, vol. LXXVII (September 1980)), where this idea is developed in more detail.

the elite possesses a common and publicized (among themselves) moral theory – namely M – to which they can appeal in order to resolve interpersonal disputes within their own ranks.[21] Of course, M and M* are different. But this presents no problem even when disputes arise between the elite and the general populace, since the elite, knowing of the correspondence between M and M*, will be perfectly content to abide by the prescriptions generated by M*. Hence, none of the bad effects Rawls envisions arising from non-public moralities will actually arise under the Esoteric Morality we are considering.[22]

Of course, this does not obviate the fact that the elite must deceive the general populace about the moral views they themselves hold: unless unusual conditions obtain, the elite must tell the general populace, falsely, that they believe M*. Such a situation is sometimes objected to on the ground that it involves serious psychological strains on the deceiving parties, who must always guard their statements and never reveal, perhaps even to those individuals who are personally closest to them, the nature of their true values. Of course, these strains will be much alleviated by the fact that M and M* prescribe the same acts, so that the elite are never required to assert they are in favor of acts that, in reality, they abhor. To the extent that these strains are a problem (and this will depend on the precise social arrangements and degree of interaction between the elite and the general populace), then they must be counted as among the costs of a two–tier system. If the rationale for a two–tier system is to increase social welfare above what it would be if everyone were to believe and attempt to follow M, then these costs must be taken into account in determining whether social welfare really *would* be higher under a two–tier system: perhaps the loss would be large enough to outweigh the gains secured through universal compliance with M. In such a case, the two–tier system would fail to secure its objective and should not be adopted, at least if other possible solutions to the Problem of Error would be less costly. It must be said, however, that

---

[21] There may be some disputes between members of the elite that must be carried out in full view of the general populace. In such cases, the elite cannot overtly appeal to M. However, they will be content to appeal to M* itself, since they know it generates the same prescriptions as M. Complexities might arise if the case in question is one in which the general populace would, through some erroneous factual belief not shared by the elite, derive an "incorrect" prescription from M* – a prescription that actually accords with what M itself prescribes (see note 13). In such a case, the elite would have to feign the same factual beliefs as the general populace.

[22] Avoiding these bad effects may not be as simple as the text suggests. So far I have spoken as though both M and M* governed the actions of both the elite and the general population. Technically, however, M* need only govern the actions of the general population (since they are the only ones subject to the Problem of Error). Nonetheless, if M* failed to address the activities of the elite, it would be difficult to persuade the general population that such an incomplete M* was the genuine theoretical account of right and wrong. Hence M* must probably be constructed to govern the activities of all. Now, it is logically possible that the actions required by M for the two groups differ. For example, it might turn out, according to M, that the general population ought never to lie, while it is permissible for the elite to lie under circuirstances C (which never arise for the general population). Hence M* might be constructed to contain two components, M* (GP) which forbids the general population to lie, and M*(E) which permits the elite to lie under circumstances C. But it would probably be more psychologically effective to construct a coextensional M* which permitted lying to *anyone* so long as they found themselves in circumstances C. Thus, the general population would know that they, too, could lie if they ever were in circumstances C. (But suppose 'circumstances C' = 'being an elite when the general population needs to be misled about the true moral code in order to avoid the Problem of Error'. An M* containing a clause referring to such a C would certainly tend to undermine the system as a Benighted Agent solution.)

this seems unlikely. The size of the elite is likely to be small, so that the number of those subjected to these psychological strains will not be large. Hence the cost to them is likely to be outweighed by the benefits secured through universal compliance with M.

Suppose, on the other hand, that a two-tier system is not advocated because of its benefits for society, but rather because it is held that the concept of morality requires usability for decision-making, or that justice requires that everyone should be able to lead the successful moral life, or that it is a good thing that right acts be done. Then what? Placed against these claims, the fact that the elite must suffer some psychological strains to support the required system seems of small or uncertain importance. To promote justice, for example, it is often necessary to make great sacrifices of self-interest; what the elite are required to do to maintain an Esoteric Morality is certainly no more costly than what justice might require from them in other contexts. The objection that a two-tiered system may generate psychological strains seems of little consequence in the context of these other rationales in favor of this solution.

Still a third objection may be raised because of the deceit itself: it may be thought that deceiving others about one's moral views is inherently immoral, and any solution to the Problem of Error that requires it must be rejected for this reason. The first thing we should notice about this objection is that it is hardly theory-neutral. Anyone who is convinced that the correct theoretical account of right-making properties, i.e., M, is consequentialist will not agree that deception is inherently immoral. Hence this person will have no moral reason to reject a system that involves deception about their moral views by the elite. On the other hand, someone who believes that M is deontological may believe that M itself includes a prohibition against deception. Such a person will have *moral* reason to reject an Esoteric Morality in which the elite must deceive the general populace. The question for such a deontologist will be now to weigh M's prohibition of deception against whatever rationale he accepts in favor of the widespread usability of morality. Suppose, for example, he believes the dictum that " 'ought' entails 'can' " requires morality to be usable by everyone, and at the same time rejects the Replacement Solution, according to which it is a constraint on the correctness of any theoretical account of rightness that it be directly usable by everyone for making decisions. A two-tier solution seems his only recourse, even if it requires forms of deception prohibited by what he believes to be the correct theoretical account of rightness. What we have here is a conflict between *ethical* reasons against a social arrangement and *meta-ethical* reasons in favor of it. It is a difficult to know how such conflicts might be resolved, but it is far from clear that the ethical considerations must always outweigh the meta-ethical ones. It is noteworthy that in many deontological codes the prohibition against deceit is only a *prima facie* prohibition at most, often outweighed by conflicting considerations that may point the other direction. By contrast, meta-ethical considerations are rarely thought of as merely *prima facie*. We cannot conclude that the prohibition against deceit, even for a deontologist, shows that Esoteric Moralities should not be accepted as the best solution to the Problem of Error. And for the consequentialist, the objection will have no weight at all.

VII. THE OBJECTION FROM COGNITIVE MANIPULATION

We have surveyed the objection to an Esoteric Morality that it requires the elite to violate the Publicity Condition, i.e., to disguise their own moral beliefs. However, it is one thing to conceal one's own moral beliefs; it is quite another to dupe others into affirming false moral beliefs. Nevertheless, it may be objected, this is precisely what the elite must do in order to bring about belief in the incorrect M* by the general population. Thus, for example, the elite must deceive the general populace into believing that an action is wrong because it involves stealing, whereas in fact it is wrong because it fails to maximize happiness. Someone who concedes that it is sometimes necessary to conceal one's own moral beliefs may well find it far more objectionable to induce incorrect moral views in others.

Once again, we should note that Esoteric Moralities need not involve systems in which a political or educational elite manipulates the moral views of the general population. The moral elite may have no power over the views of the general populace; they may merely note with approval that the population's adherence to M* leads them to do precisely what M demands. Such an elite cannot be charged with manipulation of beliefs.[23]

But what about a two-tier system in which the moral elite *does* influence the moral views of the general population by leading them to believe in M*? How objectionable would such a system be? Clearly, any serious objection to such a system will start from the premise that the moral elite is *deceiving* the general population, and the judgement that deception is wrong. As we have just seen, anyone who believes in a consequentialist M will not be moved by this objection. Moreover, even someone who believes in a deontological M that includes a prohibition against deception may find that this prohibition is outweighed by the importance of rendering morality universally usable. But whether or not it is outweighed will depend on how wrong the deception is, and this in turn surely depends on how grave a harm or disadvantage deception is to the deceived party. A relatively harmless lie must be far less evil than a lie that significantly harms its victim. In this case the harm is whatever harm is constituted by having false moral beliefs. Thus this objection, to seriously worry a deontologist, must show or assume that having false moral beliefs is a grave harm or disadvantage to the general population in an Esoteric Morality.

The question of whether holding incorrect moral views is a harm or disadvantage to the person who holds them is a difficult one. It cannot be answered definitively here, but it is worth sketching some of the considerations. Normally this question is not hard to answer, because false moral beliefs lead to wrong actions, and we may feel that it is clear enough what is wrong about wrong actions. Thus there is, so to speak, an action-oriented explanation for why false moral beliefs are to be avoided. But in the scenario we are envisioning, the false moral

---

[23] An interesting proposal, somewhat along these lines, has been suggested by Nigel Smith (see "Enchanted Forest," *Natural History*, vol. 92 (August 1983), pp. 14–20). Smith recounts the (patently false) superstitious beliefs that prevent the rural populations of the Amazon basin from destroying the jungle ecological system, and recommends "tapping" these folk beliefs in order to strengthen official conservation efforts.

beliefs lead to right actions, so we cannot criticize them on those grounds. (And, indeed, true moral beliefs would lead to wrong actions.) So the most natural ground for thinking that possession of false moral views is unavailable in this context.

But there may be other grounds for objection. According to a Kantian tradition, lying to a person is wrong because it interferes with her effective exercise of her rational agency.[24] This tradition has been picked up in medical ethics contexts, where it is said, for example, that a patient's *autonomy* requires the physician to disclose all relevant information before the patient makes any decision about a proposed course of treatment. But what is "rational agency" or "autonomy"? These are notoriously vague concepts. They may be defined in such a way that a person only counts as rational, or autonomous, if the person makes decisions on the basis of true beliefs. On such definitions, of course misleading a person about morality will undermine her rational agency and autonomy. But why should we accept *these* definitions of "rationality" and "autonomy"? Why must these characteristics depend on true belief? In the context we are considering, this question becomes critical. For it cannot be claimed that here the person possessing the false belief labors under a deficiency that will lead her to make the wrong decision, or a decision she would regret if she had true beliefs. On the contrary, if she had true beliefs in this sphere, she would make the wrong decision. Her effective decision-making is not undermined by her false views. Pursuit of this line of thought seems to lead to a dead end: we must first establish why true (moral) beliefs are important, before we can argue that rationality and autonomy, properly understood, require them.

Why, generally speaking, are true beliefs valuable? Epistemologists who discuss this issue (with respect to empirical beliefs) typically cite the importance of true belief for successful action.[25] But we are dealing with a case where, by hypothesis, false (moral) belief would lead to successful action, and true belief would lead to unsuccessful action.[26] So that rationale is unavailable to us. It might plausibly be claimed that we simply *want* to have true moral opinions (just as we might want to know if a deceased spouse had been unfaithful to us) quite apart from the usefulness of such opinions in making correct moral decisions. We want to grasp the nature of moral reality, even if we would act just as well not knowing its nature. But would we want to know this if we realized that such knowledge would lead us to act badly? At the very least this would require a difficult balancing judgment as to whether action or knowledge was most important.

A venerable tradition within philosophy maintains that one's fundamental moral beliefs constitute part of one's character.[27] Thus, someone who believes that

[24] See, for example, Barbara Herman, "The Practice of Moral Judgment," *The Journal of Philosophy*, vol. LXXXII, no. 8 (August 1985), p. 431.

[25] See, for example, Robert Nozick, *Philosophical Explanations* (Cambridge: Harvard University Press, 1981), p. 284; see also pp. 323–26. But see Alvin Goldman, *Epistemology and Cognition* (Cambridge: Harvard University Press, 1986), p. 98.

[26] Nozick, p. 321, speculates that the only way an "action can track an evaluative fact is via . . . the person's knowledge of the fact." But our case is one in which there is a counterfactual connection between the evaluative facts (specified by M) and their M* counterparts. So a person's belief in M* would enable her actions to "track" the genuine evaluative facts identified by M.

[27] Gilbert Ryle, "Forgetting the Difference Between Right and Wrong," ed. A.I. Melden, *Essays in Moral Philosophy* (Seattle: University of Washington Press, 1958), pp. 147–59.

stealing is fundamentally wrong has a different character from someone who believes that failing to maximize happiness is fundamentally wrong – even though it may be true (unbeknownst to the person) that stealing always fails to maximize happiness. A second, equally venerable tradition holds that having a good moral character is morally important in itself, quite apart from the acts it leads one to perform.[28] On this tradition, a society of people, each of whom believes the false M*, would be a *worse* society than another society in which everyone believes the true M – even though the acts performed in the two societies were identical. And even if the acts performed in the first society were better, the whole situation (encompassing both the pattern of action and the people's moral characters) might be morally worse. To decide whether it was actually worse would take a careful weighing of the relative value of good character versus right acts.

But we need to look more carefully at the claim that someone acting from incorrect moral theory has an inferior moral character. Is it really true that adherents of M* would have worse moral characters than adherents of M? It might be objected (as perhaps Kant would) that although the M* adherents are mistaken as to the *content* of their duty, it is nonetheless true that if their fundamental motive is to do their duty because it is their duty, then they are morally on a par with M adherents, whose fundamental motive is also to do their duty. But many people find this claim implausible. It entails, for example, that if Hitler genuinely believed that it was morally required to eliminate the Jews, then his moral character cannot be worse than the moral character of, say, Mother Theresa. And this seems to many people incredible. In their view, the nature of a person's moral character includes not only his desire to fulfil his duty, but also the content that he perceives that duty to have. Mother Theresa doing her perceived duty is a better person than Hitler doing his perceived duty.

But matters are more complicated than the Hitler example may make them appear. For one thing, even if one's moral character depends on the content of one's moral beliefs, it may also depend on their psychological history and status. Thus, it might be said that we cannot view a person as having bad character, even if his moral views are evil, if his coming to have those views (and maintaining them) was reasonable. So a racist who imbibes his racism from plausible authority figures, who never interacts with members of the downgraded race, and never has any opportunity to interact with them or to discover their real characteristics might be said not to have a bad character. Precisely this scenario may obtain for adherents to M*. We can imagine that they come to hold their views in the same reasonable way that adherents of M come to hold their views: e.g., both are taught their views by friends, family, and religious institutions; in both cases, plausible justifications for the respective theories are provided. So neither party believes his theory on unjustified grounds. Moreover, if M is correct, and M* is coextensional with it in this world, then the features picked out by M* as right-making are unlikely to be morally monstrous ones (in the assessment of M). At worst, they are likely to be

---

[28] Immanuel Kant, *Foundations of the Metaphysics of Morals* (Indianapolis: Bobbs-Merrill Company, Inc., 1959).

mildly evil, and at best morally neutral or even mildly good. Otherwise the coextensionality between and M and M* would not obtain. So the errors embodied in M* are not likely to leap out at any right-minded person, and we cannot fault its adherents on the ground that they have maintained their false view in the face of overwhelming evidence against it. Moreover, if the features of actions identified by the adherents of M* are morally unobjectionable (as assessed by M), then we cannot reasonably judge the characters of the M* adherents as being morally monstrous.

It seems, then, as though this objection to Esoteric Moralities is, at best, a mild one. No compelling argument that true moral beliefs are of overriding value has been put forward; certainly no argument has established that having true moral beliefs outweighs the evil of the wrong actions such beliefs would sometimes lead to in the kind of case we are considering. We saw that the moral character of a person who believes M* *may* be inferior to the moral character of someone who believes the correct M; but it is controversial whether or not this is so at all, since moral character may simply turn on one's desire to do one's duty, the difference in their characters is likely to be small in any event, and, in any case, there is certainly no guarantee that the loss in good moral character of a populace believing in M* would not be counterbalanced by the gain in right actions performed by them. The objection to Esoteric Moralities that focuses on the fact that a populace under such a Morality must have false moral beliefs is a troubling one, but under close scrutiny it doesn't have the power we might originally have expected. And from this we can conclude that the objection that Esoteric Moralities require the elite to deceive the general populace about the content of morality is at best a weak one; this particular form of deceit has not been shown to be very serious.

VIII. PROBLEMS OF IMPLEMENTATION

We have now surveyed three of the standard objections that are raised to Esoteric Moralities as solutions to the Problem of Error. We have found that, at least for *ideal* Esoteric Moralities, these objections have far less force than is commonly supposed. Several miss their mark altogether, and others depend on a comparative weighing of the importance of different desiderata (e.g., avoiding wrong acts vs. avoiding poor moral character) that may or may not show Esoteric Moralities to be, on balance, undesirable. Let us turn our attention, then, to another kind of problem that more decisively undermines this solution.

Let us start by asking whether it is really possible to implement an Esoteric Morality. The first issue here is whether or not there exist second-level rules of the kind we have been discussing. For each candidate moral system M, vulnerable to the Problem of Error, does there exist a corresponding set of rules M* which is such that attempting to follow M* would lead each decision-maker to do what M prescribes? Proponents of Esoteric Moralities tend to speak as though there are laws of nature connecting the morally significant act-types identified by M and those identified by M*. Such a law of nature might state that, for example, every act of telling a lie (wrong according to M*) is also an act of failing to maximize utility (wrong according to M). The act-types identified as morally significant by M* must be ones with respect to which members of the general populace are *infallible* – these agents must make no mistake about which acts would be of these types, even in cases where they would make mistakes about which acts are of the corresponding M-identified types.[29] But it seems extremely unlikely that, for any M of genuine interest, there exist simple correlations between the occurrence of M-identified act-types and any act-types that could serve in a corresponding M* theory. Lying does not always involve failing to maximize utility, and even if it did, agents are not always infallible in their beliefs about whether a prospective act would be a case of lying. Parallel things are true of every act-type that might be mentioned as a candidate for an M* theory. There seems no prospect of finding any laws of nature that will do the trick here, and so no prospect of finding an ideal system M*. Presumably it is precisely this assumption that has led proponents of Esoteric Moralities to focus their attention solely on non-ideal variants of this solution.

However, we should not give up so easily. Absence of the requisite nomological connections does not establish that no appropriate system M* exists. For each action that is of a type identified as significant by M is simultaneously of *many* other types.[30] In every case, at least one of these other types is one which the agent could unerringly ascribe to the act.[31] Suppose, in a particular case, that the act prescribed by M is also of (M-irrelevant) type T, the agent correctly believes that she has an act of type T available to her, and she knows how to perform this act. Then an instruction in this case to perform an act of type T would lead the agent to perform the act prescribed by M. For example, although the agent may not know which of her prospective acts is of the M-prescribed type *fully compensate an injured plaintiff*, that very act is also of the type *vote for an award of $500,000*, and she does know how to perform this act. If she wanted to vote for an award of $500,000, she would do so, and in doing so she would in fact carry out the demand of her moral code. Of course, which act-type correlates in this way with the M-prescribed type, and is also such that the agent knows how to perform it, will vary from case to case, depending on the circumstances and the agent's beliefs. Thus there will be no simple rules to substitute for M. But the rules of M* may take the form of an extended list of prescriptions to perform individual actions. Each prescribed action would be described in terms of an act-type having the feature that if the agent tried to do an action of that type, he would perform the act actually required by M in those circumstances. Such a list might appear as follows: at ten o'clock, empty the

---

[29] More accurately: the act-types must either be ones with respect to which the agents are infallible, or else such that the agent who wants to perform an act of that type will in fact perform the act prescribed by M itself.

[30] In an alternate terminology: any act of an M-significant type is on the same act-tree with many acts of different types.

[31] I assume here that if the agent is able to perform the act at all, then there is some description of it under which the agent's desiring to perform it would lead to his performance of that act. This may be too strong. There might be cases in which no *correct* description of the act would elicit its performance. (Consider the familiar finger game in which the fingers of both hands are entangled in such a way that one becomes confused as to which fingers belong to which hand. In these circumstances, wanting to *straighten the first finger of one's left hand* will elicit straightening the first finger of one's *right* hand, but no accurate description of this act will elicit it.) I shall ignore such cases in the discussion in the text; they imply that a thorough list might need to include misdescriptions of the actions to be performed.

dishwasher; at quarter past ten, pay one's bills; at eleven o'clock, balance one's checkbook; and so forth. Presented with such a list, the agent could follow it and so do everything required of him by M – even though he might not believe any of these acts to (for example) maximize utility and so would not perform them if he were instructed instead to act so as to maximize utility. Such lists could be relativized to each agent. An agent armed with a suitably designed list of this sort, and morally motivated, would perform each of the actions prescribed by M.

So appropriate systems M*, of a peculiar kind, do exist.[32] But their mere existence does not show that the Esoteric Moralities can provide a viable solution to the Problem of Error. There are several insurmountable obstacles to success. First, although for each M an appropriate M* exists, there is no reason to believe that anyone knows, or could find out, what the content of any appropriate M* is. Certainly the decision-maker herself cannot determine what the content of the appropriate M* is, for the decision-maker could only determine this if she knew what M requires in each particular case. But by hypothesis, the decision-maker would (at least sometimes) err if she tried to determine the prescription of M for each particular case. So no one who needs an M* theory to avoid the Problem of Error can construct that theory for herself. Of course, in any case where the decision-maker would err, some *other* individual might know which act was to be done, and might know under what description of it the decision-maker would be led to perform the correct act. But there is no reason to believe that, for *every* decision the decision-maker must make, there is someone who would know this. Nor is there reason to suppose that a person possessing this knowledge is always in a position to instruct the decision-maker as to what to do. There is even less reason to think that there is any one individual, or small group of individuals, who have this kind of knowledge about every act and every decision-maker subject to the Problem of Error, and who have instructional access to all these decision-makers. But this is what would be needed for an Esoteric Morality to work. Indeed, the kind of rules that M* requires – an extended list of acts – is not simple enough to be learnable in advance by any person of normal intelligence. Hence the moral elite would have to operate literally as guardian angels, hovering constantly about and advising the decision-makers from moment to moment as to what to do. Thus the difficulties in actually implementing this solution appear overwhelming.

How critical is the "implementation" problem? If the rules of M* were designed (at least in part) to serve a theoretical function – i.e., to provide an account of right-making characteristics – the difficulty I have just described would not be devastating. The rules still *would* provide this account, even if no one could determine what the content of the rules was.

But the rules of M* are only designed to serve a *practical* function: to enable decision-makers to act as M commands. The difficulty we have just seen shows that they cannot do this. There are two distinct, although related, ways to describe this failure. On the one hand, we can say that what we wanted was a practical solution to a practical problem. An analogy here might be our needing a solution to a practical problem such as taking last year's license plates off our car. To get the plates off we need a Phillips screwdriver. It is no solution to the problem to be told that a Phillips screwdriver exists somewhere in the house: to get the plates off, we need the right screwdriver actually in hand. If we cannot find it, we cannot solve our problem. Similarly, if our practical problem is to bring it about that agents with mistaken factual beliefs nonetheless do what M prescribes, it is no help to be told that a certain M* exists which is such that if these agents attempted to follow it, they would do what M demands. To get the agents to do what M demands, we need the right M* actually in hand. Since neither we nor anyone else can identify this M*, we have not solved our problem.

A second way to see the nature of this difficulty is the following. The Problem of Error arises because many agents have mistaken factual beliefs that mislead them when they attempt to follow M. To avoid this problem, it is suggested that we adopt an alternative moral system, in which M is supplemented by a suitable second-tier M*. It is demonstrated that an M* exists which is such that if these agents attempted to follow it, they would actually do what M demands. Under the new M–M* system, the agents suffer no Problem of Error that would lead them to misapply the rules they are to use in making decisions, namely M*. However, the cognitive deficiency that hindered them relative to the simple M system now simply reappears in M–M* at another level: they have traded one Problem of Error for another. The same empirical misinformation that plagues their application of M, now prevents them from seeing that M* is the correct code by which to guide their actions. They can apply M*, but they cannot see that it, rather than some alternative, is justified as an action-guide. Their false empirical beliefs have been converted into false beliefs about the moral status of M*. But the end result is that the two-tier solution has not improved their overall situation – it has only altered the location at which their deficiency impedes successful practical reasoning.

IX. A FURTHER PROBLEM

It is now clear that ideal Esoteric Moralities – ones that avoid the Problem of Error altogether – are possible in principle, but technically infeasible, given the limitations of human knowledge and memory. Esoteric Moralities fail because they assume greater knowledge among the moral elite than this class possesses or could ever possess. But suppose, contrary to fact, that some elite group *did* have the necessary information: they could construct the "rules" of M* (i.e., ad hoc lists of prescribed actions), and could communicate those rules to ordinary decision-makers. It appears that such a group would, by that very fact, possess an alternative method of securing general compliance with M. Such a group would *also* be in a position simply to convey their empirical information to ordinary decision-makers, and allow them to derive the correct prescriptions from M itself. An elite group with sufficient information to construct the rules of M*, and suitable instructional access to ordinary decision-makers, would also have sufficient information and access to teach these decision-makers (perhaps moment by moment) the facts they need to know in order to apply M itself unerringly. In other words, such a group would be in a position to implement a *Conserving Response* solution to the Problem of Error: conserving because it avoids the Problem by retaining M in both a theoretical and practical role, and enhancing the knowledge of decision-makers to the point where M itself is no longer vulnerable to the Problem. Indeed, insofar as the standard objections to Esoteric Moralities have weight, the Conserving Response would be superior to the Esoteric Morality solution, since it would be weakened by none of these flaws. For example, it would require no coercive manipulation of moral beliefs, nor any false moral beliefs at all on the part of the general population. So even if an Esoteric Morality could successfully be implemented, a superior Conserving Response solution would by that very fact be available. The upshot is this: ideal Esoteric Moralities, forms of Moderate Response solutions to the Problem of Error, are unworkable. If they could work, an equivalent Conserving Response solution would *ipso facto* also be available – and, insofar as the standard objections to Esoteric Moralities have force, the Conserving Response would be superior. We have fair reason, then, to reject ideal Esoteric Moralities as a solution to the Problem of Error.

Philosophy, University of Arizona

MOTIVE AND OBLIGATION
IN THE BRITISH MORALISTS*

By Stephen L. Darwall

My aim in what follows is to sketch with a broad brush fundamental changes involving the concept of obligation in British ethics of the early modern period, as it developed in the direction of the view that obligatory force is a species of motivational force – an idea that deeply informs present thought. I shall also suggest, although I can hardly demonstrate it conclusively here, that one important source for this view was a doctrine which we associate with Kant, and which it may seem surprising to find in British ethics, especially of the early modern period, viz., that rational agents are obligated by motives available through a form of practical thinking necessary for rational *autonomy*.

Sidgwick remarked that "the appearance of Shaftesbury's *Characteristics* marks a turning-point in the history of English ethical thought."[1] With Shaftesbury, British moral philosophy in the first half of the eighteenth century took a decidedly psychological or "internal" turn; or, at any rate, that which has had enduring interest did. By this I mean not just that, following Shaftesbury, the British moralists we still read with profit regarded what is inside the moral agent – character and motive, for example, rather than deeds and consequences – to be of fundamental ethical significance, or that they sought to make ethical thought more sensitive to psychological nuance. Both of these are true, but psychology also figured in the way writers such as Butler, Hutcheson, and Hume thought about ethics at a philosophically deeper level – at the level of the metaphysics and epistemology of morals, as well as that of substantive ethical doctrine.

I. Moral Value and Moral Sentiment

This phenomenon is perhaps most familiar in Hume's famous doctrine, taken from Hutcheson, that moral good and evil respectively consist in the capacity different traits and motives have, when appropriately contemplated, to give rise to distinctive psychological states in an observer.

> [V]ice entirely escapes you, as long as you consider the object. You never can find it, till you turn your reflexion into your own breast and find a sentiment of disapprobation, which arises in you, towards this action. . . . So that when you pronounce any action or character to be vicious, you

* Research on which this essay is based was supported by a Fellowship for Independent Study and Research from the National Endowment for the Humanities. I am indebted to discussions with William Frankena, and to W.D. Falk, who initially convinced me of Shaftesbury's importance.

[1] Henry Sidgwick, *Outlines of the History of Ethics for English Readers* (with additional chapter by Alban G. Widgery) (Boston: Beacon Press, 1964), p. 190.

mean nothing, but that from the constitution of your nature you have a feeling or sentiment of blame from the contemplation of it.[2]

Shaftesbury never went as far as Hutcheson and Hume in identifying virtue with the capacity to evoke reflective approbation; he was, however, the first to suggest the psychology that made this identification possible, and the first to use the term 'moral sense' to refer to the requisite psychological ability.

In a creature capable of forming general notions of things, not only the outward beings which offer themselves to the sense are the objects of the affection, but the very actions themselves, and the affections of pity, kindness, gratitude, and their contraries, being brought into the mind by reflection, become objects. So that, by means of this reflected sense, there arises another kind of affection towards those very affections themselves, which have been already felt, and are now become the subject of a new liking or dislike.[3]

Hutcheson (and Hume, at least in the early parts of Book III of the *Treatise*) took the psychological phenomena of disinterested approbation and disapprobation to mark off a distinctively moral good and evil, to be distinguished from "natural" (i.e., nonmoral) value and disvalue.[4] And they used this account to mount an empirical

[2] David Hume, *A Treatise of Human Nature*, ed. L.A. Selby-Bigge, 2nd. ed., revised by P.H. Nidditch (Oxford: Clarendon Press, 1978), pp. 468–69. Hereinafter referred to as *Treatise*. *Cf.* Hutcheson: "The word MORAL GOODNESS, in this treatise, denotes our idea of some quality apprehended in actions, which procures approbation, attended with desire of the agent's happiness. MORAL EVIL denotes our idea of a contrary quality, which excites condemnation or dislike." (*An Inquiry into the Original of our Ideas of Beauty and Virtue*, 4th ed. (1738), introduction; reprinted in D.D. Raphael, *British Moralists, 1650–1800* (Oxford: Clarendon Press, 1969), vol.i, p. 261.) Hereinafter referrred to respectively as *Inquiry* and *British Moralists*.

[3] Anthony Ashley Cooper, Earl of Shaftesbury, *Characteristics of Men, Manners, Opinions, Times*, ed. John M. Robertson, introduction by Stanley Grean (Indianapolis: Bobbs-Merrill Co., Inc., 1964), vol. i, p. 251; reprinted in *British Moralists*, vol. i, p. 172. Hereinafter *Characteristics*. For the first use of 'moral sense', see *Characteristics*, i. 262.

[4] The term "natural good" is Hutcheson's, and he uses it to refer to pleasure generally. Hume is also a hedonist about what he calls "good and evil," but does not use the qualifier 'natural'. Nonetheless, like Hutcheson, he distinguishes a species of *obligation* based on the agent's nonmoral good which he calls "natural" (*Treatise*, p. 498). As we shall see, the idea that there is such a species of obligation derives directly from Shaftesbury.

Although Hume follows Hutcheson in the early parts of Book III of the *Treatise* in arguing that *moral* good and evil consist in an object's capacity to evoke a "peculiar" or "particular" pleasure, the "moral sentiment," he expresses doubts later in the book (pp. 606f.) about whether the moral/nonmoral distinction is anything other than purely verbal. He repeats this theme in Appendix IV of the *Enquiry Concerning the Principles of Morals* (1751), ed. L.A. Selby-Bigge, 3rd ed., revised by P.H. Nidditch (Oxford: Clarendon Press, 1985), pp. 312–23. Hereinafter *Enquiry*. That it was *not* a purely verbal distinction was perhaps Hutcheson's most fundamental position. Every notion in Hutcheson's moral system is defined, ultimately, in terms of what he considered to be the simple moral ideas of approbation and condemnation. And it was because morality contains its own simple ideas that he speaks of a "moral sense." Thus, for Hutcheson, moral obligation and right, as well as the sense of 'morally good to elect' that led to his first formulation of the utilitarian formula "the greatest happiness of the greatest numbers," are all derivative from these fundamental simple ideas.

What underlay this difference between Hutcheson and Hume, I think, was that Hume's use of sympathy to explain why, as he believed, all virtues are either immediately agreeable or useful to those who have them or to others required the conclusion that the disinterested pleasure felt when contemplating traits likelier to be considered *moral* virtues is not essentially different from that felt in contemplating other useful or immediately agreeable characteristics such as wit. Hutcheson would have rejected both the phenomenon that Hume was hoping to explain as well as his explanation.

psychological argument that, in a sense of 'natural' different from that in which moral good contrasts with natural good, at least some "virtues and vices are entirely natural, and have no dependance on the artifice and contrivance of men."[5] Thus, using empiricist strictures similar to those Hobbes had employed, they were able to provide a partial defense of morality against the Hobbesian critique.

Hutcheson and Hume were quite self-consciously following Shaftesbury in this project. Consider, for example, the following extraordinary passage, of which Hume's famous comparison of vice and virtue "to sounds, colours, heat and cold, which according to modern philosophy are not qualities in objects"[6] must seem an echo:

> If there be no real amiableness or deformity in moral acts, there is at least an imaginary one of full force. Though perhaps the thing itself should not be allowed in Nature, the imagination or fancy of it must be allowed to be from Nature alone. Nor can anything besides art and strong endeavour, with long practice and meditation, overcome such a *natural prevention or prepossession of the mind in favour of this moral distinction.*[7]

Taken only so far, however, this general approach is but an incomplete vindication of morality against Hobbes's attack. Even if a distinctive kind of value called "moral" could be established by appropriately-situated disinterested response, this would not yet adequately explain the *hold* that morality is thought to have; it would not explain morality's binding force. It seems one thing for it to be the case that a malevolent action would provoke a response of disinterested displeasure or dislike if contemplated, and quite another for a person himself to be *obligated* not to be malevolent, at least in a sense that came to matter to many thinkers in the early modern period.[8]

Since it is an important part of my aim to tease out precisely what that sense was, I don't want to ruin the story now. Let me just say at this point that the whole matter of exactly what moral obligation is (or, perhaps more accurately, what it *could be*) was undergoing radical rethinking and revision in the period following Hobbes. Of course, Hobbes himself played an important role in this, but not because he had a particularly novel view of obligation. His impact was due more to the way his whole approach put unbearable pressure on the orthodox doctrine, including his own official view of obligation. With the appearance of Shaftesbury's

[5] *Treatise*, p. 574. Since Hutcheson believed it a fact of psychology that only benevolence in its various forms ever produces, upon contemplation, approbation and love towards the agent, he believed, unlike Hume, that all virtues are natural. Artifice may channel benevolence, but it cannot, he thought, affect the moral value of action and character, which depends entirely on whether it involves a form of benevolence or not.

[6] *ibid.*, p. 469.

[7] *Characteristics*, i.260. My emphasis. An important element in Shaftesbury's thought here is that morality cannot consist in conformity to externally imposed rules, as Locke had held in the *Essay* (*An Essay Concerning Human Understanding*, ed. P.H. Nidditch (Oxford: Oxford University Press, 1975), p. 351)). Hereinafter *Essay*. On this point, see below, Section V.

[8] Even Hutcheson and Hume, who rejected this distinction for the species of obligation they called "moral obligation," felt the need to establish a further obligation to morality. See Hume, *Treatise*, p. 498, and Hutcheson, *Inquiry*, vii.i (reprinted in *British Moralists*, i.293).

Characteristics, however, we shall see that a radical shift must have been underway. Shaftesbury crystallized that shift for the generation that followed, and, in doing so, profoundly influenced the way English-speaking philosophers have thought about obligation ever since.

II. SHAFTESBURY AND THE "OBLIGATION TO VIRTUE"

Shaftesbury's *Inquiry Concerning Virtue or Merit* was first published in an unauthorized edition in 1699, twelve years before the corrected version appeared as part of *Characteristics* in 1712. It has two books: Book I, in which it is "considered what virtue is and to whom the character belongs," and Book II, which discusses "what obligation there is to virtue."[9] After announcing this aim of inquiry at the beginning of Book II, Shaftesbury proceeds to give a complex and subtle argument that a person's *interest* is best achieved with a virtuous character – all of this without any mention of the word 'obligation' at all, until it appears for only the second and final time in the *Inquiry* in a remarkable conclusion that echoes the proto-Humean passage I quoted above.

> For let us carry scepticism ever so far, let us doubt, if we can, of everything about us, we cannot doubt of what passes within ourselves. Our passions and affections are known to us. They are certain, whatever the objects may be on which they are employed. Nor is it of any concern to our argument how these exterior objects stand: whether they are realities or mere illusions; whether we wake or dream. For ill dreams will be equally disturbing; and a good dream (if life be nothing else) will be easily and happily passed. In this dream of life, therefore, our demonstrations have the same force; our balance and economy hold good, and our *obligation* to virtue is in every respect the same.[10]

In order for the obligation to virtue to remain the same, regardless of what is true outside the agent's psyche, it must be internal to the agent. And this is Shaftesbury's view. The obligation to virtue derives from virtue's being necessary for the "balance and economy" of passions and affections in which an agent's good or interest consists.

For readers nowadays, the easy truck that early eighteenth-century British moralists had with what they considered a species of obligation consisting in the motive of self-interest may well seem strange. When we first encounter Hume speaking of "interested obligation" in the *Enquiry,* or Hutcheson distinguishing, as a kind of *obligation* "a motive from self-interest, sufficient to determine all those who duly consider it," we are apt to be puzzled.[11] Present-day readers are prepared to consider that they may also have a motive of self-interest to do what they are obligated to do, but not to believe that being in one's interest makes something obligatory. What did these philosophers mean by this?

---

[9] *Characteristics,* i.280 (reprinted in *British Moralists,* i,175).
[10] *ibid.,* i.336–37. My emphasis.
[11] *Enquiry,* p. 278; *Inquiry,* vii.1 (reprinted in *British Moralists,* i.293).

It is helpful to consider that when Shaftesbury introduces the issue he wants to address in Book II, he does so with a *disjunction*: "It remains to inquire, what obligation there is to virtue, or what reason to embrace it?" In querying what he calls the obligation to virtue, Shaftesbury is raising a question we would probably call the issue of the justification of morality. And he is proposing to answer this familiar question with a familiar (if controversial) strategy – arguing that only virtue realizes the agent's good. But why did Shaftesbury think that establishing this demonstrated an *obligation* to virtue? Why did he use the concept of obligation to raise this sort of justificatory question?

These are puzzles that arise from our perspective, as we look at early eighteenth-century texts from the vantage point of the present. But another set of puzzles emerges if one approaches Shaftesbury from the other direction. Shaftesbury's use of 'obligation' is remarkably casual; as I mentioned, he uses it only to state the question of "what obligation there is to virtue," and his conclusion: that because a virtuous life is best for the agent, he has an obligation to be virtuous. Plainly, he expected to be understood without further explanation. But if one approaches Shaftesbury through the major seventeenth-century moral and political texts, at least those that would have been most familiar to his readers, it is not obvious why he should have been understood.

III. THE SEVENTEENTH-CENTURY NATURAL LAW TRADITION

The dominant seventeenth-century view was that obligation derives from law.[12] The major British theorist of natural law, Richard Cumberland, was able to write in his *Treatise of the Laws of Nature* (1672) that "the received definition of obligation" was still Justinian's: "that bond of the law, by which we are tied with the necessity of paying any thing according to the laws of our state."[13] Cumberland noted further that 'payment' and 'his state' are "*special*, and ought, therefore, to be omitted in the general notion of obligation," making the received definition: a bond of the law by which we are tied with the necessity of acting according to it (the law).

Cumberland's characterization was accurate. The major seventeenth-century writers largely agreed that an obligation requires the existence of binding law. Since Shaftesbury does not even mention the idea of law in the course of arguing for the obligation to virtue, this only increases the puzzlement. How could he have assumed his readers would accept a demonstration of the overriding benefits of a virtuous life as establishing an obligation to virtue?

In order to see how he might have, it is necessary to appreciate fundamental changes that had, by the end of the seventeenth century, taken place within the modern natural law tradition. We can begin to understand what happened if we distinguish two different ways that the notion of necessity entered into the received view. An obligation to do something exists, it was thought, if it is something one

---

[12] What follows is obviously only the sketch of an argument that requires a great deal more detail. While I am convinced this detail can be given, I can now only express an intention to do so on another occasion.

[13] Cumberland, *A Treatise of the Laws of Nature*, trans. John Maxwell [originally *De Legibus Naturae disquisitio philosophica*, 1672] (London: 1727), p. 233. Hereinafter *Treatise of the Laws*. Selections from this are included in *British Moralists*.

must do, according to a law one *must* obey. The first sort of necessity, that which can be contained *in* a law, is relatively unproblematic, since the law itself may be written, or customarily interpreted, in mandatory terms. But what about the necessity *of* law itself? In virtue of what does law bind? And, especially, how does natural law bind? If the question is answered "in virtue of being law," then what makes a proposition law? These questions were continually being rethought throughout the seventeenth century, and in a way that led ultimately in the direction of Shaftesbury's assumption.

The modern tradition of natural law is usually taken to begin with Grotius, who defined it as "a dictate of right reason, which points out that an act, according as it is or is not in conformity with rational nature, has in it a quality of moral baseness or moral necessity."[14] Here we have the root idea that would be retained in all seventeenth-century accounts: natural law universally binds rational subjects as such. But it also goes well beyond what Grotius's successors were prepared to accept. It claims that natural law binds simply because there are truths, in the nature of things, regarding the accord or discord of acts with rational nature as such, and that these truths are evident to right reason. Right reason recognizes the necessity of an act by recognizing that its omission is discordant with the agent's own nature as rational.

Now, as we shall see, even this last idea – that something is obligatory for a rational subject just in case its omission would be discordant with his or her nature as rational – continued to be a fundamentally important one. But the question arises: what makes it a fact that a given act would be discordant with rational nature, and how are such facts known? Many of Grotius's successors could find in his writings no compelling answers to these questions, and were dissatisfied with the idea that the existence of such facts is simply evident to right reason. Much of the reaction to this problematic took the form of theological voluntarism, both of a variety that was thoroughly positivist and of a kind that was a halfway house between positivism and the moral realism of Grotius.

The latter sort of theological voluntarism was typified by Pufendorf, Nathaniel Culverwell, and the early Locke of the *Essays on the Law of Nature*. These writers were voluntarists – and, in that sense, positivists – because they held natural law to result from the will of God.[15] Rational subjects are bound by this law because they are God's subjects, and because it is God's law. But if "God's subjects" means "His to rule," then our being God's subjects cannot *explain* why we are to be ruled by Him; it is the same fact. So what explains why rational subjects are bound by God's will? The distinctive feature of theological voluntarism of the latter sort was its rejection of a positivist answer to this question. Thus Locke wrote that "all obligation binds conscience and lays a bond on the mind itself, so that not fear of punishment, but a rational apprehension of what is right, puts us under an

---

[14] Hugo Grotius, *The Law of War and Peace*, trans. Francis W. Kelsey [*De Juri Belli ac Pacis Libri Tres*, 1625] (Indianapolis: The Bobbs-Merrill Co., 1925), p. 38.
[15] Although I cannot show it here, Culverwell and Locke (though not Pufendorf) continued the Grotian idea that what is obligatory is what is in conformity with rational nature.

obligation ..."[16] This is still a kind of voluntarism, because Locke held that obligation arises from the will of superior authority. However, it rejects a positivist account of authority. God's authority differs from His power: His ability to consign His subjects to heaven or hell. Rather, this sort of theological voluntarism held that God has a right to rule because of His relation to us as creator to created. Thus, Pufendorf maintained that obligation involves the subject's recognizing that a command "falls upon him justly," and that it is because God has created His subjects with a nature enabling them to enjoy goods He has created for them, that they are justly ruled by Him.[17] The apparent idea, one which lies deep in the etymology of 'obligation', is that persons are obligated by special services done for them. And similarly, what seems to lie behind Locke's view is a position about the way creative agency acquires title to its products which is familiar from the chapter on property in the *Second Treatise*.[18] Thus, theological voluntarists of this variety supposed a moral fact to underlie and explain the obligatory force of God's will expressed in natural law.

This kind of view contains an obvious tension. Doubts about independently existing, obligation-creating moral facts which are evident to right reason are not likely to be settled by taking obligation to derive from divine will, if that must itself be supported by the moral fact of God's right to rule. The problem is not that this variety of theological voluntarism is inconsistent. It is rather that its appeal cannot arise from general metaphysical and epistemological worries about obligation-creating moral facts, but only from worries about any such fact *other than* one that creates the obligation to obey God.

The sort of theological voluntarist picture to which such general worries led was a more thoroughgoing positivism typified by John Selden, Hobbes, and the Locke of a later period (though not, perhaps, of his latest period, as we shall see).[19] Selden is little known to philosophers these days, but his *De Iure Naturali*, published in 1640, was an important and influential work. Tuck calls it "the first example of the English interest in the nature of moral obligation."[20] The reason Seiden looms large in the seventeenth-century background to Shaftesbury is that he was apparently the first philosopher to propose that the *bond* of natural law, its power to

[16] John Locke, *Essays on the Law of Nature*, ed. W. von Leyden (Oxford: Oxford University Press, 1954), p. 185. Von Leyden's introduction contains an excellent discussion of the development of Locke's ideas about natural law.

[17] Samuel Pufendorf, *De Jure Naturae et Gentium* ed. C.H. Oldfather [1672] (Oxford: Oxford University Press), I.vi.5, p. 91, and I.vi.12, p. 101. For a general account of Pufendorf on obligation to which I am much indebted, see J.B. Schneewind, "Pufendorf's Place in the History of Ethics," *Synthese*, vol. 72 (1987), pp. 123–55; see esp. pp. 143–48.

[18] John Locke, *A Second Treatise of Government*. For Culverwell's view, see *An Elegant and Learned Discourse of the Light of Nature*, ed. Robert A. Greene and Hugh MacCallum (Toronto: University of Toronto Press, 1971), pp. 39–52.

[19] Here I mean Locke's writings after *Essays on the Law of Nature* through the first edition of the *Essay Concerning Human Understanding*. This includes "Of Ethick in General," in Peter King, *The Life of John Locke, with extracts from his Correspondence, Journals, and Common-place Books* (London: Henry Colburn, 1829).

[20] See Richard Tuck, *Natural Rights Theories* (Cambridge: Cambridge University Press, 1979), p. 90. Here I rely primarily on Tuck's discussion of Selden. It is remarkable that Selden is not even mentioned in Raphael's "Bibliographical Note of Some British Writers" at the end of v. ii of *British Moralists*; nor does Sidgwick mention him in *Outlines*.

bind rational subjects, consists in a *motive,* albeit a restraining motive created by a "superior power." According to Selden, God's subjects are bound by His dictates (and these are *law*) precisely because He credibly threatens unavoidable punishment. It is sufficient for God to create binding law that He create an inescapable motive for His subjects to do what He says.

Locke reinforced these thoughts when he wrote, first, that "an understanding free agent naturally follows that which causes pleasure to it, and shuns misery," and, second, that "that is morally good or evil which, by the intervention of the will of an intelligent free agent, draws pleasure or pain after it, not by any natural consequence, but by the intervention of that power." By a moral evil, he meant a violation of an obligation – a transgression of a law, by which a punishment is annexed to it."[21] Thus, for Locke (explicitly) and for Selden (implicitly), rational subjects are obligated to do what they are unavoidably motivated to do (the first remark) by virtue of the interposition of another will (the second remark).[22]

This brings us to Hobbes. Hobbes's writings might seem the likeliest place to look for Shaftesbury's assumption that interest creates obligation. But while there are elements of Hobbes's view that push in this direction, he certainly never says any such thing. It is scarcely possible here to piece together the complex structure of remarks that Hobbes makes relating to obligation, but we can indicate briefly why any reasonable construal of his use of 'obligation' is incompatible with Shaftesbury's assumption. The major reason, to use a slogan of Hobbes's, is that, for him, "obligation is thraldom."[23] To be under an obligation is to be in *someone else's* power. Exactly what sort of power, however, is something of a question. Hobbes's definition of obligation in *Leviathan* suggests a *normative* power: "when a man hath ... abandoned, or granted away his right; then he is said to be OBLIGED, or BOUND, not to hinder those, to whom such right is granted, or abandoned, from the benefit of it."[24] The original right derives from the "right of nature" each has "to use his own power, as he will himself, for the preservation of his own nature."[25]

But in what could this normative power itself consist? Here we face a question to which Hobbes is bound by his general epistemology and metaphysics to give some answer other than that it is a metaphysically irreducible power evident to right reason. Hobbes does accept a version of the Grotian doctrine that the "law of nature" is "found out by reason."[26] And in *De Cive* he remarks both that "that is done by right which is not done against reason" and that "we ought to judge those

[21] "Of Ethick in General," p. 309.

[22] Note that a motive can be unavoidable in the relevant sense without being determining, "all things considered."

Selden also requires that the will be a "superior power." "An equal cannot bind me, for we may untie one another." (Selden, *Opera Omnia,* v. iii, ed. D. Wilkins (London: 1726)). Tuck discusses this passage at p. 92 but leaves out a crucial part.

[23] Thomas Hobbes, *Leviathan,* ed. Michael Oakeshott (Oxford: Basil Blackwell, 1960), p. 65.

[24] For a defense of the view that this is the core of Hobbes's view of obligation, see Brian Barry, "Warrender and His Critics," *Philosophy,* vol. 43 (1968); David Gauthier, *The Logic of Leviathan* (Oxford: Oxford University Press, 1969).

[25] *Leviathan,* p. 84.

[26] *ibid.*

actions only wrong, which are repugnant to right reason."[27] But by right reason he does not mean a power of intuiting normative truths. Reason "is nothing but *reckoning* ... of the consequences of general names."[28] And the laws of nature are known to reason because "they are but conclusions, or theorems concerning what conduceth to [our] conservation and defence."[29] Right reason does not set ends by recognizing normative truths; it is purely instrumental.

To square with this, Hobbes needs an account of obligation that can explain why it is instrumentally rational to do what is obligatory. The likeliest candidate is an extension of Selden's idea that obligation consists in an unavoidable motive created by another's will. In *De Cive*, Hobbes refers to what he calls "natural obligation" as a liberty "taken away by hope, or fear, according to which the weaker despairing of his own power to resist, cannot but yield to the stronger."[30] This *suggests* the following account: an obligation consists in a motive for doing something that is unavoidably conclusive, insofar as the person is instrumentally rational, created by another's will. Since Hobbes believes that no one in the state of nature has overawing power, and, therefore, that no one can create an unavoidably conclusive motive for others not to challenge him, this would explain the "right of nature." None is obligated with respect to anyone else; all are equally free.[31]

Like Selden's, Hobbes's account makes it a necessary condition of being obligated that one be subject to the will of another. This is quite foreign to Shaftesbury's idea, since it makes obligation depend on a condition external to the agent's rational will. To be obligated, the agent must be subject to a restraining bond emanating from another will. However, Hobbes also held, again like Selden, that, to create this bond, it is sufficient that the other create a situation that gives the agent a motive of a certain sort. He called this motive the "tye" or "bond" of obligation, which he distinguished from the fact of obligation itself. Only power that an agent cannot rationally hope to resist creates obligation; it does so by creating a motive not to resist that is rationally conclusive, whatever the circumstances.

---

[27] *De Cive: The English Version Entitled, in the First Edition, Philosophical Rudiments Concerning Government and Society*, ed. Howard Warrender (Oxford: Clarendon Press, 1983), p. 52.

[28] *ibid.*, p. 25. And see p. 20: "By this imposition of names, some of larger, some of stricter signification, we turn the reckoning of the consequences of things imagined in the mind, into a reckoning of the consequences of appellations." *Cf.* also Hobbes's description of "regulated thoughts" as thinking from causes to effects and effects to causes (p. 15).

[29] *ibid.*, p. 104.

[30] *ibid.*, p. 187. This is the relation we stand in to God. It is presumably on these grounds that Hobbes claims that the laws of nature create obligations when they are viewed as commands of God. See *Leviathan*, pp. 104–5.

[31] For Hobbes to hold this view consistently with his *Leviathan* definition, he must hold that voluntarily laying down a right creates the requisite motives in the agent. Clearly, he accepts the burden of defending this in the case of the mutual transfer of right that empowers the Sovereign. It seems, however, that he also believes that there can be cases in the state of nature where an obligation to perform exists and where the existence of rationally conclusive motives emanating from overawing power is not obvious (for example, where a contract has been entered into and the other has already performed). See *Leviathan*, p. 95.

IV. The Source of Shaftesbury's Assumption

Being bound in this way by another will is, however, only partly being bound from without. The agent is bound only if he or she has conclusive rational motives for acting as the other wills. Moreover, an agent can be bound in this way, even if not technically obliged, *whether or not* the motives result from the intervention of another will. Once an internal account of obligation's bond is given, it becomes possible to think of obligation as itself internal, consisting simply in the bond created by rationally conclusive motives. This is the assumption that Shaftesbury evidently expected his readers to share.

I know of three places in British ethics before Shaftesbury where this possibility is more or less explicitly taken up. One is Cumberland's *Treatise of the Law of Nature* (1672). A second is Locke's revision of his Chapter 21 on "Power" in the second and later editions of the *Essay* (1694). And the third is Ralph Cudworth's manuscripts on free will (probably written in the 1670s and 1680s), only one of which has ever been published.[32] Each is of substantial interest.

Cumberland's version is interesting both because he is apparently aware of the reforming steps he is taking even as he seeks to situate them within the "received definition" of obligation. Commenting on the Justinian formulation of obligation, he remarks that it is "somewhat *obscure* from metaphors: for the *mind* of man is not properly '*tied with bonds*'."[33] Responding to the question of what could "superinduce a *necessity* of doing or forbearing any thing, upon a human mind deliberating about a thing future,"[34] Cumberland answers that a rational agent necessarily seeks his own happiness.[35] Therefore, if an act "is certainly one of the causes necessarily requir'd to that happiness, which he naturally, and consequently necessarily desires,"[36] then it will be necessary in the requisite sense – it will be a necessary means to an end he necessarily has as rational. That an act is necessary in this sense does not entail that an agent will do it in fact, even if he believes it thus necessary – and it had better not, on the principle that 'ought' implies 'can not' as well as 'can'. "Those *arguments,* which prove our obligation, ... would *certainly prevail* [with agents], unless the *ignorance*, turbulent *affections*, or *rashness* of men, like the *fault in the balance,* oppos'd their efficacy."[37]

---

[32] As *A Treatise of Freewill*, ed. John Allen (London: John W. Parker, 1838). Excerpts are collected in Raphael, *British Moralists*, i.120–34. The remaining manuscripts are housed in the British Library. They are described in John Passmore's appendix to his *Ralph Cudworth: An Interpretation* (Cambridge: Cambridge University Press, 1951). Unfortunately, Passmore does not discuss this aspect.

[33] *Treatise of the Laws*, p. 233.

[34] *ibid.*

[35] Though not only his own happiness: Cumberland also thinks that agents can and do directly seek the happiness of others. Moreover, he believes that only considerations concerning the happiness of oneself or others can be motivating. His direct answer to the question of "what can superinduce a necessity of doing or forbearing any thing, upon a human mind deliberating upon a thing future" is "propositions promising good or evil, to ourselves or to others, consequent upon what we are to do" (p. 233).

Here, however, his argument trades on the assumption that agents necessarily seek their own happiness: "Altho' I have suppos'd, that *every one* necessarily seeks *his own greatest Happiness,* yet I am far from thinking that to be the entire and adequate End of *any one*" (p. 234).

[36] *ibid.*, p. 233.

[37] *ibid.*, p. 237.

Cumberland never abandoned Selden's distinction, which he quoted with approval, between "conclusions of reason, consider'd barely in themselves" on the one hand and what has the force of law and therefore generates obligation on the other. And he agreed with Selden that natural law must be "establish'd by God." But, unlike Selden, and like Shaftesbury, he maintained that the *naturally* good consequences of virtue and ill consequences of vice were sufficient to establish an obligation to virtue without recourse to hellfire or heavenly reward. The fundamental truth of ethics, the (single) Law of Nature, is confirmable empirically by natural reason. This is that "the endeavour, to the utmost of our power, of promoting the common good of the whole system of rational agents, conduces, as far as in us lies, to the good of every part, in which our own happiness, as that of a part, is contain'd. But contrary actions produce contrary effects, and consequently our own misery, among that of others."[38] When we discover this, we not only discover that virtue (benevolence) is the necessary means to our necessary end, we also have all the evidence we need of the existence of a God whose wish that His creatures be benevolent is expressed in the natural sanctions he has created. The evidence that benevolence is rationally necessary is also sufficient, therefore, to establish that this necessity has the "form of a law" requisite to create obligation.

The suggestion that Locke is another possible source of Shaftesbury's assumption may well be unexpected. After all, the official doctrine of the *Essay* was that "the true ground of Morality . . . can only be the Will and Law of a God, who sees Men in the dark, has in His Hand Rewards and Punishments, and Power enough to call to account the Proudest Offender."[39] Nonetheless, in his revisions of Chapter 21 (from the second edition on), Locke uses 'obligation' in a way that seems identical to Shaftesbury's. The "tendency of their ["intellectual beings'"] nature to happiness," he there writes, "is an obligation, and motive to them, to take care not to mistake, or miss it."[40]

What is particularly intriguing about the view of obligation implicit in Locke's revised Chapter 21 is that it is placed within an account of the power of *self-determination* or *autonomy*, i.e., a distinctive kind of liberty "intellectual beings" have, consisting in the power to determine their own wills by forming reflective practical judgments with motivational force. Every intellectual being as such, God included, necessarily wills his own happiness. But imperfect intellectual beings do not necessarily know what will best achieve this end, nor do they necessarily will it when they know it, since their will is determined by the greatest "present uneasiness" or desire. Nonetheless, they also possess a power of reflective consideration which they can engage "to suspend the prosecution of this or that desire," and "consider the objects of [their desires]; examine them on all sides, and weigh them with others." Through this process, they acquire reflectively informed desires they can express in a practical judgment.[41] This makes it "in our power, to

---

[38] *ibid.*, p. 16.

[39] *Essay*, p. 69.

[40] *ibid.*, p. 267.

[41] *ibid.*, p. 263. Locke, like Cudworth in his manuscripts on free will, generally reserves 'judgment' for the conclusion of a process of weighing and balancing.

raise our desires, in a due proportion to the value of that good."[42] And "when, upon due *examination*, we have *judg'd*, we have done our *duty*, all that we can, or *ought* to do, in pursuit of our happiness."[43] Thus, according to the Locke of the revised Chapter 21, imperfect rational beings have an obligation to seek the only end they necessarily seek as rational, because they have a power of reflective self-determination through which they can bring their wills into accord with this obligatory end.[44]

The idea that moral obligation is internal because it results from the autonomous rational activity of moral subjects is familiar from Kant. It is surprising, however, to find anticipations of this view in Locke's *Essay*, even if the version implicit in Locke's revised Chapter 21 differs from Kant's in several crucial respects.[45] In fact, however, Locke is far from the only British moralist to break from the earlier natural law view (which was, of course, his own official position) that obligation consists in a restraint imposed from outside the agent by another will, and argue that, on the contrary, it is a constraint that an autonomous agent imposes on itself.[46,47] It is not possible even to begin to demonstrate it here, but this is precisely the position that Cudworth takes in his manuscripts.[48] It is, moreover, the view that emerges when Shaftesbury's *Characteristics* are read as a whole, and in conjunction with his notebooks. And it is an important strain in Butler's *Sermons*.

The interest of these British moralists in the idea of autonomy and its relation to obligation is an important phenomenon, and one that has gone virtually unnoticed by scholars. Partly, this can be explained by the fact that some of the relevant published texts have been relatively inaccessible, and that some extremely important texts are still unpublished. In addition, these writers did not have a developed vocabulary to make clear what they were talking about. 'Autonomy' as applicable to individual conduct did not enter into English until Coleridge's discussions of Kant in the early nineteenth century.[49] Cudworth coined

---

[42] *ibid.*, p. 264.

[43] *ibid.*, pp. 263–64. Emphasis added, except to 'examination'.

[44] That Locke appears to be relating obligation and autonomy in a new way in his revision of Chapter 21 has also been noticed by Andrzej Rapaczinski (*Nature and Politics: Liberalism in the Philosophies of Hobbes, Locke, and Rousseau* (Ithaca: Cornell University Press, 1987), pp. 126–76). I cannot accept, however, many of the details of his account.

[45] The most substantial difference is that, for Locke, free rational activity is characterized relative to what he takes to be its given end – the agent's own happiness. For Kant, any principle of the will grounded in this end cannot be regarded as a practical law, and any action determined by it will be counted heteronomous.

[46] If, indeed, Locke ever did. I claim only that the view I have mentioned is implicit in Locke's revision of Chapter 21, not that he actually held the view.

[47] Certainly the dominant view in British ethics of the first half of the eighteenth century was that obligation was internal, and even when it was not directly tied to a self-imposed constraint of a rationally autonomous agent, there is sometimes an indirect connection made to the idea of free rational agency. Thus John Clarke: "the only sort of ties or obligations the mind of a free agent can be under, [are] the considerations of happiness or misery" (in *An Examination of What Has Been Advanced Relating to Moral Obligation in a Late Pamphlet, Entitled, A Defence of the Answer to the Remarks Upon Dr. Clarke's Exposition of the Church Catechism* (London, 1730), p. 23). The "Dr. Clarke" of the title is Samuel Clarke. John Clarke was the Master of the Public Grammar School in Hull and a fairly important contributor to early eighteenth-century British moral philosophy.

[48] This will seem surprising to those whose exposure to Cudworth is only through the passages in Raphael or in Selby-Bigge (*British Moralists*, 2 vols. (Indianapolis: Bobbs-Merrill Co., 1964)).

[49] *The Compact Edition of the Oxford English Dictionary* (Oxford: Oxford University Press, 1985), vol. i, p. 575.

'autexousy' and 'autexousious power' to refer to rational agents' "power of determining themselves" in his tome, *The True Intellectual System of the Universe* (1678).[50] Needless to say, it did not catch on.

V. SHAFTESBURY, AUTONOMY AND SELF-IMPOSED OBLIGATION

It seems clear that Shaftesbury bases his conclusion that there is an obligation to virtue on the thought that any agent has a rationally conclusive motive to have a virtuous character, since that is a necessary means to a rationally necessary end: his or her own interest. Indeed, on Shaftesbury's natural teleology, "that every creature should seek its good and not its misery is necessary in itself."[51] Rational beings are distinguished from nonrational interest-seekers, Shaftesbury thinks, by their capacity for a kind of self-reflection through which they can gain a motivating conception of their good. Unlike nonrational beings, they are not simply in the grips of naturally-given desires at any point in time. They can reflect and see their present ends as what they happen to desire presently, but perhaps would not desire were they adequately to consider their desires' etiology and the true nature of their desires' objects. Shaftesbury describes in some detail a self-reflective capacity he takes rational agents to have to take a more objective perspective on their ends; they thereby can form a motivationally effective conception of their own good, all things considered.

Now since it is generally thought to be a major achievement of Shaftesbury's to have made a convincing case both for the existence of *other-regard* as an independent psychological motive, and for the view that virtue must engage this motive and cannot be wholly self-interested, it may seem puzzling that he should have maintained that a rational agent's supreme end is his own greatest good.[52] But while Shaftesbury certainly was no psychological or ethical egoist, he was a sort of *rational* egoist.[53] Human beings are, he thought, part of an organic "system of all things," a "universal nature." So they cannot flourish as individuals apart from flourishing relationships to a flourishing whole.[54] Still, when it comes to the question of rational justification, Shaftesbury held that this is to be settled by

---

[50] *ibid.*, p. 569.

[51] This comes from what Rand calls Shaftesbury's "Philosophical Regimen," philosophical notebooks that Shaftesbury maintained from 1698 to 1712. (Benjamin Rand, ed., *The Life, Unpublished Letters, and Philosophical Regimen of Anthony, Earl of Shaftesbury* (London: Swan Sonnenschein & Co., 1900), p. 92.) Hereinafter *Life of Shaftesbury*. Cf. also p. 30, and *Characteristics*, i.80, 199, 243.

[52] Thus:

> Whatsoever therefore is done which happens to be advantageous to the species through an affection merely towards self-good, does not imply any more goodness in the creature than as the affection itself is good. Let him, in any particular, act ever so well, if at the bottom it be that selfish affection alone which moves him, he is in himself still vicious. Nor can any creature be considered otherwise when the passion towards self-good, though ever so moderate, is his real motive in the doing that to which a natural affection for his kind ought by right to have inclined him.

[53] *Characteristics*, i. 249. Certainly he was so regarded by Hutcheson and Butler. See Hutcheson, *Illustrations on the Moral Sense* (Cambridge: Harvard University Press, 1971), p. 174; Butler, Preface to the *Sermons*, [26], in *The Works of Bishop Butler*, ed. J.H. Bernard, vol. i (London: Macmillan, 1900), p. 11 [also in Butler, *Sermons*, ed. S. Darwall (Indianapolis: Hackett, 1983), p. 17].

[54] *Characteristics*, i.246.

looking to the agent's own good or interest, and not directly to the good of the whole. A helpful way to describe Shaftesbury's position would be to say that he actually held the position Butler is often supposed to have maintained in his famous "cool hour" passage: viz., that "though virtue or moral rectitude does indeed consist in affection to and pursuit of what is right and good, as such; yet, that when we sit down in a cool hour, we can neither justify to ourselves this or any other pursuit, till we are convinced that it will be for our happiness, or at least not contrary to it."[55]

Thus Shaftesbury took over the idea toward which the seventeenth-century natural law tradition had been tending: that the bond of obligation (indeed, obligation itself) consists in a rationally conclusive motive. By doing so, he was able to maintain some continuity with the modern tradition of natural law while at the same time rejecting that tradition's most central contentions about the nature of morality, as well as appropriating the notion of obligation for his own, quite different, purposes. His was an ethics of virtue, not an ethics of law, and he was sharply opposed to any view that would seek to explain the obligations of morality in terms of sanctions. Both Hobbists and theological voluntarists, he wrote in the Preface of his edition of Whichcote's *Sermons*, have "made *war* on virtue itself."[56]

Shaftesbury's role in establishing a notion of internal obligation in British thought of the early eighteenth century has generally been well-appreciated. But it has gone unnoticed that Shaftesbury also undertook to give an account of *autonomy* which is linked to his account of obligation. For Shaftesbury, obligation is, as it would be later for Kant, a constraining motive which autonomous rational beings impose on themselves. There are, of course, substantial differences between Shaftesbury's conception of autonomy and the view that Kant later advanced. An agent who looks to *his own* greatest good would, of course, be heteronomous according to Kant. And Shaftesbury had no truck with the Kantian idea that the root fact of moral experience is the thought that we are bound by a universal moral law which, because we are bound by it, we must be able autonomously to follow.[57] But Shaftesbury apparently agreed with Kant that free rational agents can only be bound by constraints that they autonomously impose on themselves. Moreover, he also foreshadowed the Kantian doctrine that moral value of character and conduct requires self-consciously moral motivation:

> If a creature be generous, kind, constant, compassionate, yet if he cannot reflect on what he himself does, or sees others do, so as to take notice of what is worthy or honest, and make that notice or conception of worth and honesty to be an object of his affection, he has not the character of being virtuous. . . . [58]

[55] Butler should be understood here as referring to virtuous pursuits in general, and not necessarily on particular occasions. This would also have been Shaftesbury's view. See Joseph Butler, Sermon XI.20, in *Works*, p. 151. [*Sermons*, p. 56].

[56] *Select Sermons of Dr. Whichcote* (London: 1698). Benjamin Whichcote was a very influential member of the Cambridge Platonists.

[57] This is what Kant calls the "fact of reason" in *The Critique of Practical Reason*, ed. L.W. Beck (New York: Macmillan Publishing Co., 1985), pp. 30, 43, 47.

[58] *Characteristics*, i.253. See also i.251 and i.256–57.

Shaftesbury praises the greater virtue of the person whose virtue is earned – who "by temper" is "passionate, angry, fearful, amorous, yet resists these passions, and notwithstanding the force of their impression adheres to virtue" by raising the affection to virtue itself through his own self-reflective activity.[59] Still, he thinks that this affection provides a *rational* motive only because of its role in the agent's overall good. For him, autonomy consists in the self-imposition of constraints of the agent's good. Virtue thus derives whatever obligatory force it has by its relation to the agent's interest, whereas for Kant the moral law is obligatory in itself, and autonomy is the free self-imposition of universal law.[60]

Shaftesbury treats autonomy extensively in two places. One is *Soliloquy, or Advice to an Author*, which is included in *Characteristics*. He nominally addresses this work to authors of books, but remarks elsewhere that this is "pretence"; his real aim "has been to correct manners and regulate lives."[61] He is concerned to show how, through the self-reflective process he calls "soliloquy," rational agents can be authors of their own conduct. The second place is a series of notebooks Rand called *Philosophical Regimen*.[62] Shaftesbury is preoccupied there with Stoic themes and texts, principally those of Marcus Aurelius and Epictetus. The most important for our purposes is Epictetus's doctrine, of which Shaftesbury develops his own version, that, while all conduct is determined by "opinion" and "fancy," rational agents have a "ruling principle" (*hegemonikon*), their own reason, through which they can critically examine and thereby rationally determine their own opinions and fancies, thus governing the determinants of action and, consequently, their own conduct.

As Shaftesbury interprets this view, the way reason operates is not, in Platonic or Grotian fashion, by intuitively grasping a metaphysically independent good or natural law to which fancy then responds. Rather, Shaftesbury associates reason with "a power of judging the fancies"[63] themselves that enables the agent to revise his beliefs and desires by gaining a conception of their place in an objective natural order.

All action results from beliefs and desires; whether conduct is self-determined or not depends on what role the self plays in determining these determinants of action. An agent who simply acts on the strongest opinion and fancy as they happen to come is "moved and wrought upon, wound up and governed exteriorly, as if there were nothing that ruled within or had the least control."[64] Simply possessing a concept of his or her overall good which the agent takes as the ultimate aim may not help, since this could itself simply be momentarily responsive to externally-given present desires. "The man in anger has a different happiness from the man in love. And the man lately become covetous has a different notion of satisfaction from

---

[59] *ibid.*, i.256.

[60] In this way, Kant's view recalls the natural law tradition's claim that obligation depends on law. However, according to him, the relevant law is one that a free rational being legislates for himself.

[61] *Characteristics*, ii.272.

[62] See note 51.

[63] *Life of Shaftesbury*, p. 174.

[64] *ibid.*, p. 114. This passage actually occurs in the context of some personal reflections, but the general point is one Shaftesbury frequently makes.

what he had before, when he was liberal."[65] To be governed "interiorly," to govern *himself,* the agent needs the capacity *presently* to take a standpoint other than that provided by present desire from which he can critically consider present desires themselves and, on the basis of this consideration, ratify or revise them or form new ones. To use a term of present-day discussion, he needs a more objective standpoint.[66] And according to Shaftesbury, the requisite standpoint is that of a being who exists through time in a natural order.[67]

Shaftesbury includes as an aspect of reason the capacity to objectify perspective.[68] By reflecting on themselves as natural beings with desires and beliefs that arise through various and sundry processes in an objective natural order, rational agents can form a conception of which objects will "hold good"[69] for them or "bear [them] out,"[70] and thus be part of their good through time. Shaftesbury describes in some detail a self-administered therapy available to rational beings ("soliloquy" or "self-converse") through which they can form a conception of their "real good" over time, by querying the sources of desire, the nature of their desires' objects, and by considering what they would want, all things considered, over time.

A major element in this process is bringing desires to consciousness by literally giving them voice. "There is nothing more useful in the management of the *visa* ... than to have a sort of custom of putting them into words, making them speak out and explain themselves as it were *viva-voce,* and not tacitly and murmuringly, not by a whisper and indirect insinuation, imperfectly, indistinctly, and confusedly, as their common way is."[71] The rational agent becomes his own audience in this soliloquy. By "a certain duplicity of soul," he can "divide himself into two parties": an orator who speaks from the standpoint of his present desires and an auditor who can listen to his remarks more objectively.[72] The auditor can then attempt to identify the desire and situate it within a psychological context, thereby undermining threats to autonomy posed by "sly" desires whose motive force depends on "insinuation" and secrecy.

> Thus I contend with fancy and opinion, and search the mint and foundery of imagination. For here the appetites and desires are fabricated: hence they derive their privilege and currency. If I can stop the mischief here and

---

[65] *Characteristics,* i.192.

[66] I refer here, of course, to Thomas Nagel's use of this notion. See, e.g., *The View From Nowhere* (New York: Oxford University Press, 1986).

[67] He needs a more objective standpoint than his own present standpoint, which may simply be in the grip of his desires, to grasp their nature, causes, and objects. However, the standpoint of rational choice for Shaftesbury is still the individual's own standpoint, albeit as existing through time, and as informed by an objective grasp of nature and his place in it; it is not the standpoint of one person among others, or the standpoint of the universe as a whole.

[68] "Every reasoning or reflecting creature is by his nature forced to endure the review of his own mind and actions," *Characteristics,* i.305. This passage suggests that objectification is entirely involuntary for rational agents, but Shaftesbury's whole point is that often taking a more objective standpoint is something the agent voluntarily does. *Cf.* "One would think there was nothing easier for us than to know our own minds, and understand what our main scope was ..." (*Characteristics,* i.113).

[69] *ibid.,* i.201.

[70] *ibid.,* i.218.

[71] *Life of Shaftesbury,* p. 166.

[72] *Characteristics,* i.112.

prevent false coinage, I am safe. 'Idea! wait awhile till I have examined thee, whence thou art and to whom thou retainest. Art thou of Ambition's train? or dost thou promise only pleasure? Say, what am I to sacrifice for thy sake? What honour? What truth? What manhood? What bribe is it thou bringest along with thee? Describe the flattering object, but without flattery; plain as the thing is, without addition, without sparing or reserve.[73]

The objective auditor thus turns critic and "addresses [the identified desires] familiarly without the least ceremony or respect"[74] in order to assess more objectively their relative importance in the agent's overall good.

Shaftesbury never explicitly mentions obligation in his description of soliloquy and self-determination, but it is implicit in his discussion. First, it follows from his view that an agent's obligation depends on his or her overall interest that a person is obligated to do what he or she would do if rationally autonomous. Second, the metaphor of self-government (and implicitly, of self-imposition of obligation) runs throughout his discussion of soliloquy, especially in the *Philosophical Regimen*. "How go I? This is a matter, and the only matter. This is of concern. This is mine, and at my peril. – How do I govern? The world? – No. But how do I govern MYSELF?"[75] It is important to appreciate that Shaftesbury does not mean by self-*government* the same weak sense of determination in which he also says that the will is "governed" by fancy and opinion. It is central to his idea that the self can take different standpoints *and* that it can, and *must* for genuine self-government, recognize the *authority* of the more objective standpoint of the agent's real interests over time. The "internal auditor" who constructs and expresses this perspective must "with an air of authority erect himself our counsellor and governor."[76] This is "the superior part which disciplines, instructs, and manages these subjects," and which has "authority and command."[77] Rational agents thus are capable of self-government in the more robust sense that, by taking the standpoint of their own objective interests over time, and recognizing the authority of judgment from that perspective, they can bind themselves. There is thus a link between Shaftesbury's assumption that obligation consists in a rationally authoritative motive and his view that self-governing rational activity involves a kind of practical thinking through which obligation is self-imposed. An autonomous agent imposes an obligation *in*

---

[73] For a measure of Epictetus's influence on Shaftesbury, compare the following from the *Discourses*: "For, just as Socrates used to tell us not to live a life unsubjected to examination, so we ought not to accept a sense-impression unsubjected to examination, but should say, 'Wait, allow me to see who you are and whence you come'..." (Epictetus, *The Discourses as Reported by Arrian*, trans. W.A. Oldfather, v. ii (Cambridge: Harvard University Press, 1985), p. 85.) *Cf.* also Epictetus's advice to "talk to yourself" (ii.97) and to "become your own pupil and your own teacher" (ii. 349). And Shaftesbury: "By virtue of this soliloquy he becomes two distinct persons. He is pupil and preceptor" (*Characteristics*, i.105–6). See Frederich A. Uehlein, *Kosmos und Subjectivität* (Freiburg/Munchen: Verlag Karl Alber, 1976) for a helpful discussion of Epictetus and Shaftesbury.

[74] *Characteristics*, i.123.

[75] *Life of Shaftesbury*, p. 102; see also p. 270.

[76] *Characteristics*, i.112.

[77] *Life of Shaftesbury*, p. 169; see also p. 171 ("the principal and commanding part") and *Characteristics*, i.122–23.

imposing a motive on himself; he does this by placing himself subject to motives he has from the standpoint he must acknowledge as authoritative in order to govern himself.

The idea that the obliging force of morality must be an internal motivational force is often associated with a Humean critique of rationalism in ethics. There is, however, a kind of ethical rationalism that agrees that obligation must be internal in this way. The most well-known example of this position is Kant's view that rational agents are obligated only by laws that they can create motives to follow through rationally autonomous self-imposition. But, as we have seen, Kant's view is by no means the only instance of the general thesis that rational agents are obligated by motives that they create for themselves by a form of practical thinking necessary for self-determination. This was Shaftesbury's view, and he is only one representative of a wider tradition in British ethics before Hume. It is ironic, then, that Shaftesbury's *Characteristics* should have played such an important historical role in solidifying the notion of internal obligation on which Hume's critique of rationalism would later trade. What lay behind the identification of obligation with motive for Shaftesbury and his tradition was their view of obligation's relation to an autonomy made possible by practical reason – a view that looked forward more to Kant than to Hume.

Philosophy, University of Michigan

NATURALISM AND PRESCRIPTIVITY*

By Peter Railton

Introduction: Setting the Problem

Statements about a person's good slip into and out of our ordinary discourse about the world with nary a ripple. Such statements are objects of belief and assertion, they obey the rules of logic, and they are often defended by evidence and argument. They even participate in common-sense explanations, as when we say of some person that he has been less subject to wild swings of enthusiasm and disappointment now that, with experience, he has gained a clearer idea of what is good for him. Statements about a person's good present themselves as being *about* something with respect to which our beliefs can be true or false, warranted or unwarranted. Let us speak of these features as the *descriptive* side of discourse about a person's good.

Discourse about a person's good also has another, *prescriptive* side, for to make or accept a judgment that something is good for someone is in some sense to recommend that thing to him and to those who care about him. Such a recommendation need not be overriding – there often is more to be considered in any given deliberation than the good of one particular individual. But someone who spoke in earnest to others about their own good, and then was simply puzzled when they took his remarks to be any sort of recommendation, would betray a lack of full competence with such discourse.

Philosophers have been struck by the difficulty of understanding how evaluative language, such as discourse about a person's good, could be at once essentially descriptive and essentially prescriptive. To be sure, there is no difficulty in seeing how a descriptive statement might come to function prescriptively. Suppose that I am looking for a lawyer and I overhear you say that Hoolihan always wins his cases. Your statement can function as a recommendation – once I have heard it – even though its content appears to be flatly descriptive. Its commending force appears not to reside essentially in the content of the statement itself, but rather depends upon a context in which my interest in finding a successful lawyer is already independently given.[1]

Similarly, there is no difficulty in seeing how a prescriptive judgment might come to function descriptively. A child soon learns that those things that an adult

* I would like to thank Paul Boghossian, Richard Brandt, David Copp, Stephen Darwall, William K. Frankena, Allan Gibbard, Donald Regan, Judith Jarvis Thomson, and David Velleman for discussion of some of the material contained in this text. I would also like to thank the editors of this volume for their assistance and patience.

[1] Are there prescriptions whose action-guiding force for agents depends upon no interest at all? There could be if a substantive theory of rationality were correct, for then there would be commands of reason that depend upon no interest or motivational state of the agent. However, part of the circumstances that constitute the setting for the problem discussed in this paper is a sense that no substantive theory of rationality can be made to work.

goes out of the way to label 'good for you' have certain characteristic features. When a child hears his parents prescribe taking a medicine, saying that it will be 'good for you', he effectively acquires the information that something unpleasant is in the offing. It would, however, be odd indeed to say that 'unpleasant' is part of the meaning of 'good for you'.

One can, then, use a description to recommend, or use a prescription to convey information. Discourse about a person's good seems to presuppose something more: an inherent, necessary connection between the content of the description and the force of the prescription. Yet G.E. Moore's "open question" argument has convinced many philosophers of the impossibility of finding a connection of this kind between good and any property captured entirely in descriptive, non-evaluative terms.[2] If any such property were constitutive of the meaning of 'good for so-and-so', the argument runs, then a statement identifying this property with a person's good would be a mere tautology, analytically true, and no more sense could be made of questioning it than of questioning the statement 'The good of a person is identical with that person's good'. But even if we consider 'The good of a person is identical with that person's pleasure' (which, of all such equations, has had the most philosophical advocates), it seems clear that to question this statement would not be absurd and would not betray a simple failure to grasp the meaning of its terms.

Very grand claims have been made on behalf of Moore's argument. Moore himself thought it to show that all attempts to define 'good' or to identify it with some natural property would involve outright fallacy. Such claims seem much too strong.[3] We can, however, say at least this much: application of the argument to every purported analysis of 'good' yet given has shown none of them to be utterly incontestable, so that none is obviously successful in stating an analytic truth.[4]

Moore believed that the failure of descriptive analyses of 'good' was no barrier to capturing what we above called the descriptive side of talk about good, because he held that 'good' refers to a non-natural property with which we have direct acquaintance by a kind of intellectual intuition. But most contemporary philosophers are unhappy with the Moorean idea of non-natural properties that are intuitively known, and many have concluded that the failure of descriptive analyses of 'good' raises fundamental questions about the status of value judgments. After all, it seems clear that most judgments of the goodness of particular things are synthetic statements, not tautologies. But, typically, synthetic statements concern natural properties, and our knowledge of their truth or falsity derives from experience. If all known attempts to identify the property of being good with some or other natural property have failed – as Moore's "open question" argument might

---

[2] See G.E. Moore, *Principia Ethica* (Cambridge: Cambridge University Press, 1903), esp. pp. 15ff. Strictly speaking, Moore's argument was applied not to conceptions of a person's good, but to good itself. For reasons we need not go into here, Moore believed treating "good for so-and-so" as a basic category to be inherently confused; see *Principia*, pp. 98ff.

[3] For an important early discussion, see W.K. Frankena, "The Naturalistic Fallacy," ed. Philippa Foot, *Theories of Ethics* (New York: Oxford University Press, 1967).

[4] I say 'obviously successful' because it remains possible that once some existing analysis has been fully understood and assimilated, and once all accidental connotations of the notion of 'good' have been stripped away (assuming such a thing to be possible), the analysis could emerge as incontestable.

might be used to argue – then where in the world does the property of being good fit, and how on earth can we come to have knowledge of it?

One philosophical response to these quandaries has been to deny that discourse about goodness is genuinely referential, despite the descriptive character of its surface grammar.[5] This *non-cognitivist* response seeks to remove any mystery about the two-sidedness of discourse about goodness by developing an interpretation of it as essentially prescriptive, but not fundamentally descriptive. The most straightforward version of non-cognitivism is expressivism, which claims that judgments of good express (but do not report) commendation.[6] Like exhortations or exclamations, judgments about goodness lack a descriptive content that could make them have truth-value or be objects of knowledge (hence the label non-cognitivist).

Sophisticated expressivist views allow that some secondary descriptive content may, through association, accrue to judgments about goodness – as exhibited a bit perversely in our earlier example about children and medicine – although, at bottom, the discourse remains non-cognitive. One of the tasks facing expressivists is to provide a systematic reinterpretation of discourse about a person's good in order to show how essentially expressive, non-cognitive language could display on its surface thoroughly descriptive, cognitive grammatical and logical behavior. Numerous technical problems beset such reinterpretations, and no one has as yet offered an expressivist account that satisfactorily preserves all the cognitive features of discourse about value.

Yet, whatever its technical problems, expressivism represents a powerful philosophical response to the problem posed by the "open question" argument. It holds out the promise of providing a fundamental explanation of value discourse, allowing us to see it as playing a distinctive role in language. This role involves the use of language to signal the presence of certain attitudes, and to exert thereby a kind of conversational force – to influence and negotiate, to shape attitudes and alliances, and to promote consensus where, on the one hand, consensus is desperately needed if groups are to function well, and where, on the other hand, consensus is quite unlikely to be produced entirely on the strength of flatly descriptive, observable matters. Further, expressivism takes to heart the point, prominent in much modern philosophy, that we must guard ourselves against being duped by taking linguistic forms at face value. It offers instead an epistemically respectable account of the role and character of value discourse that renders it an intelligible phenomenon and does not merely reify its categories.[7]

---

[5] An alternative approach is to accept the descriptive grammar of discourse about good at face value, but then to say that since nothing answering to its descriptions – nothing with the required connection between descriptive character and prescriptive force – could exist, statements about a person's good are always false. For an example of such an "error theory," applied to the moral case, see J.L. Mackie, *Ethics: Inventing Right and Wrong* (New York: Penguin, 1977).

[6] For two historically important examples of expressivist accounts of value discourse, see A.J. Ayer, *Language, Truth, and Logic*, 2d ed. (London: Gollantz, 1946), ch. 6, and C.L. Stevenson, *Ethics and Language* (New Haven: Yale University Press, 1944).

[7] For an impressive example of the explanatory power of expressivism, see Allan Gibbard, *Wise Choices, Apt Feelings* (Harvard University Press: forthcoming).

An alternative philosophical approach to the theory of value, the one I will be examining in this paper, also seeks an epistemically respectable explanation of value discourse. Yet the direction in which it moves is, in one sense, the opposite of expressivism. For it treats the cognitive character of value discourse – its descriptive side, as we have called it – as essential to it, and then seeks to account for the prescriptive force of value judgments as arising from the substantive content of such judgments. Unlike Moore's cognitivist position, however, the approach in question does not treat value properties as non-natural and *sui generis*, and therefore avoids the problems confronting Moore's account of the semantics and epistemology of value. Instead, the approach we will consider attempts to locate value properties among features of the world that are accessible to us through ordinary experience and that play a role in empirical explanations. It therefore treats value properties as *natural* properties, and so is a form of *naturalism* about value.[8]

Just as an expressivist faces the problem of showing how essentially non-cognitive uses of language could have the cognitive character of actual value discourse, the naturalistic cognitivist faces the complementary problem of explaining how an essentially descriptive use of language could have the prescriptive force of value discourse. Once again, the difficulty is not in finding a way in which descriptive discourse could, in appropriate contexts, be used prescriptively. As we have noted, that would be easy enough. The difficulty is in locating a tight, "internal," and necessary – or quasi-necessary – connection between the particular content attributed by the naturalist to judgments of value and some appropriate commending force. The principal concern of this paper will be with that difficulty, and with a possible strategy for contending with it. Some version of this strategy is available to various forms of naturalism, but it is most readily and conspicuously available to a certain class of hedonistic naturalists, who hold that the experience of happiness – viewed as a kind of psychological state – is the only thing intrinsically good for a person.[9] Although I do not find hedonism the most plausible naturalistic doctrine about a person's good, I do think it underrated, and it does nicely exhibit the strategy I wish to discuss.[10]

However, before discussing this strategy (in Section III), a few preliminary remarks about value (Section I) and naturalism (Section II) may be in order.

---

[8] I certainly do not mean to have given a definition of 'natural property' or 'naturalism' in this way. More will be said about naturalism in subsequent sections. For now, let me note only that what seems to me to be of interest in naturalism is not a metaphysical doctrine about what sorts of things are part of – or not part of – "Nature," but rather a methodological stance reflecting our experience of the ways in which useful predictive and explanatory theories have been achieved. Anyone who would be a naturalist in this methodological sense must regard it as a matter for inquiry, not definition, what sorts of properties can figure in developed, explanatory empirical theories – that is, what sorts of properties are "natural."

[9] I use the expression 'happiness' rather than 'pleasure' in characterizing hedonism because of the unfortunately narrow connotations of the latter. I do intend 'happiness' to pick out a class of experiential states.

[10] For a view I find more plausible, see Peter Railton, "Facts and Values," *Philosophical Topics*, vol. 14 (Fall 1986), pp. 5–31.

I. VALUE: A PERSON'S GOOD

We are here occupied in this paper with one species of value, that which is realized in a person's own good, sometimes called his well-being or welfare. This sort of value should be distinguished from many others. A life, after all, can be good for many things. It can benefit others; it can advance knowledge; it can serve as a model of how not to behave. We are interested in the way a life can be good for the person living it, and intrinsically so.[11] That which has intrinsic value has value in its own right, for its own sake. Nothing need be added or done to such a thing in order for this value to be realized.

In particular, the sort of intrinsic good we will discuss is *nonmoral* value, that component of the good a life may hold for the person living it which is logically independent of the moral qualities of that person.[12] For example, pleasures that are morally deserved, morally undeserved, and morally indifferent all have something in common that enters into the determination of how well or ill a life goes for the person leading it. This shared thing is the nonmoral value of pleasure. Some may wonder whether anything could possess intrinsic value if it really were morally deficient, but even so stern a moralist as Immanuel Kant believed there to be sufficient distance between how well someone's life goes and how virtuous he is to make necessary religious postulates that would secure the happiness of morally good lives.[13]

II. THE NATURE OF NATURALISM

Two Kinds of Naturalism

Since I propose to discuss a naturalistic approach to the particular species of value that constitutes a person's intrinsic nonmoral good, some initial explanation is needed of what naturalism in value theory might amount to, and why one might pursue it. (A caveat: I cannot claim to speak for more than one contemporary naturalist.)

Naturalism can be a doctrine about either method or substance. *Methodological naturalism* holds that philosophy does not possess a distinctive, *a priori* method able to yield substantive truths that, in principle, are not subject to any sort of empirical test. Instead, a methodological naturalist believes that philosophy should proceed *a*

---

[11] I will not try to say with any rigor what it is for the value realized in a life to be good *for* the person living it. It seems uncontroversial in present-day philosophy that, at a minimum, in order for something to be good for a person, that person must exist at the time of realization. By this criterion, it could be part of my good that I have certain experiences or engage in certain activities, but it could not be part of my good that people think well of me after my death. Aristotle believed that one's *eudaimonia* could be affected – at least for a certain length of time – by events occurring after one's death (*Nicomachean Ethics*, book I, chapter 10), but that may be a reason for thinking that we should not without qualification translate *eudaimonia* as "a person's own good" or "happiness."

[12] According to an important tradition in moral philosophy – utilitarianism – intrinsic nonmoral value is not only independent of moral value, but prior to it, part of its very foundation. This is a view I find compelling, and one which makes our discussion especially relevant to the foundations of ethics. However, I will not attempt to argue for such a view here. Our question about the possibility of naturalism lies within the theory of nonmoral value itself, and does not presuppose any particular moral theory.

[13] Immanuel Kant, *Critique of Practical Reason*, trans. L.W. Beck (Indianapolis: Bobbs-Merrill, 1956), pp. 128ff., and *Religion within the Limits of Reason Alone*, trans. T.M. Greene and H.H. Hudson (New York: Harper and Row, 1960), p. 5n.

posteriori, in tandem with – perhaps as a particularly abstract and general part of – the broadly empirical inquiry carried on in the natural and social sciences.

Substantive naturalism, in contrast, is not in the first instance a view about philosophical methods, but about philosophical conclusions. A substantive naturalist advances a philosophical account of some domain of human language or practice that provides an interpretation of its central concepts in terms amenable to empirical inquiry.

How are these two forms of naturalism related? One need not be a methodological naturalist in order to advocate substantive naturalism, and, indeed, substantive naturalistic interpretations have at times been defended by the claim that their statements have the status of analytic truths, arrived at by *a priori* conceptual analysis. A substantive naturalist of this stripe – an "analytic naturalist" – is unlikely to be a methodological naturalist, for methodological naturalists have characteristically viewed interpretive tasks as substantive, rather than merely formal, and have therefore denied that interpretations can be defended by entirely *a priori* means.

Equally, a methodological naturalist need not arrive at substantive naturalist conclusions. A philosopher adopting a naturalistic method might conclude, for example, that expressivism offers the best account of what is going on in discourse about value, and hence that value judgments do not possess cognitive meaning, naturalistic or otherwise.

The two forms of naturalism are therefore not essentially connected. Although, as it happens, the contemporary naturalism with which we will be concerned here is both methodological and substantive, its primary allegiance is owed to methodological naturalism. It is not a view driven by metaphysical considerations about what sorts of entities do or can exist, and so it does not start out with a definition of 'natural property' meant to divide the realm of possible being into the Real and the Unreal. Rather, our naturalist is impressed by the fact that claims about the world which have, historically, been deemed by philosophers to be *a priori* true – the principle of sufficient reason, the Euclidean structure of space, the restriction of mechanical interaction to local contact, the nonexistence of vacua, and so on – have, with distressing regularity, been revised or abandoned in the face of emerging scientific theories. What is striking here is not that allegedly *a priori* philosophical statements which were believed true in the eighteenth century are now rejected, since, after all, many of the *a posteriori* statements of eighteenth-century science are also now heartily disbelieved. The striking thing is that the development of scientific theory has shown us how claims which seemed logically or conceptually true when matters were viewed in a strictly philosophical way could nonetheless come to seem empirically false as a result of the effort to construct powerful explanatory empirical theories. In such cases, it often seems possible in retrospect to account for the *sense* of logical or quasi-logical necessity that attended certain claims in this way: the conceptual categories embedded in language at any given time characteristically present themselves as fixed and definitive – for example, the history of linguistic revision that lies behind existing categories typically is no longer visible to contemporary users of the language.

Methodological naturalism owes its inspiration, in part, to the thought that, although the remedy for the inadequacies of eighteenth-century science seems to have been the ever-more-ambitious pursuit of systematic science, the inadequacies of eighteenth-century philosophy have not been remedied by an ever-more-ambitious pursuit of systematic philosophy. It seems to the methodological naturalist, therefore, that philosophers who can see from a historical perspective the danger of becoming entrapped by treating evolving linguistic categories as fixed should resist the temptation to view philosophical inquiry as somehow methodologically prior to science, and should instead attempt as best they can to integrate their work with the ongoing development of empirical theory. This is not a recommendation of philosophical passivity, but instead an effort to identify a more productive direction for philosophical activism to take.

Thus, when the naturalist with whom we will be concerned puts forward his substantive naturalistic theory of value, he does so as part of an attempt to develop a good explanatory account of what is going on in evaluative practices involving claims about a person's own good. Our naturalist's central claims hence are, at bottom, synthetic rather than analytic. This would be so even if he put forward his naturalistic interpretation using *reforming definitions*, for a reforming definition is revisable as well as revisionist, and must earn its place by facilitating the construction of worthwhile theories.[14]

The "Open Question" Argument Revisited

One important consequence of the fact that our naturalist's interpretation of discourse about a person's good is put forward on methodologically naturalistic grounds is that Moore's open question argument no longer applies directly to it. For the naturalist's interpretation is based, however indirectly, upon experience, and does not purport to be strictly analytic or utterly incontestable – indeed, it presents itself as remaining open to further challenges.

Our naturalist's interpretation is hedonistic; that is, he claims that the experience of happiness alone constitutes a person's intrinsic nonmoral good. This claim is put forward as part of a methodologically naturalistic project, for example, as a reforming definition or an *a posteriori* statement of property identity. What would such a claim be like?

A more familiar example may help. Consider the scientific identification of water with H_2O. It was, of course, a significant empirical discovery – not a result of *a priori* analysis – that water is a compound of two parts hydrogen and one part oxygen. If it be said that this claim now has the status of a definition, then surely it is a reforming definition, for an important revision in thinking about water – and about chemistry in general – was required in order to deny water the status of an element, and to introduce the principle of distinguishing chemicals by their molecular composition rather than their macroscopic features. Competent eighteenth-century speakers could learn the meaning of 'water' as it occurred in ordinary language, and could later be introduced to the meaning of 'H_2O' as it

[14] For discussion of the use of reforming definitions, see Richard Brandt, *A Theory of the Good and the Right* (Oxford: Clarendon, 1979), esp. pp. 3–16, 23.

occurs in chemistry, and still find the question whether water is H_2O *conceptually* open. So, for them, the identity statement 'Water is H_2O' would fail the "open question" test. This did not, however, rule out the identity statement, because it was not among the ambitions of scientists making this statement to state a conceptual truth.

Of course, once 'Water is H_2O' has been introduced as a reforming definition – for example, in the teaching of chemistry – then the expression 'Water is H_2O' becomes true-by-virtue-of-meaning in a clear sense, and so the question of whether water is H_2O becomes, in this sense, conceptually closed. But this reforming definition could itself be altered or dropped under the pressure of further empirical discoveries or theoretical developments, and so it does not really purport to close the question with conceptual necessity.

In a similar way, a hedonistic naturalism based upon *a posteriori* identity claims or reforming definitions would not purport conceptually to close the question of whether a person's good is identical to the experience of happiness. And because conceptual closure is not among its ambitions, the "open question" argument could not properly be used to refute it, either.

Revisionism

Even if Moore's "open question" argument cannot be deployed directly against an interpretation of discourse about a person's good that does not purport to express analytic truths, a significant critical function may still be served by pressing Moorean questions against such interpretations. For it would be a challenge to any theoretical identification or reforming definition of P in terms of Q to argue that there is something central to the notion of P that does not appear to be captured by Q; this would make the question "I can see that this is Q, but is it P?" genuinely compelling, not just barely possible. How troublesome such open questions may be will depend, of course, upon the character of the alternative accounts in the offing for P – and also upon whether we think P is clear enough as it stands, or conceptually basic, or so unlikely to be amenable to clear, unambiguous explication in terms we find less problematic that we are prepared to do without any analysis of P at all.

Since almost any notion P found in natural language will draw its meaning from multiple sources, and will have taken on diverse functions – and possessed diverse relations to other concepts – at various points in its evolution, it is to be expected that any rendering of that concept intended to make it sufficiently clear to suit purposes of theory-construction will be, to some degree, revisionist. So it was with water and H_2O, and so it will be with any significant evaluative concept. This revisionism means that some open questions will remain. It lies among the tasks of a philosophical theory to shed light upon the ways in which a discourse has functioned and evolved, and to motivate the particular rectification of discourse effected by theory. To accomplish these tasks, a theory must explain how those features upon which it fixes afford the most compelling understanding of the discourse.

Our evaluative notions bear the stamp of their origins in religious, teleological conceptions of the world. This might lead one to skepticism about such discourse.

F.P. Ramsey, for example, wrote, "most of us would agree that the objectivity of good was a thing settled and dismissed with the existence of God."[15] Yet the question of what, if anything, our talk of good might amount to in a secular setting seems to me not so easily answered. Ramsey is surely right that giving up the existence of God, or of a universal teleology, is unlikely to leave our evaluative notions unaffected. One consequence is that any secular account of value is bound either to assert that our value judgments are systematically false – because they are based upon false or meaningless presuppositions – or to be revisionist in some way about the meaning of value judgments. And, once again, revisionism virtually guarantees that some Moorean questions will remain open. How damaging this is will depend upon how much is lost of the original notions, and how important it is to us to be able to carry on with some substitute for the original notions.

Revisionism may reach a point where it becomes more perspicacious to say that a concept has been abandoned, rather than revised. No sharp line separates tolerable revisionism and outright abandonment, but if our naturalist wishes to make his case compelling, he must show that his account of a person's good is a rather clear case of tolerable revision, at worst.

Most philosophers in this century, aware of the centrality to human thought and practice of evaluative notions, have wanted to avoid outright abandonment of value discourse and have shied away from claiming that our value judgments are systematically false, and so have opted for some sort of revisionism. Non-cognitivist views such as expressivism represent a form of revisionism about the underlying semantic character of value discourse. (Further, depending upon the success of the non-cognitivist reconstruction of value discourse, more extensive and substantive revisionism may also be required of the non-cognitivist.) The contemporary naturalist we will consider here is prepared to contemplate some degree of revisionism about the meanings that have been attached to evaluative terms as part of his effort to construct a theory of value discourse that will preserve its cognitive character.

Is the Naturalist's Account Scientistic?

Now it is fair enough at this point to ask "What is all this talk of 'theory construction'? And what thought animates the naturalist's attempt to assimilate the assessment and attribution of value to empirical inquiry and judgment?" One might fear that the naturalist is somehow seeking to objectify value and agency in such a way that he can turn over to the physical and social sciences the business of judging what makes a good life. More broadly, the worry here is *scientism*, which perhaps can be thought of as the view that everything worth knowing or saying about the world and our place in it – with the possible exception of some colorful emoting – belongs to scientific theory. Scientism is a remarkably crude and hasty view, which no doubt owes whatever hold it may have on the contemporary imagination to the impressive gains of scientific knowledge in comparison to other areas of inquiry. But what argument can be offered to show that every meaningful part of human inquiry can simply be turned over to science? Thomas Nagel puts a

[15] Ramsey, *The Foundations of Mathematics and other Logical Essays*, ed. R.B. Braithwaite (London: Kegan Paul, 1931), pp. 288–89.

similar worry concerning a "test of reality":

> ... it begs the question to assume that this [scientific] sort of *explanatory* necessity is the test of reality for values.... To assume that only what has to be included in the best causal theory of the world is real is to assume that there are no irreducibly normative truths.[16]

Yet a naturalist, especially a methodological naturalist, need not proceed in the hegemonic spirit suggested by talk of a "test of reality." His perspective can instead be experimental: let us see how far we can go in understanding a domain of judgment and purported knowledge by applying to it a form of inquiry based upon empirical models, and asking where the judgments and knowledge-claims of this area might fit within a scheme of empirical inquiry. A non-hegemonic naturalist pursues his interpretive and explanatory project without assuming in advance that his success or failure will decide the genuineness of a domain of discourse, and so his approach need not be question-begging. It is obvious to most of us that assessments of value are bound up with a great many empirical considerations. What is less obvious is how far these empirical considerations might take us. The effort to answer this question, not to legislate other approaches out of philosophy, is the primary concern of a non-hegemonic naturalist.

Moreover, the non-hegemonic naturalist is responding to the current situation in philosophy, where historically important alternative approaches to value, such as rationalism and intuitionism, no longer seem promising. And though there are some more or less well-defined non-naturalist approaches to areas of value afloat today, it remains unclear how these views are to explain our epistemic or semantic access to value, or to account for the supervenience of the non-natural upon the natural.

To this, one can reply: "Well, look at mathematics. There is no obvious account of how epistemic or semantic access, or objectivity, is possible in mathematics. And naturalism is certainly not a clear success at accounting for mathematical knowledge. So why look only at naturalistic models; why not consider others?" Why not, indeed? Our non-hegemonic naturalist has no quarrel with the idea that we will not be able properly to assess naturalism or its competitors until each is fairly well developed. He simply follows a philosophical division of labor in attempting to see how far a naturalistic approach can be carried. If it is entirely out of place to bring an empirical approach to the business of making and warranting value judgments, then this should become more conspicuous the harder naturalism is pushed.

Reductionism

Our naturalist believes that the distinction between prescriptive and descriptive uses of languages does not preclude his project. Does it follow that he must therefore in some sense be a *reductionist* about value, someone who believes that the content of statements of value can be captured by statements which contain no expressly evaluative terms?

---

[16] Thomas Nagel, *The View from Nowhere* (New York: Oxford University Press, 1987), p. 144.

He needn't be, for he may hold that value properties are *sui generis* natural properties, though perhaps he would also hold that they supervene upon descriptive properties, such that no two states of affairs could differ in their value properties without also differing in their descriptive properties.[17] But the naturalist who would vindicate the cognitive status of value judgments is not required to deny the possibility of reduction, for some reductions are vindications – they provide us with reason to think the reduced phenomena are genuine. The successful reduction of water to H_2O reinforces, rather than impugning, our sense that there really is water. By contrast, the reduction of "polywater" – a peculiar form of water thought to have been observed in scientific laboratories in the late 1960s – to ordinary water-containing-some-impurities-from-improperly-washed-glassware contributed to the conclusion that there really is no such substance as polywater. Whether a reduction is vindicative or eliminative will depend upon the specific character of what is being reduced and what the reduction basis looks like. Even the reduction of water to H_2O was in part revisionist, as we noted, of both common-sense notions and previous chemistry. No general assumption can be made that reduction must be eliminativist or otherwise undermining.

The vindicative reduction of water to H_2O has another feature worth remarking upon here for the sake of parallelism with what our naturalist is attempting to achieve in the domain of value. Because the form of the reduction of water to H_2O is that of an identification, it makes no sense to ask of a causal role assigned to water (as in "This erosion was caused by water") whether the causal work is "really" being done by water or by H_2O. There can be no competition here: the causal work is done by water; the causal work is done by H_2O. In a similar way, if a naturalist in value theory identifies value with a – possibly complex – descriptive property, then it would make no sense to ask of a causal role assigned to value (as in "He gave that up because he discovered that it was no good for him") whether the causal work is "really" being done by value or by its reduction basis. The causal work is done by value; the causal work is done by the reduction basis.

As a result, the naturalist in value theory is able to make use of naturalistic accounts in epistemology and semantics to explain access to value properties, for the identification he furnishes can afford the ground for the requisite causal-explanatory role for value. For example, a naturalistic epistemology may require that, if p is to be an object of knowledge, then the fact p must be part of an explanation of our belief p. If value is identical with a – possibly complex – property which can appropriately participate in the explanation of our beliefs, then it can be an object of knowledge. And once again, it will make no sense to ask whether it is the reducing property or the value property that explains the beliefs in question – if the identification holds, then each does.

---

[17] For examples of nonreductionist, naturalistic accounts of moral discourse, see: Richard W. Miller, "Ways of Moral Learning," *Philosophical Review*, vol. 94 (October 1985), pp. 502–50 and Nicholas Sturgeon, "Moral Explanations," ed. D. Copp and D. Zimmerman, *Morality, Reason, and Truth* (Totowa: Rowman and Allanheld, 1986).

[18] I borrow this term from David Copp.

Confirmationalism

One last initial matter about our naturalist concerns his relation to a position that might be called *confirmationalism*.[18] The confirmationalist, as I understand him, is a particularly one-dimensional sort of naturalist. He holds that, to warrant acceptance of an account of the good, it suffices to confirm empirically the existence and explanatory efficacy of that notion of the good. The confirmationalist therefore believes that the importance of the current debate about whether or not so-called "moral explanations" can be genuine is this: once it can be established that some property that we have designated 'moral' can play an explanatory role, then we will be justified in accepting that property for normative guidance.

But here is a quick argument against the confirmationalist. Suppose a puckish naturalist, exasperated with the "Personal Health" column in the *Times,* identifies the property of being intrinsically good with the property of being *cholesterol-laden.* There is no problem now about showing that good in this sense exists (there are things laden with cholesterol) and has an explanatory role (the fact that a foodstuff is cholesterol-laden can help explain how its presence in the human diet leads to heart disease). So, if the confirmationalist is right, shouldn't we now regulate our lives in accord with this fatty notion of a person's good?

Obviously, confirmationalism thus baldly put is not a plausible form of naturalism. For to find an explanatory role for a property that simply is stipulated to be identical with goodness would not, in itself, tend to show that this property affords a satisfactory interpretation of 'good'. Good has a distinctive role in deliberation and action, and it must be shown that the reducing property is a plausible candidate for this role. "Being cholesterol-laden" would appear to have no hope of being seen as a tolerable revision of our concept of good.

We can put the point another way with more direct reference to naturalism. On various naturalistic theories of reference, the reference of a term is partly constrained by which actual phenomena were present – and, perhaps, playing a causal role – when a term has been introduced or used. The puckish confirmationalist would have to show that a common property uniting a great range of the uses of the term 'a person's own good' is "cholesterol-laden." Similarly, on various naturalistic theories of reference, certain stereotypes and truisms are associated with given expressions, and also serve to constrain its possible reference. For 'good,' it is a truism that anything intrinsically good for a person is desirable for its own sake. And it further is truistic, as John Stuart Mill noticed, that the pre-ferences of an experienced individual give some evidence about what is desirable for him. But however much we may be drawn to foodstuffs containing cholesterol, it would be unavailing to contend, on the basis of actual preferences, that it is the cholesterol in these foodstuffs that we desire, regardless of how they taste.

Now we can begin to see how the naturalist must proceed. To achieve a vindicating reduction of good, he must identify it with a natural property (or complex of properties) that, to a significant extent, permits one to account for the correlations and truisms associated with 'good' – i.e., is at most tolerably revisionist – and that at the same time can plausibly serve as the basis of the normative function of this term. The confirmationalist's view of things is correct only insofar as it would be part of a vindicating naturalistic reduction to provide evidence for the existence of, and for our access to, the reducing property as a part of empirical reality. Whether that part deserves to be called 'good' is a larger matter.

Can a property (or complex of properties) be found that both meets naturalistic conditions on existence and access, on the one hand, and possesses the requisite normativity, on the other? Let me try to indicate how such a project might be undertaken, and where some of its difficulties might lie, by considering one version of a hedonistic theory of a person's good.

III. A Strategy for Naturalism: An Analogy

The general strategy for naturalism about a person's good that I will be discussing involves the linking together of five elements: (1) locating a (possibly complex) property that is claimed by an *identificatory reduction* to underlie the cognitive content of discourse about a person's good; (2) providing evidence to the effect that this property plays an *explanatory role* of an appropriate sort to warrant saying that the property is both (potentially) empirically accessible and actually exemplified in our experience; (3) providing an account of how this property, given its character, could come in a non-accidental way to play a significant *normative role* in the regulation of human practices corresponding to the normative role played by the concept of a person's good; (4) developing an argument to the effect that the account this property affords of a person's good is, if revisionist, at worst *tolerably revisionist*; and (5) developing a further argument to the effect that recognizing this property as underlying discourse about a person's good would not undermine the normative role of such discourse, so that the reduction is *vindicative upon critical reflection*. An example of – what I take to be – a simpler and less controversial case may help illustrate how these elements could be linked together. After a brief introduction to the case, we will take up the five elements of the strategy in order.

Consider attributions of the property of being *fit to sail* or *seaworthy* to a boat or ship. Judgments of seaworthiness unquestionably have a commending function, a prescriptive side. Moreover, there has been significant historical variation in the sorts of vessels deemed seaworthy and the sorts of features entering into deliberation about seaworthiness. There is, for example, a history of mariners seeing ships as "lucky" or "unlucky," or as possessing a spirit or personality. Moreover, in some maritime traditions, a boat is not thought fit to sail unless it has been properly blessed, or painted with eyes so that it can see its way. Finally, it often is a matter of protracted controversy whether a given boat (or design) is seaworthy. These considerations – commending function, historical variation, and persistent controversy – might tempt one to adopt a non-cognitive analysis of discourse about seaworthiness: when a mariner calls a boat unseaworthy, on such an analysis, he is not describing some independent characteristic of it but rather expressing his attitude of disapproval toward setting sail in it.

At the same time, however, discourse about seaworthiness is fully cognitive in its surface grammar, and the property of seaworthiness figures in the conclusions of inductive inferences from evidence and in the premises of deductive explanations of the behavior of sailors and ships. Further, among the many ways in which a vessel might be commended, judgments of seaworthiness offer a distinctive kind of recommendation – it would be quite a different matter to commend a boat as fast, or handsome, or capacious, or efficient. Finally, although judgments of seaworthiness show cultural variation and are frequently contested – especially when a boat is of novel or unusual design – considerable consensus can typically be found at a given time within a seafaring community about the classification of a large number of cases. Of course, when one picks a point in time and looks at relatively isolated maritime traditions, it is not difficult to see judgments of seaworthiness as determined to a significant degree simply by assessments of how similar a vessel is to familiar designs. But when one looks at how traditional conceptions have evolved over time, or at contemporary judgments of seaworthiness within the global community of sailors and marine architects, it is evident that designs once deemed unseaworthy because they were unorthodox have established themselves as seaworthy through a history of successful navigation under demanding conditions. All of these considerations point away from a strictly non-cognitivist account of seaworthiness, and point instead toward the idea that judgments of seaworthiness represent an effort to report certain genuine properties of vessels.

(1) *Identificatory reduction.* At this point a naturalistic account of seaworthiness can be brought into play. A naturalist might argue that what underlies talk of seaworthiness is a set of physically realized dispositional properties of vessels, properties which constitute such features of a vessel as its stability, water-tightness, structural strength, steerability, and so on. This complex set of dispositional characteristics he would deem the reduction basis of 'seaworthiness', and he would marshal evidence about the evolution of judgments of seaworthiness over time to argue that talk of seaworthiness – either within a given maritime tradition, as folk designs evolve, or across maritime traditions, as shipbuilding has become more explicitly experimental – tends within contextual limits to track these dispositional characteristics.[19] Of course, any attempt to identify those properties which discourse about seaworthiness tends to track becomes extremely complex once one confronts historical changes in (folk and scientific) theories as well as conflicts of interest of the sort that are found within a maritime community over matters of design, safety, and so on. Still, the naturalist argues, we can see in our evolving discourse about seaworthiness a pattern in which judgments of seaworthiness *not* connected to the dispositions of vessels that constitute stability, water-tightness, and so on – e.g., judgments that more closely reflect sheer fidelity to traditional ways of doing things – tend to be supplanted by judgments that do reflect these dispositions, as manifested in the performance record of actual vessels. The naturalist therefore offers as the first element of his five-part strategy a reductive account of seaworthiness in terms of certain dispositional features of vessels. If we assume that physical theory affords further reduction of these dispositional features to underlying structural and compositional properties of vessels, then these

---

[19] The useful term 'track' I have borrowed from Robert Nozick's discussion of epistemology in *Philosophical Explanations* (Cambridge: Harvard University Press, 1981).

structural and compositional properties would be the ultimate reduction basis of talk of seaworthiness.

(2) *Explanatory role.* The second element of the naturalist's strategy has in part already been realized. For if dispositional – or structural and compositional – features of vessels can help provide empirical explanations of the actual performance of boats and thereby of the evolution of boat design and discourse about seaworthiness, then we have an argument for attributing reality to these features and seeing them as natural properties within our ken. This argument could be strengthened by showing the explanatory value of the dispositional features constituting the reduction basis in engineering science in general.

(3) *Normative role.* Because those who go to sea have an interest in staying afloat and navigating successfully, even – or rather, especially – under adverse conditions, there is little difficulty in understanding how a discourse that tracks those dispositional features of boats that account for stability, water-tightness, and so on, could come to play a significant role in regulating the practice of mariners. The interest involved is so strong and so nearly universal within a seafaring community that it is easy to see how the term 'seaworthy' could come to seem to have something like "intrinsic commending force."

Yet we do not wish to attribute to discourse about seaworthiness more prescriptivity than it actually possesses. The commending force of judgments of seaworthiness is not genuinely intrinsic, for there are rare times – for example, when looking for ships to scrap, or to scuttle for an artificial reef – when one is quite uninterested in seaworthiness, and the judgment that a vessel is seaworthy will not count as a positive consideration. What is needed is no more than a reliable, intelligible connection between judgments of seaworthiness as they typically are made and the commending force they typically have. The naturalist's reductive account, along with an account of the characteristic interests and practices of seafarers, would enable us to accomplish this.

(4) *Tolerable revisionism.* In light of the history of judgments of seaworthiness, is it tolerably revisionist to identify seaworthiness with physically realized dispositional properties? After all, in various maritime traditions, the fitness of a boat to sail has included a number of alleged immaterial characteristics. It may be possible to use physically realized dispositional properties to account for some of the immaterial properties attributed to boats in past judgments of seaworthiness: a boat's unluckiness may be attributable to unusual or difficult-to-detect defects in design or construction that render it accident-prone;[20] a boat's personality – its fickleness, say – may be attributable to an asymmetry in shape or weight distribution; and so on. But other immaterial properties – such as having been properly blessed – may correspond to no underlying physically realized dispositional attribute of a boat, and so may have to go by the board in the naturalist's reduction. A certain amount of the notion of seaworthiness, as it has

---

[20] In one famous case, a freighter deemed to be jinxed in virtue of its record of bizarre collisions was found to have an accidental cross-connection in its steering, which caused aberrations only under rather special conditions. Obviously, many of the ships deemed "unlucky" were innocent of special defect in design or construction, but suffered from poor seamanship or mere chance.

figured in actual maritime practice, will therefore be revised out of it by the reduction.

Would such a revision change the subject? That seems unlikely. The sort of revision involved is typical of changes that have taken place in a very wide range of properties that figure in commonsense theorizing. Animistic and spiritual concepts, once quite important in commonsense explanations of the behavior of (what we now would deem) inanimate objects, have largely been reduced to a metaphorical role. Indeed, in my idiolect the notion of seaworthiness is so closely tied to physically realized dispositional features of boats that it involves some strain to think of "luckiness" or "being blessed" as part of a boat's seaworthiness.

Given that the central preoccupation of discourse about seaworthiness seems always to have been the capacity of a ship to navigate successfully in a wide range of weather, and given that the reduction basis for 'seaworthiness' proposed by the naturalist involves those dispositional features of a vessel which would figure in an explanation of this capacity, it seems to me plausible to say that the naturalist's account of seaworthiness is at worst tolerably revisionist.

(5) *Vindication upon critical reflection.* Suppose that mariners were to be given this naturalistic reduction of seaworthiness, and suppose that this reduction satisfactorily embodied the four elements already discussed. Would it undermine the normative status of judgments of seaworthiness to see them as tied to physically realized dispositions – or structural and compositional features – that help explain the capacity of vessels to navigate successfully in a wide range of weather?

Why should it? The strong and nearly universal interest of mariners in staying afloat would be met by ships that are more rather than less seaworthy in our naturalistic sense. The elements of the notion of seaworthiness that would have gone by the board would almost certainly not strike most of those who judge whether ships are seaworthy as so central to the notion of seaworthiness that, were they to be lost, the practice of making and relying upon judgments of seaworthiness would lose its point, or take on a dramatically different point. Instead, once the reduction had fully been contemplated, it would seem bound to vindicate the practice.

To see more clearly why a vindication of the practice seems to be the result, we can ask how a reduction of seaworthiness might fail to yield vindication. Suppose that the success and failure of ships at sea were – as we are told the success and failure of decisions about stock-market investments are – almost entirely a matter of chance. Boats deemed seaworthy – like brokers deemed brilliant – would simply be those that have, by chance, accumulated a record of success. Then a reduction of the notion of seaworthiness to (something like) "past good luck" – with no predictive implications – would not vindicate the practice of making judgments of seaworthiness. Instead, upon critical reflection, judgments of seaworthiness would seem to involve attributional fallacies of a sort familiar in cognitive psychology, and the pretense that ascriptions of seaworthiness pick out significant features of vessels that explain their differential survival at sea would be deflated.

By contrast, the naturalistic reduction considered above, which indicates how discourse about seaworthiness has tracked (though not without a large number of fluctuations) actual, persistent dispositional characteristics of vessels that support non-accidental explanations of differential survival, would, upon reflection, vindicate that discourse's attributive pretense.

Hedonism

Let us now consider briefly how the hedonist might adopt this five-element strategy in his account of a person's good. I should say again that I focus upon hedonism not because I find it the most plausible doctrine about a person's good, but because it enables us to construct a relatively straightforward (and not entirely implausible) example of the strategy at work. Let us take the five elements in order.

(1) *Identificatory reduction.* The sort of hedonist we will be considering identifies the good of a person with his being in a distinctive experiential state: happiness. A person's well-being, on this view, is increased to the extent (and only to the extent) that he has more extensive or intensive experience of this state. The hedonist claims that this psychological property underlies our discourse about a person's good.

It has often been remarked, against hedonism, that when we reflect upon what is desirable for its sake we find a plurality of ends, not happiness alone. Why say that talk of a person's good has tracked happiness, rather than some broader constellation of ends?

Our hedonist offers the following reply. We have supposed happiness to be a distinctive experiential state. Let us suppose, further, that anyone who has experienced both happiness and unhappiness will have a settled preference, other things equal, for the former. Then the hedonist might propose the following simple model for the evolution of desires. When a given set of desires leads us to act in a way that brings with it the attainment of happiness, these desires are positively reinforced; conversely, when other desires lead us to act in ways that lead to unhappiness, they are negatively reinforced. Over time, for any given individual and relative to the range of behaviors he undertakes, individuals will tend to possess and act on desires that have brought happiness in the past. Quite likely, most of these desires will have immediate objects other than happiness, and many will involve intrinsic interest in ends other than happiness. What evolves in the individual, then, is a set of desires, including intrinsic desires, that can be explained in part as tracing a path oriented toward the experience of happiness, even though individuals often do not aim at happiness.

A similar evolution can, according to the hedonist, be found at the social level as well. Across societies and across time within a society, significant variation can be found in the range of behaviors and activities deemed to be part of an individual's good. The hedonist wishes to account for these variations and changes by noting the quite different circumstances that tend to promote the experience of happiness in different societies, and by noting the effects of changing beliefs about the likely consequences of various behaviors. At the same time, there are a great many similarities across societies and time, and so the hedonist draws our attention to the widespread agreement that certain activities or states, such as eating and drinking, or having friends and lovers, contribute to a person's good. In general, the hedonist's idea is to explain inter- and intrasocial variations and constancies in discourse about what is good for individuals as tending to follow those circumstances or activities in which the experience of happiness is produced – or seems likely to be produced according to prevailing beliefs.

(2) *Explanatory role.* If the hedonist's account of the evolution of discourse about what is good for individuals is correct – and I do not claim that it is – then he has already found an explanatory role for the property of being happy: it helps account for the sorts of things we desire and deem desirable. Here it is important to see that the explanation's informativeness depends upon our hedonist's substantive conception of happiness. Were he to treat happiness as "the satisfaction of desire," then it could not play this particular role in explaining the evolution of desires, for that role depends upon the shaping of desire by the experience of happiness.

If the hedonist's explanations are to some degree successful, then that will suffice to warrant calling happiness, so conceived, a natural property. It is a complex matter to assess the explanatory claims of the hedonist, and the naturalist should be content to leave such assessment largely to the development of psychological theory – does psychological theory find that it makes use of a substantive, experiential conception of happiness in accounting for human behavior? Let us suppose for the sake of argument that it does, and therefore that worries about the reality and naturalness of the hedonist's reduction basis can be met.

(3) *Normative role.* Elements (1) and (2) of the hedonist's task required that he give us reason to think that there really is such a thing as substantive happiness, and that discourse about a person's good appropriately tracks it. For element (3), it is necessary that he give us reason to think that this very thing, substantive happiness, has the capacity to play the normative role of a person's intrinsic nonmoral good. To accomplish this, a sufficiently tight, "internal" connection must be found between the experience of happiness and an appropriate recommending force.

Such a connection can be effected by the very feature of substantive happiness that underlies its explanatory use: what the experience of happiness itself is like. On a substantive conception of happiness, such as the one appealed to by our hedonist, the connection between happiness and what we find motivating is not logically tight. It is not definitionally true on such a conception, as it is on some non-substantive conceptions of happiness, that we find happiness desirable. However, our hedonist can argue that the connection is as tight as need be; he claims it is psychologically (or perhaps even metaphysically) impossible for a person to have the peculiar experience that is happiness and not be drawn to it.

Such a connection with commending force is, as seems appropriate, tighter than in the case of seaworthiness. For it is psychologically possible to be aware of what seaworthiness consists in and yet remain uninterested in it. The greater tightness in the case of the hedonist's reduction of a person's good reflects, I think, our commonsense view of the different degrees of prescriptivity of these two areas of discourse.

(4) *Tolerable revisionism.* The hedonist's proffered explanation of the evolution of desires leaves us with the expectation that his account of a person's good will involve some degree of revisionism. We possess, according to his proffered explanation, intrinsic desires for a range of things other than happiness, and so

when we consult our intuitive views about whether happiness alone is good in itself for a person, the answer appears to be no. Although the hedonist has no problem in convincing us that a person's happiness is among the things good in themselves for him – here intuition readily concurs – the hedonist faces great difficulty in convincing us that happiness is the only thing intrinsically good for a person.

The most characteristic philosophical counter to hedonism is to construct examples or thought-experiments that serve to make us ask whether we would indeed want considerations of our own happiness alone to govern our choices. Such an appeal to intuition can put considerable pressure on the hedonist's claim to be, at worst, tolerably revisionist. How might our naturalistic hedonist respond?

To defend a claim of tolerable revisionism he must, in some direct or indirect way, capture most of the central intuitions in this area, and must do something to lessen the force of those which he cannot capture. If this sounds more like old-fashioned philosophy than new-fangled naturalism, that is as it should be. For the naturalist is trying to show that assessments of a natural property can have the appropriate character to take on the familiar normative function of 'good' in our deliberative practices.

Perhaps the most central intuition about a person's good is the one directly captured by the hedonist: if anything is good for a person, the experience of happiness is. But with regard to other ends that, intuitively, appear intrinsically desirable, the hedonist must follow a more indirect route, via his claims about the psychology of desire. If diverse intuitive views about what is desirable for its own sake can be explained in a unified way by invoking a substantive conception of happiness – along with variation in belief and circumstance – then the hedonist can claim that, despite appearances, these other ends owe their hold upon us to the role they have played in the creation of happiness. Thus, the hedonist claims, to take our theoretically-unexamined intuitions at face value would be to misunderstand the character of our own motivational system.

To make this claim more plausible, the hedonist must rehearse in detail the sort of argument made earlier to defend the claim that our discourse about an individual's good tracks happiness. Suppose, for example, he finds philosophers (and others) at some particular juncture in history claiming that end E, distinct from happiness, is part of an individual's intrinsic nonmoral good. He would then attempt to show that the sorts of activities that typically followed from an intrinsic interest in E in that society were such as to yield – or to seem likely to yield – substantive happiness. By comparison, he could consider other societies in which intrinsic interest in E would have no characteristic tendency to produce – or seem likely to produce – substantive happiness, and show that in such societies E typically is not regarded as intrinsically desirable. For example, individual autonomy, which in contemporary Western societies is sometimes held up as an intrinsic good, has been said not to be deemed a good at all in other, more communitarian societies.

In this way, the hedonist would attempt to convince us that the usage of 'good' – our practice of identifying things as good to have or to seek – has been driven fundamentally by the property of substantive happiness, so that we should not be captivated by the surface diversity of our intuitive notions about good. Our initial confidence that ends other than happiness figure in their own right in a person's good might in this way be undermined by reflection upon how those other ends came to seem desirable to us.

Moreover, the hedonist may continue, counterexamples based upon dramatic departures from the circumstances under which our desires were actually formed may, on reflection, seem less compelling and thus less a barrier to the amount of revisionism involved in hedonism. Thus, the now-familiar science-fiction example of the experience-machine – a machine which affords to those who will but plug into it an experiential life indistinguishable from leading any sort of life one might wish, all in the comfort of the neurological unit of one's local hospital[21] – cannot, according to the hedonist, afford a crucial test against experiential conceptions of the good, because it draws upon intuitions about what we want for its own sake which were developed in settings where the drastic split the machine effects between experience and reality does not typically exist.

And so the hedonist shifts from the task of indirectly capturing intuitive judgments (by showing how they can be explained within a hedonistic scheme) to the task of explaining away intuitive judgments (when they cannot be fit within this scheme). To explain away an intuition is not always to show that it is somehow ill-grounded; instead, it can be a matter of showing that the intuition is really about something else. Thus, to return to the experience-machine example, the hedonist may agree that there is much we think would be lost in a life spent hooked up to microelectrodes rather than out in the world, making and doing. But he would urge us to recall that we are concerned in the present discussion with an account of that area of value which concerns how well or ill an individual's life goes for him, his own intrinsic nonmoral good. My life would certainly lose various sorts of value or significance if things I took myself to be doing were not, in fact, happening. Thus, it would diminish the value and significance of my acts of sending off money to aid Central American peasants if this money never reached them. But suppose that I would never in the normal course of events learn whether or not this aid reaches them. Could it be said, the hedonist asks, that how well my life goes for me is a function of whether, utterly beyond my ken, someone in Miami is pocketing the money I have sent for an agricultural co-operative in El Salvador?

This is not to say that it should not matter to me whether my efforts are genuinely availing, but only that a distinction must be made between those elements of what is important to me that depend upon their contribution to how well my life goes and those elements that have to do with other forms of value or significance my life might have for myself or others. These other forms of value or significance may matter greatly to us, and we may therefore be unable to accept the idea of confining our lives to the pursuit of our own well-being. This way of putting it should, however, make it clear that such wider concerns need not undermine hedonism as an account of precisely what "our own well-being" consists in.

[21] For a seminal discussion of an experience machine, see Robert Nozick, *Anarchy, State, and Utopia* (New York: Basic Books, 1974).

I will not attempt to say whether the hedonist's attempt to respond to intuitive counterexamples is generally effective, since I seek only to exhibit an available theoretical response. And, in any event, we now must move on to consider another kind of argument that hedonism is not tolerably revisionist, an argument that is itself theoretical.

According to a well-developed tradition in the theory of value, internalism, it is essential to the concept of intrinsic goodness that nothing can be of intrinsic value unless it has a necessary connection to the grounds of action. The need for such a connection is defended as truistic – we simply could not make sense of a claim that something is someone's intrinsic good if that thing could not afford that person positive grounds for action. An account of intrinsic good that purports to be no more than tolerably revisionist must, it is argued, capture this truism.

A complication, however, is that this truism has at least two readings, depending upon whether the grounds of action are taken to be *motives* or *reasons*. The difference between these readings may not be important on an instrumental, broadly Humean conception of rationality, according to which reason does not itself establish the ends of an individual but rather operates to help an individual effectively pursue ends already given by his desires and other ends, so that reasons are themselves always grounded in motives.[22] But the difference can be crucial on substantive conceptions of rationality, such as Kant's, where a motive may fail to create a reason, and a reason may be present even in the absence of motive.

According to our hedonist, the experience of happiness *is* intrinsically motivating – anyone who is capable of such an experience will, once he has tasted it, want more rather than less of it, other things being equal. Does this suffice to accommodate the internalist truism?

Difficulty arises in at least two cases, both of which depend upon adopting rather powerful, non-instrumental conceptions of reasons. First, suppose there to be rational agents – perhaps even humans – who cannot experience happiness. Now on some conceptions of reasons for action, nothing could count as a reason for action unless it would, necessarily, engage the will of *all* rational agents as such. But if there are some rational agents who cannot experience happiness, then there are some rational agents whose will would not be engaged by happiness in the manner that our hedonist envisages, and this would disqualify happiness as a reason for action for any rational agent. Second, suppose that the possession of a motive does not *automatically* generate a reason for action. Then even if all rational agents were capable of happiness, the intrinsically motivating character of the experience of happiness would still not provide the guarantee necessary – according to the second reading of internalism – that happiness will always furnish an appropriate reason for action.

The question now becomes whether these two possibilities are genuinely damaging to the hedonist's claim of tolerable revision. Perhaps they are not. With regard to the first possibility – that rational agents might exist who are incapable of

---

[22] I follow a standard practice in calling this sort of instrumental conception of rationality 'Humean'. I do not mean to claim that this conception is, in fact, the whole of Hume's.

experiencing happiness – the hedonist can argue, not implausibly, that the compelling idea underlying internalism is that a being X's good must be such as to engage X positively, at least once X has full understanding and awareness. Is it further necessary, in order that something be X's good, that this thing similarly engage all rational beings, no matter how arbitrarily different those beings are from X? To give up this further condition may be revisionist with regard to a certain philosophical conception of intrinsic good as "rationally commanding" on a substantive view of reasons. But it is doubtful whether this philosophical conception is somehow contained within the truism that internalism takes as its starting point and that must be accommodated by any tolerably revisionist account of a person's good.[23]

A similar response is available to the second possibility – the possibility that, on a substantive conception of reasons, a motive may fail to produce even a *prima facie* reason for action. As long as the hedonist is able to draw upon a respectable philosophical conception of reasons – the broadly Humean account – to accommodate the internalist truism, then the fact that he is at odds with an alternative (and, it must be said, rather esoteric) philosophical conception of reasons need not be a sign of more-than-tolerable revisionism. Moreover, the hedonist might claim, it may be important in avoiding significant revisionism that one *not* entirely accommodate this alternative philosophical account of reasons. It is, for example, truistic that if a course of action promises great unhappiness or pain, then an agent has a *prima facie* reason to avoid it. A philosophical conception of reasons which would permit us to assert that the prospect of great unhappiness or pain could fail to count at all as a reason for an agent may have such difficulty convincing us of its correctness as a theory of reasons that it cannot be used to undermine hedonism.

(5) *Vindication upon critical reflection.* To ask whether a reductive account of a discourse is vindicative is to ask, roughly, to what extent the discourse can retain its pre-reductive functions – descriptive and normative – when exposed to critical reflection with the reduction fully in view. Our discussion of revisionism is relevant to answering this question, because what is at stake in assessing the extent of revisionism is the degree of fit between the reductive account and the pre-reductive discourse. If the fit is reasonably close in many essentials, then there may be a good chance that the reductive account will be vindicatory.

---

[23] At this point, it might be argued that in adopting a broadly Humean account of reasons and abandoning stronger notions of "rational command," the hedonist has already adopted a form of skepticism about intrinsic good, skepticism of the kind that philosophers have often attributed to Hume himself. According to this argument, the idea of "rational command," though esoteric, was in fact discovered by philosophers to be a logical presupposition of ordinary discourse about good. When the hedonist gives it up, he in effect engages in a quite extensive revisionism, so much so that he changes the subject.

The hedonist, for his part, can reply that he is unconvinced that the philosopher's idea of "rational command" is at the core of ordinary discourse about a person's good, and that, in any event, the fact that the doctrine of "rational command" leads to so powerful and revisionist a conclusion as skepticism about intrinsic good should suggest that this doctrine stands in need of much greater support than it has thus far received. The need for support will be larger still if the hedonist can make good his attempt to give a naturalistic account of prescriptivity.

But the issue of revisionism cannot be decisive, for vindication depends upon more than fit. A closely-fitting reduction might reveal the nature and origin of an area of discourse to be such that we are led to change our views about whether the phenomena to which that discourse purports to refer are genuine, or about whether we are willing to allow the properties which that discourse effectively tracks to regulate our decisions normatively. In the case of a hedonistic reduction of a person's good, success in claiming tolerable revisionism might be matched with failure at vindication if, upon critical reflection, we found the prospect of happiness vs. unhappiness or pleasure vs. pain so insignificant that we would no longer be inclined to give considerations of our own good much, if any, consideration in deliberation.

It is important to see that there would be no logical absurdity in accepting the hedonist's reduction of discourse about a person's own good as well as his claim that happiness is intrinsically motivating, while at the same time believing that happiness, however attractive it may be, is not worth seeking. If other ends can be pursued, they can be put forward as more worthy of pursuit than one's own good or happiness. Alternatively, one might survey the scene of human motivation and opportunity and conclude that nothing, not even one's own good, is really worth seeking.

In the case of seaworthiness, vindicative reduction was achieved by pointing to an almost-universal interest that the reduction served at least as well as the pre-reductive notion: the interest of those at sea in staying afloat. Is there some similar interest in the case of one's own good? Yes, although the term 'interest' seems excessively mediating. From all appearances it matters to people – no matter how clearly or dimly they see things – whether or not they are happy or unhappy, experiencing pleasure or pain. We must be careful here to remain faithful to the substantive character of our hedonist's account of happiness. We cannot, for example, claim it as definitional that happiness matters, i.e., that that which left us indifferent would not, by definition, be happiness. Instead, we must rely upon (what the hedonist must hope is) a deep fact about us and about the quality of the experience of happiness (or of pain): no one who has that experience (an experience like *that*) can be altogether indifferent to it. We are such, and the experience is such, that we are moved in a way that does not depend upon possession of any particular ideology, interests, or attitudes. This resilience of the attractiveness of happiness and the aversiveness of pain is what underwrote the hedonist's confidence that he had discovered a sufficiently tight connection between the underlying descriptive content attributed by his reduction and the commending force that accompanies genuine acceptance of a judgment that something is good for one. This resilience is now used to underwrite the hedonist's confidence that, even if his account of a person's good is tolerably revisionist and somewhat deflationary, it remains true that acceptance of it would alter neither the appeal of happiness nor our willingness to allow considerations of our own happiness to figure importantly in our deliberations, so that the reduction he has effected can be substantially vindicative.

Conclusion

We have seen a five-element strategy that the naturalist who accepts hedonism might follow in order to accommodate both the descriptive and prescriptive side of discourse about a person's good. How successful this strategy may be depends, of course, upon how compelling the arguments for hedonism are, and here I have limited myself largely to setting these arguments down without evaluating them. A further question is whether this strategy can be generalized to non-hedonistic forms of naturalism, since at crucial points appeal has been made to (what the hedonist has alleged to be) the specific character of happiness and its interaction with human motivational systems. It seems to me that certain other forms of naturalism about a person's good – in particular, those that appeal to the reduction basis of informed desires[24] – may be able to follow this strategy, while others, lacking a suitable connection to motivational systems, almost certainly cannot. My chief aim, however, has been to suggest how something thought by many to be, in principle, beyond the reach of cognitive naturalism might, nonetheless, be possible for at least one form.

The hedonist who would be a vindicating reductionist, then, must satisfy both the confirmationalist demands for a real, accessible property, and also the further demand that the property he fixes upon be able to explain and capture – within the limits of tolerable revisionism – the prescriptivity of discourse about a person's good. Naturalism of the sort discussed here therefore is not a way of avoiding difficult issues about prescriptivity or stopping us from asking familiar normative questions, but a way of thinking about such issues and questions – a way that seeks to come to terms with normative institutions while accepting the challenge of showing how these institutions might have epistemic standing in a domain where genuine cognition is possible for beings like us.

Philosophy, University of Michigan

---

[24] For an example, see Peter Railton, "Moral Realism," *The Philosophical Review*, vol. 95 (April 1986), pp. 163–207, and "Facts and Values."

COMMUNITIES OF JUDGMENT

By Allan Gibbard

Walk across a campus on a beautiful fall day and observe what a conversing species we are. Chimpanzees can be taught to talk a little, in sign language. Put educated chimpanzees together, though, and they turn out to have nothing to say to each other. We humans are different; we can even find silence awkward.

Language does many things for us; conveying straight information is the most obvious. I want to stress. though, some of the ways that talk adjusts our terms for living together. What I say will be speculative and some of it will no doubt be wrong, but I suspect it is not completely off-base. Much of talk we can see as securing and adjusting terms of association – terms, among other things, of cooperation and mutual restraint. In part, this is a matter of governing our feelings toward each other. Feelings tend toward action; they can make for social glue or social bombshells. Nature, in the form of Darwinian evolution, has given us various ways to mesh feelings, and some of these. I think, are a matter of language.

What goes on with talk? Crucially, language lets us represent together situations we are not in at the moment. Without language, we cannot all respond to the same absent situation, or at least we cannot show that we are doing so. Without language, then, terms of association for a situation can only be adjusted in the situation itself. Think of one dog barking at another encroaching dog, or two dogs cautiously sniffing each other on neutral territory. With language, in contrast, I can do things like this: I can tell you about a colleague who leaves town right after the last class of the term, and the unnerving confrontation I had with him. You can react: you can evince a feeling of shock or withhold it. you can give what he did or what I did an emotively charged label, or you can talk about when it might be all right to go away during the term and when it isn't. My feelings about the situation respond to yours and yours respond to mine, and so if things go smoothly, our feelings converge. We work toward common attitudes toward staying around during exam period or not.

Let me call large parts of our talk and thought 'normative', and use the picture I just sketched to give a theory of normative thought and language. I apologize for rushing through things I try to lay out more fully elsewhere.[1] First, let me try to identify normative language in a fairly theory-independent way. We can talk of what it *makes most sense* to do, or to believe, or even to feel. Does it make most sense to say nothing to the brilliant colleague who talks too harshly to students? Does it make sense to feel aggrieved at the chairman who, with eminent senior faculty, tolerates things he will not tolerate among junior faculty? When does it make sense

---

[1] See especially Allan Gibbard. "Moral Judgment and the Acceptance of Norms," vol. *Ethics*, 96. no. 1 (Oct. 1985), pp. 5–21.

to accept a statistical hypothesis? Let me call words and thoughts that could be put in terms of this phrase "it makes sense to" *normative*. The phrase "it is rational to" sometimes acts as a learned variant of this phrase, and some philosophers have spoken of propriety, or fittingness, or warrant, or of "ought" in some sense. Instead of saying it *makes sense* to feel aggrieved, for instance, we can say the aggrieved feeling is warranted, or fitting, or proper. We can say that the person ought to feel aggrieved.[2] Experiment and I think you will find that phrases like these can do a great deal of work.

Now the proposal I want to explore is this: take a person who uses the phrase "it makes sense to," or says something we could gloss with that phrase. He tells me, say, that it makes sense to feel angry at my colleague for what he has done, or that it makes most sense to tolerate it. The phrase "it makes sense to," we could say, conveys a primitive normative notion. Our problem, then, is to understand what the notion is. We should explain the notion, I propose, by explaining the state of mind it enters into. We should explain talk about what it makes sense to do, to think, or to feel by explaining the kind of state of mind such talk expresses. And that state of mind I shall call "accepting a norm." If you tell me "It makes sense to let things ride," you are expressing your acceptance of a norm that, as applied to my circumstance, says to let things ride.

The explanation so far places all the burden on explaining what it is to accept a norm. Here I want to turn naturalistic; I want to explain accepting norms as something evolved creatures like us might do. Here, then, is a speculative ecology of norm-acceptance: we are evolved, highly social linguistic creatures, and I have already said something about what language can do for us. It helps adjust terms of association. Animal life is full of *bargaining situations*: situations where all can gain from cooperation or mutual restraint, but where the gains could be distributed in many different ways. Think of dominance hierarchies: deferring to you over a good food source beats getting into a fight; so does sharing the food and so does being deferred to. Mutual restraint has advantages for both of us, but they can accrue more to you or more to me. Now if we are coordinated in our actions and expectations, we reap the advantages of mutual restraint: if, say, we both expect me to defer to you, we avoid a fight. If we are uncoordinated, in contrast – if both you and I expect the other to defer – we get a costly fight.

In thinking evolutionarily, we read benefits as enhanced reproductive prospects: roughly, prospects of having grandchildren. Mechanisms evolve that enhance reproductive prospects, and some of these will be mechanisms of coordination in bargaining situations. Dominance hierarchies and territorial behavior are biologists' stock examples. Now my speculation is this: as our ancestors evolved, life became too complex for rigid, stereotyped coordinating mechanisms to work. At the same time language was evolving, and language allowed for a more flexible, delicate coordination.

How might this work? Well, suppose there were a special kind of state of mind, a state of mind directed toward acting such-and-such a way in such-and-such

---

[2] Some of these phrases present the feelings as permissible, some as mandatory. I skip over the difference.

circumstances. (The point will be to identify this state of mind with accepting a norm.) Suppose the state of mind carried with it the following tendencies: First, someone in that state of mind tends to act that way in those circumstances. Second, a person in that state of mind tends to avow it, and his avowals influence others to share the state of mind. Then discussion will tend toward consensus – toward sharing the state of mind. Consensus in turn will lead toward acting as the state of mind directs.

Call this state of mind, then, "accepting a norm." Accepting a norm involves both tendencies to avow it and tendencies to act on it. Avowals make for mutual influence, and tend toward other people's accepting like norms. Accepting like norms tends toward everyone's acting on them. If the norms direct a coordinated pattern of action, all this leads to coordination.

I. Diverse Communities

Other things besides mutual influence might promote consensus in the norms that a group accepts. Suppose people are responsive to demands for consistency. Consistency limits how much a person can shape the norms he avows to suit his private purposes. He has to be willing to apply them to himself as well as to others. Think, too, about higher order norms: norms for the acceptance of norms. One thing that might move a discussion away from deadlock is a challenge to someone's credentials. A person can be asked what puts him in a position to judge. We could expect people to begin to have answers. They could begin to develop views about what makes for good normative judgment, and in response to demands for consistency, these views could be elaborated into epistemologies of norm acceptance. At this point, I have carried my story beyond the ancestral ecology of norm acceptance, but I am talking about things that we ourselves can do with mental equipment shaped by our ancestral ecology. One thing we can do is tell epistemic stories, and to elaborate them in response to demands for consistency. We can develop norms to govern the acceptance of norms.

Now if the sketch I have drawn is on the right track, we should expect to find an elaborate psycho-social dynamics of norm acceptance. Various pressures of advantage bear on the norms a person will find plausible, and so will the influence of people around him. The result will be some degree of consensus and some degree of disagreement. We should expect, though, more agreement within a group that discusses intensely than between groups that are conversationally isolated from each other. We should expect like pressures of advantage to tend toward the acceptance of like norms. Normative judgment, on the picture I have sketched, is partly individual: people stake out positions and avow them. In part, though, it is communal: we discuss together, and we rehearse mentally for discussions together, influenced by earlier discussions. To some degree, a group will form a community of judgment, and different groups may form different communities of judgment, at odds with each other.

That sets the stage for the things I want to discuss in this paper. Let me ignore the individual aspect of judgment, the disagreements among people within a group, and think about diverse communities that can each achieve a consensus. The groups can think about each other, and they may interact. They may need to develop joint norms to govern the terms of their interaction. My goal in this paper is to ask about norms of accommodation among diverse communities of judgment.

The communities of judgment we live in are fuzzy and overlapping. Some of them are large and some small; some are intense and others diffuse. Now with different groups, we come to say different things, and I want to ask what the stories we tell can have to do with each other. In a small, intense community we can talk through, among other things, the lives of outsiders and our dealings with them. That way, for one thing, we develop our thoughts about life in our own community: how, we can ask, shall our norms extend to exotic circumstances? What does that tell us about those norms, and about our reasons for accepting them? These intimate discussions may also help us to live with the outsiders we are discussing, and figure out how to work toward broader communities of judgment on at least some topics. Our larger groups disagree irreconcilably on some matters. Still, we can talk other matters through, and we need to. On a restricted range of topics, agreement may be in the offing and worth pursuing – even though, on other topics, discussion looks futile. Agreement on restricted topics keeps peace. It helps groups cooperate. At its best it enriches people's live by broadening their understanding, their sense of humanity, and the richness of their friendships.

My point in running through these truisms is this: the character of normative judgments, I am claiming, is partly a matter of their role in discussion. Different discursive roles, then, should make for normative judgments of different kinds. We need to ask, then, about avowals that we make differently from one group to another. Some judgments we avow with intimates, but leave aside as diverse groups work toward a joint community on other topics. Acceptance, on the account I have sketched, has something to do with avowal. What, then, of these judgments that we avow in one group but keep off the agenda in others? Do we fully accept them? Are they judgments of rationality, or do they have a specially modest status? What, too, of judgments we avow on their own terms in larger groups, but tell special stories about in smaller groups? How does my story look when communities of judgment form, on the one hand, a pastiche of loose public groups, and on the other hand, intimate groups of fellow searchers for truth and meaning in life?

We choose our communities of judgment, in a sense, and gains and losses bear on the choice. Life in a messy and dangerous world depends on being able to form broad communities of judgment on a restricted range of norms – norms that enable us to live together. To thrive, though, we need more intimate communities as well. In these communities we can exercise our normative capacities and try to make sense of life and its possibilities. There is a complex story to be told here of practices and their costs, of coherent possibilities and the pressures that bear on them – and I can tell very little of it. In this paper, I try to broach some of the things that need to be explored. Partly, indeed, I just want to point to the questions. There should be a story to tell here, if the picture I have been sketching is at all true.

II. ISOLATION AND REPRESSION

In many realms of thought, feeling, and action, groups do not need to agree with one another. Some topics do not need to be discussed. They can do without joint community, and no group loses much. Faraway groups used to be fully isolated, but now, of course, isolation is always a question of topic and degree. Groups can have separate norms, say, for how they treat their own members, and they may be fairly indifferent as to how people in each other's groups are treated. Groups can accept separate norms for belief, separate norms for feelings, separate aesthetic norms, and the like. If their interactions are sparse enough, that may mean no great loss for anyone.

Isolation, as I am characterizing it, is a matter of cost: groups are isolated on a topic if they can disagree on it without much loss. I mean losses here as the groups themselves assess them. Whether much is lost through disagreement depends partly, of course, on how the groups can interact or avoid interacting. Judgments of loss, though, can change as well by themselves. It might, say, cost a religious group sorely, by its own lights, to have infidels as neighbors. With revised standards of cost, they might no longer find this costly. At that point, they would have achieved isolation on points of religion: they still have infidel neighbors, but that is no great cost.

People need intimate groups, and not only widespread understandings. Isolated thinking is disorienting. On any topic, then, a person needs other people with whom to think, but for many topics he has some choice of who those others shall be. He can discover fellow spirits, people whose judgment rings true for him. He can work with them to develop his normative views. Within the chosen group, discussants can brand views of outsiders irrational. They can do so without confronting the outsiders whose judgments they dismiss. On any topic a person needs some community, some discussion – but perhaps on some topics he can choose his group.

On other topics, a group is imposed by circumstance. A person needs consensus within that group; the alternatives are sad or worse. Without the right community, he may lose chances at cooperation. He may face ruinous conflict or war. Or the price may be that he is alienated from people he could value. In some cases, for some purposes, people must agree or pay. The range of matters on which one needs agreement will, of course, be greater with people close at hand than with those far away. Those close at hand are close in various ways – as family members, as neighbors, as friends and fellow spirits, as co-workers. Different relations will demand agreement on different matters, with varying urgency. A person may participate in a host of vague and overlapping communities of judgment in different realms. Some of these groups will be more the result of his choice than others.

I take up isolation chiefly to set it off from other ways one group can exclude another from its community of judgment: costly conflict, repression, a *modus vivendi*, and full toleration. When disagreement hurts, groups can cope in various ways. They may just accept the costs. They may talk further and work toward a community that has so far escaped them. They may turn to repression. Or they may work for tolerance or a *modus vivendi*, agreeing on ways of coping together with their disagreements. Much of life, of course, tangles these strands.

Groups are *isolated* on a topic, I proposed, when none of them lose much from thinking about it in separate ways. Then they face little pressure to work toward a joint community of judgment on the topic. Now we can ask what status the judgments of an isolated group will have if they are coherent. There are a whole range of possible answers, if I am right. The group may have a story of why the other group are poor judges of the matter. They may make their judgments parochially, confining their conversational demands to their own group and ignoring the conversational demands of others. Or they may accept a relativistic story – a story of why the judgments of each group apply fairly well within that group and apply badly to other groups. A story of one of these kinds can always be found, if the group wants to bother: a story that excludes others from the discussion. The constraints with teeth on the story are ones of gain and loss – and where groups can discuss in isolation, even those lose their bite.

What, then, when isolation is not to be had? Sometimes one group can repress another, and so it still has no need to work toward common norms. By repression, let me mean coercion of a special kind: coercion held illegitimate by the people coerced. Repression in this sense is possible, then, only when people accept norms of legitimacy, norms governing complaint. Normative agreement can coordinate, but egoistic norms coordinate poorly. Egoistic coordination is intricate and unstable.[3] A more effective device is to agree on norms for complaint – norms that are not directly egoistic. People then expect complaint if they cross certain lines. If, though, people are at odds over what norms for complaint to accept, then trouble looms. Some may then be coerced and find this coercion grounds for complaint. That is repression in the sense I shall adopt: coercing people in ways that they themselves find illegitimate.

Not all coercion is repressive in this sense. People may welcome coercion; even when they do not, they may think it legitimate. An egoist may think it fine to try to steal, and all right for others to try to keep him from stealing. Neither stealing nor threats against it are ground for complaint by his doctrine. Threats against him are then coercive but not repressive: he treats both the threats and their evasion as legitimate.

So much for what repression is, as I am using the term. Must we avoid it, then? Even in this wide sense of the term, repression is always a bad. It shifts the basis of normative discussion, and it subverts a valuable kind of respect we may have for each other. Normally we talk as if each is free to choose as he is persuaded. Threats are out of the picture; they do not apply to the alternatives anyone treats as eligible. When repression threatens in earnest, this sense of autonomy is lost, and that is a sad cost. Respect itself is perhaps a feeling or attitude, but there are kinds of behavior that show it. There is a kind of respect that is shown by leaving people free to act in the ways that they think it would be illegitimate for us to prevent. This is not the only kind of respect, and perhaps it is not the kind that chiefly matters. It is, though, one kind that matters. Acting on it consists in avoiding repression.

Still, there is a limit to what anyone will tolerate in others, given the choice. A thug might insist he had a right to his thuggery, and then we shall repress him if we can. We want to extend this kind of respect to people, but not at all cost.

---

[3] For the classic discussion of egoistic bargaining and coordination, see Thomas Schelling, *The Strategy of Conflict* (Cambridge: Harvard University Press, 1960), ch. 2.

Sometimes, then, alternatives are bleak. On various topics for various groups, no community of judgment can be had, at least at a decent price. Groups then may think in separate ways, perhaps at no great cost. At times, though, the costs are substantial or even appalling – above all, when groups are at odds over norms for complaint. Then one group may try to repress another: it may coerce others in ways those others find cause for complaint. Still, repression is sad: tolerance shows a kind of respect, a willingness to treat people in ways they themselves find legitimate. It is part of our discursive nature that we find this respect important. We repress only at a price.

Now repression may be out, of course, even apart from this. A group may lack all power to repress, or repression may be possible only at the cost of ruinous struggle or costly policing. Then either groups bear the full costs of thinking their separate ways, or they find ways to accommodate their differences.[4]

It is schemes of accommodation that chiefly interest me in this paper. So far, though, I have been taking up ways of doing without them. Sometimes groups can stay isolated, at least on certain topics. Sometimes one group can repress another. I looked at repression for two chief reasons: partly to point to a cost that schemes of accommodation can avoid – the loss of a valuable kind of mutual respect – and partly to get away from the easy assumption that repression must always be rejected. Repression always has sad costs, but sometimes the costs of alternatives are greater. Schemes that avoid repression at lowered cost, then, are well worth seeking out. Tradition provides us with some, and I want to go briefly into their structure.

III. Covenants with Hell

William Lloyd Garrison, the abolitionist, denounced the American Constitution of his day as a "covenant with death and an agreement with Hell."[5] The Constitution accommodated slavery, and slavery was Satanic. Now we can agree with Garrison about slavery, and still not think that all who accepted the Constitution had bargained away their souls. We can agree that the Constitution was an agreement with Hell, and still think that men of good will can and sometimes need to make such agreements. Abolitionism, after all, stood no chance in the South; even a full lifetime after the Constitution was adopted, the North was hard put to end slavery in a bitter war. During that lifetime, economic power had shifted toward the North. Until its end, the North could only have lived with slavery or lived apart. Hell would burn on, covenant or not, but the Constitution might one day prove an engine to quench its flames.

Between right-thinking people and slaveholders, I suppose, there could be little community of judgment on slavery. For a time, though, I am saying, right-thinking people could share a constitutional order with slaveholders. On what basis? The Constitution allowed a *modus vivendi*: shared norms for cooperation in the face of deep disagreement, where one side at least would repress the other if it could.

---

[4] My discussion of accommodation in this paper draws heavily on Rawls and his explanation of a "political conception of justice." See especially John Rawls, "Justice as Fairness: Political Not Metaphysical," *Philosophy and Public Affairs*, vol. 14. no. 3 (Summer 1985), 515–72.

[5] *Encyclopaedia Britannica*, 11th ed., s.v. "Garrison, William Lloyd."

Now how could that work? The two groups could have developed quite separate communities of judgment on how to deal with each other within a constitutional order. They could each have treated norms of cooperation purely as instruments for advancing their separate goals. A more widespread community of judgment on constitutional arrangements, though, stabilized those arrangements – and stability, I am saying, at first was a good thing. People could not be brought to agree on the morality of slavery, but in discussion with each other, they might develop ways of living together under norms that were the best anyone could hope for. That would constitute a *modus vivendi*.

Now the psychology of accepting norms runs deep in us, if I am right. Normative discussion can elicit the whole syndrome I have called accepting norms. That holds, I suggest, even if the topic is sharply delimited and talk proceeds against a background of grave disagreement. It holds even if each side would repress the other if it could. The psychology of working toward common norms in these special circumstances may resemble the more ordinary psychology of moving toward consensus on norms.

Now in life, the chief quandary here is when to accept norms of accommodation and when to stand firmly against them. A vast potential for accommodation is in us, and sometimes its realization can be appalling. Sabini and Silver discuss how initially naive and more or less decent women hired as guards at the Ravensbruck concentration camp turned to inhuman monsters.[6] Zimbardo and co-workers simulated the brutality of prisons with Stanford students who were screened for psychological normality.[7] Still, at times, there is no acceptable alternative to a workable compromise.[8] Compromise may then be stabilized by developing norms of accommodation: common norms on sharply restricted topics. These norms may need all the psychic support that better norms can have in better times. Peace depends above all on stable expectations, and here as with other bargains, expectations are steadied by normative commitments and normative appeals. Peace then rests on a rough quasi-moral consensus on rules for groups dealing with other groups they find evil.

The rules take on a moral aura, even when, by normal standards of decency, they look absurd. Think of non-intervention among states: Breaches of this rule jump to mind, but the rule governs much of what states do, and it is embraced with fervor and cant. We are even told that the people have a right to decide their own way of life – when the ones who are deciding are a dictator and his henchmen, or a small, determined party, or a large group that oppresses other groups. One interesting question is what stands behind this cant. Why should such talk grip us? That is a socio-psychological question, a question of the dynamics of norm-acceptance.

Another question is how to regard this grip, this moral aura. Is it an illusion to be resisted? On this score, the case for accepting a norm like non-intervention is

---

[6] John Sabini and Maury Silver, *Moralities of Everyday Life* (Oxford: Oxford University Press, 1982), 83–84.

[7] See discussion *ibid.*, pp. 77–83.

[8] On dilemmas of compromise, see David Luban, "Bargaining and Compromise: Recent Work on Negotiation and Informal Justice," *Philosophy and Public Affairs*, vol. 14, no. 4 (Fall 1985), 397–416.

strong. Norms of non-intervention are stabilizing, and they are more or less attainable. They are not the best possible norms for world affairs, but they may be the best on which a rough consensus of governments can be reached. We can try to nudge the world toward a better consensus. Minimal standards of human rights hold out some hope, and we should press for their recognition. In a better world, there would be machinery for enforcing them. International standards of democratic control would be even better; they would truly allow the people to decide. In the meantime, we are stuck with non-intervention: we need to cultivate respect for the principle, even when states violate human rights, and even when they are far from democratic.

My own chief question here, though, is what we are doing when we do accept norms of accommodation. What status do we give the terms of a covenant with Hell? In a sense, we accept the terms; we embrace them in a widespread normative discussion, and they work toward the same kinds of ends as many other norms: mutual restraint and, within tight limits, cooperation. We see arrangements as fair or unfair, equitable or inequitable. By our normal standards, though, talk of fairness here is wildly out of place. The norms of accommodation we cling to and defend have little to do with the way we think things really ought to be. Can this be a coherent state of mind?

As groups work toward joint agreement on norms of accommodation, members need an account of what they are doing. Within each group, people need to say what status the norms have, and what the norms have to do with the norms they accept within their own group. Now from what I have been saying, it should be clear what the best story is. Norms of accommodation, people can tell each other locally, are norms for circumstances of a special kind, the circumstances in which a *modus vivendi* is needed. They are norms for groups living in deep disagreement, when one group would repress the others if it could but no group can do so at a price it finds worth paying. In a *modus vivendi*, then, norms of accommodation are norms of the second best: divergent groups can work toward a community of judgment on these norms when they see that no agreement is in the offing about what is best.

As they work toward widespread agreement on norms of the second-best, people can tell different stories within their own groups and between them. A local group must keep track of what really matters, and of how a better world would be arranged. That is part of making sense of life and of members' dealings with each other. Their norms of accommodation, they must say, are the right norms for coping with the stubborn disagreements they face with other groups. In the wider world, on the other hand, they must avow the norms of accommodation everyone needs, the norms whose global acceptance is in the offing. They must insist on these norms or accommodate their views to the views of others. They must enter into a widespread normative discussion on its own terms, engaging their normative faculties. Perhaps they also can tell the story of second-best virtues globally, for there may be enough agreement between groups on how to measure the benefits that flow from the norms of accommodation. Whether or not, though, people can tell this story globally, they must either tell it locally or live with norms that clash.

As for the local norms, perhaps they too can be avowed coherently by one group to another. Even when this intergroup avowal is coherent, however, it cannot be insistent. Groups must distinguish between urgent business and eventual business. Some things a group might hope to convince others of eventually, whereas other things urgently must be established. In this sense, discussants must bracket their views of what is most worth achieving, so as to carry on the urgent discussion of how it makes sense for groups to accommodate each other in the face of deep disagreement.

Life with a *modus vivendi*, then, requires two things: first, in urgent discussions between groups, it requires setting aside norms on which no accord is in the offing. These norms can still be pushed locally, and pushed with fervor and conviction. Between groups, though, they are not seriously on the agenda. Second, it requires avowing norms of accommodation wholeheartedly to everyone. The avowal can be backed by a story of why these norms are valid as second-best norms, but it is the avowal, not the story, that does the chief work. For the most part, discussion will work by direct appeal to the norms of accommodation themselves. Norms of accommodation, after all, get their hold on us in the same way as other norms, through the psychosocial dynamics of normative discussion. The story of why they are valid as second-best norms does something else: it reconciles the norms of accommodation with local norms – norms that express a fuller view of life and what matters in it. The story thus makes for coherent local discussion with norms of both kinds in play.

Let me back up, then, and review. Living together is often a matter of bargaining, but raw bargaining is unstable. Human bargaining is pervaded by moral claims; even when the claims are transparently self-serving, bargainers feel called upon to make them. So it is with bargaining to a *modus vivendi*: the norms that emerge take on a broadly moral aura – even when each party finds evil in the others.

My earlier account of normative discussion explained these phenomena. Bargaining involves normative discussion: working out, partly in community, what norms to accept as applying to a situation. The psychic mechanisms in play have a biological function of coordination, and that includes the coordination that stabilizes bargaining. Even when disagreement runs deep, these mechanisms can work us toward a partial community of judgment on delimited subjects. They work to create some intrinsic attachment, some real normative governance for the norms that emerge.

My question was whether we could understand our resulting state of mind as coherent, and express it in a coherent normative story. We can, I proposed, if we explain norms of accommodation as second-best norms, as norms for coping with deep and perilous disagreement. We can then tell consistent stories locally and globally. We can develop norms of accommodation in global discussion, invoke them, and rely on their intrinsic appeal. Still, we can admit openly, on occasion, that these norms are not directly the ones that matter. We can admit that we appeal to them for want of a better alternative.

IV. TOLERATION

Real toleration, I want to say, is more than a *modus vivendi*, but it has a similar structure. A *modus vivendi* is accepted only because the alternative is ruinous conflict, and all groups find the scheme preferable. Mutual toleration, too, involves a scheme of accommodation that all groups prefer to its alternative. What binds them to the scheme, though, is that it allows them to live in a kind of mutual respect.

Repression has its limits: it may be that no group can repress all the others, and if some group can, the repression may have great costs, from war, to policing expenses, to lost cooperation. Some costs of repression, though, are more subtle. They are matters of what we can mean to each other, and so of what life can mean to us. I have spoken of a kind of mutual respect repression loses, and tried to explain what that might mean. Respect is a feeling or attitude toward others: an attitude, among other things, that prompts a person to try to rely on honest persuasion in dealings with them. It prompts him to try to treat others in ways they themselves will find legitimate. This holds especially for coercion: respect keeps a person from coercing others unless they themselves find the coercion legitimate. Respect, so defined, is not something one can always show toward everyone, no matter how they are prone to respond. It is wrenching, though, to act toward a person against his protests, voiced or silenced. It is wrenching to turn away from a normal stance of hearing protests and working toward understanding.

The problem is not one for delicate liberal sensibilities alone. Tyrants repress opinion, and so do whole social groups. Their very determination suggests a drive for accord. If the real thing cannot be had, at least a forced semblance is wanted.

Toleration is a scheme to achieve this kind of mutual respect in the face of disagreement. In favorable conditions, groups at odds can work toward a community of judgment on restricted topics, and develop norms of accommodation. The initial pressures may be those of a *modus vivendi*, and those pressures may go on helping to sustain the arrangement. Part of the reward of accommodation, though, is this kind of mutual respect, and in time that itself may seem enough to justify the accommodation. Groups then have achieved toleration.

Again we can puzzle what status could be claimed, coherently, for norms of mutual tolerance. Here, though, an answer is ready at hand. Norms of mutual tolerance, we can say, have roughly the same status as the norms of accommodation involved in a *modus vivendi*. They too are norms for a special circumstance of living in disagreement. They are norms whose acceptance might be in the offing in a wider group, a group stuck in disagreements on other norms. Again, a local background story can be told about why the norms are valid. The story reconciles these norms with the more local norms through which life and its significance are understood. Here, though, the story rests not on the overt costs of conflict, but on the importance of a kind of mutual respect. As with other norms of accommodation, these norms of tolerance gain their hold in the usual way, through the sociopsychic mechanisms that make for normative discussion – discussion in the wider group – and for normative governance.

People can come to delight in their variety. Then the problem of tolerance disappears. At that point, groups no longer hold back from repression because it shows disrespect; they welcome what they might have repressed or tolerated. Still, for everyone there will be things he wishes no one did. If others do these things anyway and claim the right, he may want to be tolerant. He may wish, say, that there were no believers in astrology, and yet want such beliefs tolerated. He does not delight in the variety astrology adds, and so if he allows the beliefs regardless, perhaps he is tolerating them. He *tolerates* something, as I am proposing we use the term, if (i) he prefers people not to do it, (ii) the people who do it would think it illegitimate for others to stop them, and so (iii) he refrains from coercing them, out of a wish to live in mutual respect.

At least since John Stuart Mill, a chief ambition of political philosophy has been to develop a test for legitimate coercion. It is urgent that some such test draw wide adherence, or at least that we agree case by case. Norms promote coordination in the broadest of senses, and shared norms of legitimacy and complaint do so most of all. For a particular kind of society, there may be a standard for legitimate coercion that almost all can accept. Of course, once again, consensus and stability are not everything, but we may hope for something even better: a formula that draws adherence and, furthermore, merits it.

We should not think, though, that we can simply oppose all repression, or that the right formula is easy to decide. Almost inevitably, some disagreements will make for hard choices. In what range of ways are parents to be free to treat their children as they think best? Shall we act against discrimination in distant places? Against blood sports and other forms of cruelty to animals? We may find schemes for mutual respect in the offing on terms we find scarcely acceptable. There is value in relying on persuasion, in not coercing people in ways they find illegitimate. This makes for the normal free interchange we thrive on. To achieve the widest mutual respect, though, we may have to give up too much. We may sometimes be stuck with a complex survey of what is gained and what is lost from particular attainable schemes.

Our problem then is to decide how wide a community to try to achieve on a basis that all accept as legitimate. Our community of tolerance may not be the widest we could have achieved, for some things we may still find intolerable. We may, though, end up tolerating things we would repress, if only we could succeed in doing so and still achieve respect for each other in a wide enough group.

Suppose that in fact, though, a system of tolerance is in the offing. How shall we now regard its norms of accommodation? An accommodation may be tolerant and still be unjust. There is nothing incoherent about thinking both that we shall achieve accommodation – that we shall come to coerce each other only in ways we have also come to think legitimate – and that some of the coercion will really be illegitimate. Once we have achieved toleration, once we regard our accommodation as a reasonable price for living in mutual respect, we then shall think our norms of accommodation just. In advance of the consensus, though, or before we ourselves form a part of the consensus, can we agree?

The question here is one of the authority we accord our future selves as normative judges. We and others, talking in the widespread group, will be affected by the talk and come to accept certain norms of accommodation. The usual sociopsychic dynamics of consensus formation will have worked on us. Eventually, we will be prone to avow those norms, and those norms will govern our sentiments. The question is: do we now in advance think that all this will make us good normative judges? Do we now accord authority to ourselves as we shall be as a result of discussion – a global discussion in which we work toward accommodation? This is a question of what epistemic norms to accept, what norms for according authority. If we think we shall be good judges, then we think the norms we shall come to accept are valid.

Now it would be extravagant to deny all normative authority to ourselves as we shall be as a result of discussion. It would be extravagant to think that widespread discussion worsens us as judges of the norms of accommodation that apply to our circumstances. Our normative sensibilities as they are now have in the past been shaped by discussion and accommodation. If we think that further discussion and accommodation would deprave our judgment, why trust our judgment now?

That does not mean that we take any accommodation widespread discussion might produce as valid. We start with tentative judgments of what is fair and reasonable, as well as tentative judgments of what would make us good normative judges – of what would make us good assessors of norms of accommodation. Tentatively, we must accord some authority to ourselves as we would be after global discussion. We think in advance also, though, that any such authority would be vitiated if the judgments we came to make were palpably wild. For some scenarios of how discussion might go, we are sure in advance that we would have gone astray. For others, we shall be at a loss in advance to know what to say. Still if we are to keep our normative moorings at all and stay coherent, we need to accord some authority to ourselves as we would be after global discussion. Valid norms for accommodation to our circumstances – valid norms for accommodating the disagreements that will survive discussion among different loose groups – are to be known in part by the hold they will have on us as a result of discussion among those groups.

V. Review

We think as individuals, but partly, too, we think in groups. As separate groups discuss, separate communities of judgment can develop. These rough communities could disagree even if everyone were ideally coherent – that, I take it, is what the history of attempts to prove otherwise suggests. A person has some choice of who shall make up his community of judgment, and in an indirect way, the gains and losses that stem from the choice bear on what norms it makes sense for him to accept. Communities come in degrees and they can form on different topics. Part of the art of life is to develop widespread, loose community on some topics and more intense, local community on others.

For simplicity, I spoke as if groups lay at two poles. At one pole, we need to discuss if we are to make sense of life at all: we need to think together about what matters and how. We need this discussion just to keep our normative moorings. At the other pole we confront big, loose groups, groups that we have to get along with somehow. In these widespread groups, large disagreements are bound to stick, at least for now. People may find each others' outlooks bizarre and unhelpful. Now I glanced first in this paper at cases where no common norms are needed. Sometimes groups can isolate themselves from each other – on limited topics, at least. Sometimes one group can succeed in repressing another. Often, though, neither isolation nor repression is possible, or repression is possible but its costs are too high. Some of these costs are straight costs of policing and of resistance to policing. Other costs are more subtle: repression goes against an important kind of mutual respect, the respect that consists in not coercing people in ways they think illegitimate.

The promise lies in having local norms on some topics and joint norms on others. How this might work is what I chiefly wanted to study. Even in deep disagreement, groups can work toward a widespread community of judgment on norms of accommodation. They can develop joint norms on how to cope with their disagreements. I spoke of two such cases, a *modus vivendi* and toleration. The difference lay in the cost of failure, in the kind of costs that lead each subgroup to prefer those joint norms to none at all. With a *modus vivendi*, each group would repress the other if it could. were it not for the overt costs of policing and resistance. Tolerance comes when groups are at odds on some matters, but they tolerate each other for the sake of a kind of mutual respect. Each group would accept the joint norms even if the overt costs of repression and resistance could be minimized. They treat their norms of accommodation as a scheme to achieve the goal of living together without anybody's being coerced in ways he thinks illegitimate.

In life, the chief quandary is when to accept norms of accommodation and when to reject them. We feel their pull, but still, shall we think we are being taken in, affably seduced when our guard should be up? Or shall we think we are only being reasonable? On these questions, I had only a little to say. The alternatives, conflict or repression, always have important costs. Sometimes, though, these costs are worth paying; sometimes the price of an achievable accommodation would be too high. We will not always choose mutual toleration even when it is attainable.

My chief puzzles here, though, were not when to accommodate; they were about the ways we can accept norms of accommodation when we do. These norms have a dual aspect: in the widespread group where we develop them, we accept them in their own terms. The ordinary psychic apparatus of norm-acceptance is at work, and norms of accommodation come to strike us as evident. We discuss, we influence each other, and we find things plausible or implausible. We develop joint standards of fairness or unfairness between otherwise disagreeing groups. To enter fully into widespread discussion, we need to think we are working toward well-founded conclusions: we must accord authority to the things we will eventually come to accept. Otherwise, we lose some of the advantages of our human normative makeup. For coherence, though, we also need a local story of what we are doing. We need a story that will fly within intimate groups, the groups we use to keep our normative moorings. We need to say how our norms of accommodation fit into norms we can recognize as valid in our most earnest, unconstrained discussion with fellow spirits. This local story, I proposed, can rest on the idea of the second-best: our norms of accommodation, we can say, are the best attainable basis for avoiding the costs of conflict and repression. They are norms for living in deep disagreement on other norms when no better widespread consensus is in the offing. Norms of accommodation, in short, take hold of us in two ways: in their own terms in widespread discussion, and as necessary instruments of accommodation in a more probing, intimate setting.[9]

Philosophy, University of Michigan

[9] Some of the material in this paper comes from work done while the author was a Visiting Fellow at All Souls College, with support from a Rockefeller Foundation Humanities Fellowship.